How Now, Butterfly?

A MEMOIR OF MURDER, SURVIVAL, AND TRANSFORMATION

Charity Lee
WITH BRIAN WHITNEY

WILDBLUE
PRESS

WildBluePress.com

HOW NOW, BUTTERFLY? published by:
WILDBLUE PRESS
P.O. Box 102440
Denver, Colorado 80250

ISBN 978-1-948239-64-6 Trade Paperback

ISBN 978-1-948239-63-9 eBook

Cover design © 2019 WildBlue Press. All rights reserved.

Interior Formatting/Book Cover Design by Elijah Toten
www.totencreative.com

How Now, Butterfly?

INTRODUCTION

I named my firstborn, my son Paris, after a hero in the *Iliad*. Paris was a sheepherder who was actually a prince of Troy banished at birth. His mother, Hecuba, loved him unconditionally, yet she knew, because of a dream she had before he was born, she had given birth to the torch that burned her city down. She *knew* her son was a threat.

One day while Paris was with his sheep, isolated in his own world, three goddesses appeared to him and asked him to settle a disagreement about who was the most beautiful among them. Among his choices was Hera, goddess of home and family; Aphrodite, goddess of love; and Athena, goddess of war and wisdom. Paris chose love over family, wisdom, and war. My hope was my Paris would always choose love.

I obviously didn't read the original story close enough. Clearly, I chose to read it to reflect my perception of how one should make choices in the world with the hope it would influence his perception of who to be in the world.

Paris chose Aphrodite, love, not because he believed in love, but because it gave him something he wanted, Helen, a king's wife. Much like my Paris made a choice, not because he believes in love, but because he thought it would give him what he wanted: the ability to bring about death and my destruction.

Paris' choice led to the destruction of Troy. People died, in the most horrific ways, because of his choice that fateful day. The prince in the epic poem did not end up a hero. He ended up locked behind the walls of Troy as all of Greece came after him. His own people would not hide him "since he was hated among them all, as dark death is hated" (Iliad).

In my story, the hero-who-is-no-hero kills the princess. My son grew up privileged, well-educated, in a home with a mother who loves him to the moon and back. Yet, despite affluence and affection, Paris, at the age of thirteen, tortured and murdered his little sister Ella, to bring his fantasy of causing another's death and my destruction into reality.

Paris of Troy was a weak narcissist, but my son Paris is both a narcissist, a sociopath, and possesses worrisome paraphilias. I wasn't given Hecuba's prophetic dream. There were not any of the movie-esque warning signs in his childhood which clearly pointed out he was a threat who would destroy my world. As he entered adolescence, I worried he might hurt himself, but I never worried he would hurt anyone else. Especially not Ella. He loved her.

So I thought.

I was wrong. My mistake led to the destruction of my daughter and the destruction of my world.

Now I believe him when he says he has his inner "wolf" caged deep inside him; I just don't believe in his ability to keep that wolf caged when he no longer lives in a regimented world. He is scheduled for release back into the wild in the not-too-distant future, possibly sooner if he's paroled. I also believe I am the only one who is authentically scared by that knowledge.

Perhaps you want to ask me why it is time to tell my story to the world, from my perspective, in my own words, my way, to whoever chooses to pick it up and read it. Why twelve years later do I feel it necessary to walk down this painful path again to write this book? Why haven't I just moved on? Because while the painful path never ends, it is possible to progress down it.

I have progressed to the point when it is time to bring these tragedies, which attempt to hold me down, to leash. I cannot banish them. Trust me; I have tried every way I know to do so. I cannot wish them away; wishes are for fairy tales. My life is no fairy tale. So I learn to tame them.

I expose them. The only way to banish darkness is with light.

Hopefully by the time you read this, I will have progressed a bit further down the path.

My hope is someone else learns something from the tragedies and triumphs contained in these pages.

What is, is, but what never should have happened has turned into the exact thing which needs to happen after any tragedy: something ugly that happened turned into something wonderful and beautiful; something happened that may mean nothing in the long run, but turned into something that brings meaning now; something that allows love to transcend hate; something that allows for creation instead of destruction.

When your life is destroyed, when your reasons for being are taken from you, words are inadequate to describe the pain, the level of devastation; the utter despair and darkness that ensnare and confuse your thoughts, your actions, your very soul. It's impossible to describe the wish to die, desperate to escape the nightmare you find yourself living; hoping death brings peace. If not peace, hopefully brings nothing. No pain. No love. No feeling at all. Feeling nothing felt preferable in the darkness of my reality.

When I wrote the bones of what turned into this memoir, I was dealing with excruciating emotional, spiritual, physical, moral, maternal, psychic conflict resulting in paralyzing pain. And so much more. Like PTSD. Complicated grief. Bi-polar disorder. Addiction. Anxiety.

And all of their incapacitating side effects. Insomnia. Hypervigilance. Paranoia. Self-medication. Suicide attempts. Extreme mood swings. Isolation.

My children were suddenly gone after my son announced himself a sociopath by murdering his little sister. I was under investigation by a legal system which viewed me with suspicion rather than compassion. I was accused of, and believed to be responsible for, turning my son into a murderer; I was accused of not protecting my daughter, the ultimate sin a mother can commit; I was assigned full responsibility for my daughter's death. By everyone, including myself.

When I began to write these words, I was watching my daughter rot. Every day, before I fell asleep with her at the funeral home, I traced with my fingers knife wounds that covered her body, every day in the same pattern, every day until she was handed to me in a cardboard box.

I was watching my son turn from the then boy I loved to the now man who both enjoys and could not care less about what he did to his sister, our family, to me. But who cares very much about what he did to himself.

I survived despite the odds stacked against me from birth; I survived to prove to my son he has no say in my destruction, but despite his wishes has almost everything to do with my creation. While I am sure it was not his intention, I met myself, my true self, yet again. For the first time, despite it all, I liked who I met.

When I was writing these words, I created The ELLA Foundation, a nonprofit to aid those whose lives have been affected by violence, mental illness, or the criminal justice system. ELLA speaks just like my Ella did, for herself, for itself. ELLA speaks for me and both of my children. ELLA speaks for all those in pain due to violence, loss, mental illness, incarceration, stigma, and lack of understanding or acceptance.

All the while, I was absolutely losing my fucking mind. Over and over and over again. So ... I wrote more, and more, and then more still.

This memoir is my way of reminding myself I am human; my way of reminding you that you are human. We are not saints. We are not monsters. I, we, don't have to be heroes. We just have to be ourselves, come what may.

We have to be human.

When you deal with someone who does not deem themselves human, someone who deems himself some sort of evolved superhuman, someone who is exceptionally smart, cunning, and capable of acts you are able to observe but could never perform, how do you find the truth in that?

How do you let go of that? How do we find the meaning, the lesson, the truth, in the worst someone can do to us? In the worst we can do to one another?

How do we even know that meaning, lessons, and truth exist any more than we know that justice, freedom, love, right, wrong, and hate exist? Does any of this really exist, really mean anything? It may not, but in order for us to continue to strive to make a world in which all these things continue to exist, it has to. Because in reality....

The only thing that truly exists is what we hope exists.

The ability to love despite the ability to suffer. The ability to forgive despite the ability to destroy. The ability to ask the question "Why?" despite the fear of doing so. The ability to create emotion, reason, and meaning out of suffering, destruction, lack of understanding.

The ability to move forward knowing we will never have the answers to those questions we really think we need answers to.

Unlike Hecuba, I have not escaped my nightmare life. I constantly struggle to know what to do next, how to survive each day, how to live again.

Ella and I used to read *How Now, Brown Cow?* We started looking at one another when either one of us was stumped about a problem, a situation, a dilemma and asking, finger on chin, "How now, Butterfly?"

Every day now I have to ask myself, "How now, Butterfly?"

This memoir is taken from my journal entries, memories, dreams, and experiences not of this world. Writing this is one of the ways I survived in order to begin to live life again.

I've learned to grow tulips from shit.

I wish you all the best, love, and light while you garden.

—*Charity Lee*

This book is dedicated to:
Paris Lee—for showing me what love is
Ella Lee—for showing me how love acts
Phoenix Lee—for showing me love really does conquer all

"You wouldn't believe it. It's like a wonderful nightmare."
"Sure," I said. "I'd believe anything. Including nightmares."

The Sun Also Rises – Hemingway

CHARITY LEE BENNETT
JANUARY 22, 2007
JOURNAL ENTRY: ONE WEEK
PRIOR TO THE MURDER

This morning, eating breakfast with the kids, I read the story of Janie de la Paz in the local paper. She is, was, a four-year-old girl killed in a drive-by shooting. She was in bed. Asleep. Twenty-three shots were fired into her house. A bullet went through the wall, into her head. As I read the article, I sat at the breakfast table with my kids. I am so grateful we live in a safe neighborhood. I may have made my mistakes, I may be facing tough times, but I have my kids. We are together. We are safe. We don't have to deal with random, senseless violence.

At least there is that.

I've never been much for New Year's resolutions, but earlier this year I made one. Reading about Janie reminded me of it. It was simple. One I know I can keep.

My vow is to make 2007 better than 2006. I will treat others decently; I will be treated decently. I will be happy with what I have: my kids, my friends. I feel as though I finally remember who I am and what I can do. I am Charity. I know who I am. I know I am good. I know I am strong.

PARIS LEE BENNETT
FEBRUARY 4, 2007, 11:29 PM
9-1-1 CALL

This is Abilene 9-1-1. What is your emergency?
Hello?
Abilene 9-1-1, go ahead.
I—I accidentally killed somebody.
You think you killed somebody?
No, I know I did. My sister.
Okay, where's your sister now?
She's in the bed.
Is she breathing?
No. I've looked. (Gasping, crying). I feel so messed up.
Okay. Calm down, okay? I want you to stay on the phone with me, okay?
Mm hm.
Now, what's your sister's name?
Her name is Ella. Ella Bennett.
How old is Ella?
Four.
She's four years old? How old are you?
Thirteen.
Is she bleeding anywhere?
Yeah, she's bleeding all over the bed. (Pause) Because I stabbed her.
Okay. What did you stab her with?
A knife.
Where did you stab her?
Lots of places.

FEBRUARY 27, 2007: MORNING

Twenty-three days have passed since my son stabbed my daughter to death.

My Ella Bella, my beautiful butterfly, is gone.

She died a horrible, violent death by her brother's hands—my son's hands, my Paris' hands. It does not matter if I am awake. It does not matter if I'm asleep, although I don't sleep anymore. Awake or asleep, life is a nightmare. I have become severely depressed. I am thirty-three years old and my best friend has to hand feed me, which she insists on doing because I've lost thirty-five pounds in thirteen days. All the pills the doctors give me don't help . . . but they could kill me. There is that.

I can hardly think, just write. I have no answers, and nothing makes sense. I have no idea how to make it through this. Part of me wants to disintegrate while another part says I have to, I must, make it through one more day.

But why?

What is one more day going to bring except more pain? I have too much anxiety to go out to public places. Even if I wanted to go out, I wouldn't. Not anymore. People are unbelievable. A woman, a complete stranger, a soccer mom, walked up to me in the grocery store yesterday, my first outing since I lost my children, and looked me straight in the eye and said, "I know who you are! I know who your son is. He should be drawn and quartered. You should be forced to watch! He is a monster and you raised him!"

All I could choke out was, "I don't know who you think I am, but you need counseling," my voice shaking. I could barely walk but somehow, I made it out of the store, cart abandoned, integrity intact. I sat in my car and sobbed, screamed at the top of my lungs for an hour.

What have I done to deserve so much pain and loss? I am a good mother; we all make mistakes. How am I going to make it through this?

I love my son.

I hate my son.

He doesn't seem concerned about how I am; he doesn't seem to care about anything really. He displays no emotions around any of this. The worst thing for him about this entire situation is how bored he is. He complains to me about it often. He's angry I'm not allowed to bring him books. All he seems to care about is Paris. While he sits in there, bored, I'm out here in Hell. I am harassed by the media. I am interrogated by the police. I am investigated by Child Protective Services. All of them depose me and investigate me, to try to find what it is I've done to turn my son into the boy who killed his sister. They won't believe Paris wasn't abused. They won't believe Paris was loved. They want an explanation for how he could turn into a monster. So do I.

I need an explanation for how he turned into the boy who killed his sister.

I want my Ella Bella back. But that can never happen. I want Paris to be happy, sane, and healthy. I can't have that either. He is no longer mine. He will grow up in jail or a mental institution.

Even if he could come home, I can never allow him to come home to me. I am scared of my own son.

Yet I visit him every day. I'm organizing a book drive for the jail. I am his mother. He is my son, and he's still just a boy. Who else will watch out for him if not for me? I follow a uniform down the dingy, fluorescent-lit hallway in the back of the Taylor County Detention Center at 5:30 every afternoon to a visitation cell. I need to see my son every day. He is the only child I have left. I need to know he is ok, still here, that I have not lost them both. I'm glad the guards are there and can see us through the glass when they put me alone in a room with Paris. I am scared of my son.

The first time I saw him after he killed Ella, he wore an orange jumpsuit and sat in a plastic chair, preternaturally calm.

He's still, calm like this throughout most of our visits. After my son stabbed my daughter to death he called a friend, talked for six minutes; told her he did something that might make me mad. He didn't tell his friend what he'd done. Was Ella in bed, dying, while he called that friend? He hung up and then, finally, called 9-1-1. Could Ella, my butterfly, have been saved?

Is my son telling the truth? Was it deliberate, or did he really have a psychotic break, like he claims?

Thirteen years ago, I gave birth to a boy who would grow up to kill his own sister. Did I give birth to evil? Is there something I missed in raising him that caused this? Or is it genetics?

Why Ella Bella? Why? She gave me such joy. She was my girl. My diva. My extrovert who loved everyone. Especially her brother.

Paris was fine twenty-eight days ago. I would have sworn it. An average kid who loved his sister. He was pissed at me because I scolded him for spending all his money at the mall, but he still let me kiss him goodbye when I left for my shift at the restaurant. But, then, somehow Paris convinced the sitter to leave, how that happened I still don't understand, and he killed Ella.

He called 9-1-1 at 11:30 that night.

The police came to my work at 12:30 am. We were cleaning up the restaurant after the Super Bowl crowd, and they brought me into the manager's office to tell me what happened. It took them a few minutes to say what they came to say. First they told me Ella was hurt, so of course I wanted to rush out of there and get to where she was. When they told me she was dead, I fainted. When I came to, I asked where my son was. That is when I heard, for the first time, the words "your son murdered your daughter."

The detectives wanted to know my son's history. I told them the history of the boy I thought I knew; an inaccurate history based on my perception of who I thought Paris was.

Paris, although still in middle school, went through the process of fingerprinting, photos, and interrogations on his own. When I asked to be taken to him, I was told he did not want to see me. I didn't see him until late the next day; I didn't even get to see a copy of the police report for weeks. But I did have to sit in my car for six hours that night, a sweatshirt over my head as cops and the media asked question after question while the neighbors stared at me or at my house with yellow crime scene tape.

I kept thinking, "My daughter is in there, dead. My son killed her. This does not make sense. This is not happening. My daughter is in there, dead. My son killed her. This does not make sense. This is not happening." Over and over and over. Each time I repeated this mantra, my brain fractured, the shards becoming too small and too hard to hold onto.

Today when I saw him, Paris was quiet and scared. He told me, again, about the hallucinations he had the night he killed Ella. He put his head on his arms on the metal table between us, and looked at me with big, soft-brown eyes and, with what I worry might be faked emotion, said, "Mom, she was a burning demon. I didn't know. I didn't know." But he doesn't cry. I want to believe him, that he killed my baby because he had a psychotic break. I want to believe he's sick. I want to believe he's just sick, and not evil.

I've heard this story from him many times now. He fell asleep next to Ella but woke up and saw a demon with a pumpkin head that was on fire. He says the demon made a horrible cackling sound. Terrified, he started to hit, choke, and then stab it. He says he attacked the demon to protect Ella from it. He told the police he didn't realize it was Ella until it was too late.

I miss her fat legs. I miss the way she said "Charity." I miss listening to her sing and I miss dancing with her. I miss her Princess Barbie teeth. I miss sleeping next to her in bed, even the times she woke me up with her tossing and sleep talking. I miss how she threw her leg over my back and her arm around my neck and said, "Oh, Mama, I love you so much." I miss her "yo' mama" battles with her brother and me. I miss her quirky fashion statements and her asking me if she looked "slexy." I miss showering with her, smelling strawberries and almonds in her blond curls as they dried afterward. I miss her laugh and I miss the sound of her voice. I miss asking her what she learned at the end of each school day. I miss being bossed around and told what to say. I miss watching cartoons with her on Saturday mornings.

Most of all I miss hugging her and doing all our kisses: hippo, Eskimo, butterfly, and Mama kisses.

Everything that meant everything is gone. Forever. How do I learn to live in a world where the murder of your daughter by your son is possible? How do I find purpose in my life now that my purpose in life is gone?

My children are gone.

And it is all Paris's fault. How is it possible to love and hate my son in one fell swoop? As my grief, depression, and anxiety increase, so does my resentment toward Paris. I will never see my daughter again. That is Paris's fault. I will never be able to mother Paris again. That is Paris's fault. I live in hell and I'm coming apart at the seams. That is Paris's fault. My children were my reason for being and now those reasons are gone. That is Paris's fault.

There is nothing in this world as precious to me as my kids. How will I ever find anything this precious again? How will I find a reason for being, a reason as compelling as my two kids? There is none.

FEBRUARY 28, 2007

Last night was one of the worst nights I have lived through since everything happened. I want Ella. I want to believe Paris. But something about him is off. It's like I'm talking to an entirely different person, not the affectionate, funny boy I know. It's hard to take what he says at face value.

After writing, I went to bed and had a very vivid dream, too real. It was more than a dream; it was a message. I don't remember every detail, but I woke up feeling everything that has happened in my life was destined to happen, that all of my life experiences are somehow interconnected. If just one detail of my life, of that Sunday, would have been different, Ella might still be with me.

I woke up feeling my task is to find the meaning of all this and do something with it. But what am I supposed to do with this pain, this confusion and despair, the overwhelming grief, the fear? How can this level of pain have any meaning or purpose?

Ella is watching over me. I believe this in no uncertain terms. She is still with me. Last night, my time with her, it was real. This was not just a dream.

I found myself in a huge white house perched on the edge of a cliff, in a library. I am frantically looking through books trying to find an answer to why Ella is gone, why Paris is a killer; an answer to how I am supposed to make sense of all this, fix all this. I am desperate, ripping books from the shelves, throwing them to the floor when I don't find my answer. Then, I am outside, in a chair by a pool. The air is moist and warm. It cocoons and comforts. Ella sits on my lap, whispering into my ear, "Hey, Mama, you know I love you, right?" Her little body is sturdy, very solid. Her breath is warm on my ear, her arms are around my neck, squeezing. She's peering intently into my face, her extraordinary eyes—translucent in the light, hazel with sparkling flecks of gold in the center—emanate a wisdom, a calm, which is new. I bury my face in her blonde curls. She smells exactly like I remember: strawberries and almonds. I just hold her. Smell her. Love her. She tells me I won't find my answers in a book this time. She tells me I will only find the answers in my heart, my soul.

Then I woke up.

Ella wants me to know that if I am to make any meaning out of this nightmare, I must stop trying to figure it out intellectually. I must dig deep into my soul. Use my heart, not my head, to figure this out, to find a purpose behind this horror.

Thank you, Ella. You are truly my guardian angel.

If I were more eloquent I could, perhaps, find a way to use words to better express how this much loss feels. But could I really? I doubt there are adequate words to describe the state of my soul.

Last night was another horrible night.

The local newspaper reported the District Attorney will officially pursue a Capital Murder charge against Paris when the grand jury convenes.

Reading those words did something to me; something I am not sure makes sense. Those words helped me make it through my shock. Those words helped cement to me that this is real.

My brilliant thirteen-year-old, my skateboarding Goth kid who still watches cartoons, he really did murder his four-year-old sister. He really did murder my daughter. There's no way to pretend he didn't. The headline, in black and white, burrowed its way into the wounds made by Paris. I broke down. Sobbing. Retching. Unable to stand. Throwing things. A-screaming-at-the-top-of-my-lungs type of breakdown.

I finally collapsed into the truth that my son is a murderer, a capital murderer. It has been written; so it shall be.

I talked to Ella. I prayed to God. I begged God to allow me to continue to feel connected to my daughter, so that her spirit can continue to give me strength to go on, to walk in peace, to buffer my soul. This is a nightmare, truly, and I don't know how I've made it this long. All I can attribute it to is Ella. When she's with me, my right arm tingles, as though she has her hand on me, holding me up.

I know my prayer worked because when I awoke today my sense of calm has returned, even though the nightmare has not gone away. It is, in fact, growing. After reading the local news, I searched the internet. The life and death of my daughter has become a national news story. It's been picked up by CNN, Fox News, and MSNBC. This is going to be a long and painful process. The media will swarm Abilene, and my house, when the trial begins. I will keep the media from my son until he's eighteen. He's sick. He needs privacy. He needs help.

In the meantime, I now sit in my house and wait to visit Paris, and then I'll go to Seymour to spend the night at my mother's.

This house is ruined for me. I can't stand to be in any of the rooms except maybe my bathroom; even there I have to leave the curtain open to shower because I am afraid Paris will walk in and kill me. I walk into the kitchen and I catch sight of Paris, picking up the butcher knife. I walk down the hallway and I see Paris going into my bedroom, to the bed I shared with Ella. I see Ella sleeping, Paris standing over her. I try to picture Ella alive and happy but so many times my brain goes to the darkest places, bringing up images of her dying slowly, in pain and terrified, or pictures of her body after her death.

At least I can go to my mother's house now. We're talking again, working things out. But, really, I'm going so I can be with my little sister. She's only a few years older than Ella. To be honest, it's hell to be around her, she reminds me of what I have lost. But she is a child and I'm her big sister. She was so close to Ella. Children suffer too.

MARCH 4, 2007

My Ella Bella has been dead one month today.

Every day I grow more depressed. I went to visit my sister last night but woke up at 4:30 am with the compulsive need to be in this house. I didn't wake up anyone, just left. I don't want to be anywhere but in Abilene, in this house, with Ella.

When I arrived this morning, the door to my bedroom was shut tight, and my cats, Leo and Clair were in the room. I experienced such a strange feeling when I saw the door, because there is no way the cats could shut that door by themselves.

I don't know how I am going to make it through this. All I feel is utter despair or mind-numbing depression. I have brief moments of calm, but they usually don't last more than a few hours.

Quite often, I find myself talking to Ella and even praying every now and again. It helps in small ways, but not always in ways that last.

I miss you, Ella Bella. More every day. Please stay with me. Give me the strength to go on in this life without you.

During our visit today, Paris told me he had another hallucination last night.

This time Ella was lying on his bed at the Juvenile Detention Center. She had her back to him, facing the wall. She didn't move or speak; the bed was covered in blood.

I was horrified he experienced this hallucination. But maybe it is Ella, wanting me to know he is sick.

This sounds insane, but I still have to say it: I think Ella shut my bedroom door to let me know she is still with me, and then she went to Paris. I think she showed herself to Paris so he would tell me he saw her, and I could see he *is* mentally ill. How can I harbor rage against my thirteen-year-old son who is battling his own mind to such an extent he can murder his own sister? All I felt as he told me of this hallucination was sadness and compassion. He is scared he will turn into a "psycho homicidal maniac" because he has no control over his own brain. He lives in fear of himself.

I know how it feels to be afraid of yourself. If you can't be safe in your own head, how are you to be safe anywhere?

Each day I pray. I pray I continue to be given the strength to walk forth another day. I pray I continue to be given the gift of feeling my daughter's presence. I pray to continue to live in the love I have for my son and not give in to the anger and resentment that I also feel. I pray to make it through the night with my daughter at my side and, when I awake, I will continue to feel her presence once again.

My prayers were not answered. It has been one day, yet eternity has passed. My feelings are blunt. But not numb. I wish I were numb. I wish I were dead. All of this would be over for me and Paris would be the only one left. He would be all alone.

Part of me wants to inflict the same pain on him he inflicted on his sister and me. But would he even care? Could he feel that sort of pain? He's so different now than the Paris I knew. The Paris who would hug me and smile at me. Once upon a time I thought I mattered to him, but now I don't know.

Another part of me wants to live, to continue to be his mother, but I don't know how to do either of those things.

I live a life composed of hell and nightmares.

It's hard to think or talk about that night. Or those first two weeks, when I didn't sleep unless I was next to Ella.

The police had Ella for a few days, as they processed her body at the crime lab in Fort Worth, then she was sent back here, to a funeral home in Abilene. Her father, who never was a meaningful part of her life, decided now was the time to step in and try to take her body back with him to Alabama. I refused. Her memorial and ashes would be here, with me, where she had known love. Our funeral home would not release Ella without my consent.

Nor would they cremate the body without a signed release from him. This went on for two weeks, as my attorneys fought with his lawyer. The kind people at the mortuary would let me visit Ella whenever I wanted. They had her in a private room, on a padded table. There were flowers and I brought in a stuffed animal. She looked like Ella, but she did not feel like Ella. They had put her back together as best they could. She was dressed in clean clothes, most of her defensive and stab wounds hidden. Makeup covered the contusions on her face. Her beautiful hazel eyes were closed.

The staff gave me privacy. I would lie down on the table next to Ella; I'd trace some of her wounds and sob myself to sleep. I knew logically she wasn't there. But I couldn't let her go. She began to change, physically, her nails growing, her skin in the very first stages of decomposition.

Finally, after he was told he would be sued for past unpaid child support unless he got the hell out of town, Ella's father released her body for a cremation.

Now I sleep at home, with her ashes. I'm still not ready to release her.

MARCH 7, 2007

Ella Bella has been dead thirty-one days. My son still lives in the juvenile detention center. I pass my days in fear and grief.

I torment myself with wondering how she felt when she died. Did she know she was dying? What was she thinking as she died? Did she know it was Paris, her adored big brother, who was hurting her? Could she imagine that he could do such things to her? Could she imagine that anyone could? Did she call for me? Scream for me? Did she think I had abandoned her?

I pray she did not feel pain for long and that she thought of her mother who loves her. I pray she did not think I had abandoned her. I hope the stories of angels are true and angels carried her soul out of her body, ending her pain. I pray she could feel her mother's love and it gave her comfort at the time of her death. I pray she is able to stay connected to me so I may feel her with me from time to time. I pray for the strength I need to work through this nightmare.

Time has new meaning. Thirty-one days is eternity. It drags on horribly, slowly. I am cut off from my feelings. They are there, but I know I cannot get too close to them. If I do, I will disintegrate into sea mist like the little mermaid Ella loved to read about. Of course, it was when the mermaid became sea mist she was able to feel joy again.

Every moment I walk on a tightrope of contradictory emotions I can't fall off because all the landing places lead to more pain. I try to focus on my love for my son because if I fall off that side of the tightrope, I fall into a pit of anger, hatred, and wanting Paris to suffer, as I know my Ella Bella did. If I focus too much on Ella and my love and loss of her, I fall off that side into a deep abyss of desperation and grief, wishing and waiting for death to occur.

So I balance the pole and keep walking—desperate not to fall.

I hold Paris' hands when I see him. They are the same hands I've held since he was a baby. I used to kiss those hands. I used to play games with those hands. I used to have tickle wars with those hands.

When I hold them now, I hold the hands that brutally stabbed my daughter to death. I don't know what to think of those hands anymore. I love them. I hate them. I am scared of them.

As much as I miss my Ella, I have a hard time pulling up memories of the four years we had together. This tortures me and I feel guilt at my inability to remember more right now. I am so foggy. I have had signs she is still with me, but I haven't felt her with me these last couple of days. The tingling in my arm has been absent. I feel alone.

These are problems I have no power to fix. I cannot bring my Ella back from the dead. I cannot make Paris mentally whole again. I can no longer mother either of my children the way I do best. I don't understand how I get up and breathe every day. It grows harder.

Ella—I need you to stay with me a while longer. I need to feel your presence. I fear I cannot make it through this life without you or your brother. This is not the life I dreamed of for us. Especially you, my Ella Bella. I have no idea where your brother's life will lead. I have a life that is up for grabs because it is full of misery and murder. What if I don't have the strength to keep living it?

I am so sorry, Ella Bella. I failed you as a mother. I was not here to protect you.

I did not know I needed to protect you from your own brother.

MARCH 8, 2007: MORNING

I went to counseling today. Lawyers keep telling me not to see any therapists, that anything I say can be used against me, or Paris. I'm not sure how saying over and over again that I am in fucking hell is going to get anyone in any further trouble, but I've found a pastor to be my counselor. His records cannot be subpoenaed because it is pastoral counseling. He does not have to keep notes, just listen.

I'm not as numb as I thought: grief and pain are my constant companions.

I am now at the jail to visit Paris. I'm sitting in the waiting room, trying not to hyperventilate; there's a live-feed news truck outside. I don't know if it is here for me, or because the Texas Youth Commission may be indicted by the Feds for guards beating and raping the children —the TYC in charge of the juvenile facility where Paris will eventually be transferred. It doesn't matter why the truck is here. It doesn't change the fact I'm having a panic attack at the thought of being stalked by the media again.

MARCH 8, 2007: EVENING

I completely lost it tonight during my visit with Paris. He was indicted by the grand jury today. Capital Murder. There is no end in sight.

After seeing the therapist and then the news truck outside the center, I couldn't help but sob for most of the visit. There was a puddle of my tears on the table by the time I left. This is not what I want to do when I visit Paris, but I couldn't stop. Paris kept squeezing my hands in a show of support when I'd cry. I appreciated it, but at the same time, those are the same hands that killed his little sister and ruined all our lives. I try not to look at his hands because, when I do, I see blood on them now.

As we talked he preened in front of the small window, hoping to catch a glimpse of the reporters. "Do you think they can see me?" he asks.

He doesn't seem to care they are telling his story because he's a villain and did something evil. It seems all he cares about is they are talking about him.

In the room next door, there was a girl visiting with her dad. They were arguing, loudly, for a long time. The father was aggressive and yelling at her, "You're a slut! You're a whore! You deserve to be in here!" I finally went over and told him to shut up. He was ruining my time with my son, but I was also worried about the girl. She is in juvie because she skipped school and smoked weed. She didn't kill one of her siblings.

How do I manage not to yell at Paris for what he has done?

MARCH 8, 2007: NIGHT

I am exhausted. I have deep dark circles under my eyes. I have minimal motivation to do anything at all. I smoke constantly.

Tomorrow I go to get the last picture Ella drew, a butterfly, tattooed over my womb. I want something created by her hand on my body permanently. The picture was in her pre-school "journal," the one her teacher gave the kids for them to write out or draw their thoughts and feelings. Ella's earnest, meaningless scribbles, which she would point to and say, "This says I love you, Mama" . . . it breaks me to remember these moments, but I want more. She is forever in my heart and thoughts, but I need more.

How do I go on? How now, my butterfly?

Her teacher and principal have agreed to let me keep reading books aloud to her class every Friday, and so I do. I read and I leave. These moments provide one of the few things these days that give me a sense of continuity. The teacher and I think it's good for the kids to see me since they lost Ella so abruptly. She was friends with everyone, and they miss her.

I also go because children have a much better way of dealing with death than adults. They just tell you what they think. They don't stutter for the right words. They do not look at me like it's my fault Ella is dead, or Paris is a murderer. They ask me if I miss Ella and tell me they do, too. One even told me I should keep her toys and play with them when I need to smile.

Those kids, Ella's friends, they don't understand death. I don't try to explain it to them. I don't understand it either. But for these few precious minutes every week, I'm given unconditional affection, whether I have the answers or not, and I give them some sense of security (however false it is) that life goes on and stability exists.

I can't send Paris books, because the authorities consider it special treatment, so I've engineered a book drive for the entire juvenile detention center. It was finally approved, thanks to Shea, an aide of one of the state reps from Abilene. I am happy it will happen, but I'm also angry. Part of me wants to help Paris any way I can, but another part of me wonders why I should do anything for him after what he did. Why anyone should.

Nothing I do can help Ella. Nothing will ever bring her back to me. She is gone forever. Four years with her was not enough. A mother isn't supposed to outlive her children. Her child isn't supposed to be brutally murdered by her own brother. A mother isn't supposed to feel hatred toward her son. Supposed to doesn't mean shit.

The pain, grief, and contradictory emotions I feel will walk with me to the end of my days. I will never be the same again. I will never see Ella again. I will not watch her grow up. I don't know what will happen to my son. Either I will watch him grow up incarcerated or, at some point, I will lose him, too.

The days of my future appear dark. I don't know how to find the light anymore. My kids were my light and they made my days bright. I wish I could shut my eyes and make this go away. I wish there was a way to go back to what I had. Most of all, I wish I could have my Ella back.

But this is one instance where I don't have to be careful what I wish for. No matter how hard I wish these wishes will never come true.

MARCH 9, 2007

The emotional extremes I go through daily exhaust me. This morning I woke up depressed; closer to noon, I felt wound too tight. The first thirty minutes at the tattoo parlor, I felt I would burst. After Ella's butterfly tattoo was finished, I felt calm and peaceful, so I went to the bookstore to find a new book to read to her class. But then, when I went to visit Paris, I became very angry again.

Some days after I leave him, I hate him. Today he acted bored and smug. He kept drumming his fingers on the table and looking around the room. He asked me what I did in the free world, as if I get to do whatever I want while he is locked up, as if I am not locked in this nightmare because of him. It is his damn fault he is not free. He murdered my daughter.

He talked about wanting to get a tattoo to remember Ella by also. At that point the only thing I could feel was intense rage. What right does he have to remember my daughter? She would not be just a memory if it were not for him. She would be here with me, where she belongs, not dead. If not for Paris, I would not be living this nightmare.

Tonight, I hate him. I am plagued constantly by thoughts of what happened in that room: the pain Ella must have felt, the thoughts that went through her head, the terror. I don't even know when she died. Did she die while he talked on the phone with his friend? Did he kill her before he made that phone call? Could she have been saved?

He says he went to bed with her. He never did that before. He says suddenly he's lying next to a burning demon, that he's terrified, that he choked her first, then stabbed her, then pushed her away, then stabbed her in the back.

If that is the truth, why was there only one spot on the mattress covered in blood? If he was scared of what he said was a hallucination, how did he have the courage to reach out to strangle her, then get close enough to stab her to death? And of course, the biggest question, why would he bring that knife into the bedroom with him in the first place?

I hate my son.

Why has no one ever witnessed Paris having a hallucination? Hearing voices? Why do these things only occur when Paris is alone? At night?

Why did I give birth to a monster? Why is she dead and he's allowed to live and torment me?

I hate my son.

I hate my son.

I hate my son.

I hate my son.

I hate my son.

I miss my Ella.

Tonight, I can't stop thinking of how beautiful her eyes were when the sunlight hit them. Or how she wanted me to hold her when she went to bed, but when she was ready to sleep, she would move to the other side of the bed. When I got back in bed, she would cuddle up next to me—she was always so warm. Or how her nose would wrinkle when she was mad. Or how she would lean over and put her hair in the pool. Or how she liked to help me cook. Or what a slow eater she was. She would rather talk than eat. I remember what it feels like to nurse her. I remember how she liked to sit in my office trash can when she was a baby.

I miss my Ella. I miss my Ella and I want her back. That will never happen, and I'm stuck with Paris whom I love and yet grow to hate more every day. At times I find myself wishing he would kill himself. What right does he have to continue to live after murdering his own sister and destroying every happiness I have known?

All I have left of Ella are my memories, which are clouded with thoughts of how she died. My photos. Her green tutu. Her Converse skater shoes she loved, just like her brothers. Her toy animals she would play vet with. Her cat Oreo. A box filled with the ashes of what was once her beautiful life-filled body. None of that compares to what is was like to have Ella.

I hate my son. I love my son. How am I supposed to survive the pain of a heart divided?

What the fuck am I going to do? All I want to do is lie down on the floor and cease to exist.

MARCH 10, 2007

Weekends are not good for me. They never have been. I do not know what to do with myself when I have a lot of free time. Now that my kids are gone, I have nothing but "free" time.

During my visit with Paris today, I told him if I'm putting forth the effort to help him, then he has to put forth some effort, too. I'm beginning to pull away from him. As time passes it grows more difficult for me to not show my anger, to bite my tongue, to remain calm.

Right now, I'm just worn out.

Sometimes while I'm with him, or at random moments in the day, I focus on a spot on the floor and fill a large part of my mind-space with the image of me lying flat on my back on that spot, shutting down my organs one by one, willingly.

I imagine leaving my body and feeling a lightness of spirit I have not felt since the time I was five years old and found hundreds of caterpillars. It is one of my favorite memories, a memory from a time before my father was murdered. I woke up early one morning, and went outside to the weeping willow tree in the backyard. I loved the sound it made when it was windy; I thought a tree nymph was shaking her hair over me. I realized the trunk was covered with hundreds of caterpillars— the cute, fuzzy brown and gold ones. I ran back to the house for a big coffee can and spent the morning carefully capturing caterpillars. When I was done, I left the can in the shade of the screened-in porch. And promptly forgot about them. The next morning, I went to go check on them and found they had burst from the can. They covered the screens of the porch, which was now a moving patchwork quilt of color. It was beautiful. Life broke free. Life finds a way to break free of capture and confinement.

At some point, I always have to tune back in to reality.

My friend Robin came to town tonight, so I spent the evening with her and her mom. We talked about history and politics, things I haven't talked to anyone about for a long time. It was nice not to talk or think about the last five weeks of my life. Tomorrow she is going to help hang my butterfly lights, get boxes for the book drive, and go visit Paris with me.

So, I guess today ended up all right. I suppose I should be grateful for that, but all I want is to have Ella back.

I love you, Ella Bella. Wherever you are, I hope you know that and that you are at peace. I miss you.

MARCH 11, 2007

It seems that every day since Ella died lasts an eternity. No matter how short the days really are, they feel like forever. There are moments I wonder how long I can endure. I miss Ella so much. I yearn for her.

Every time I see a little girl with her mother, I want my Ella back. Every time I see Paris, I hate him a little more.

Today, he was a monster. He talked to Robin and me about a book he's reading, in which a father took revenge on two men who hurt his little girl. Paris said it reminded him how I always said I would only kill if someone hurt Ella. But yet I didn't. I reminded him I'd said I would only kill someone if they hurt my children, and that I was left in a difficult place since he was the one who killed her.

Why would he say something like that to me? It's as though he is trying to stab me with a knife made of words. He told us about other parts of the book, describing only the violent scenes. I listened in horror. He had a little smile on his lips as he spoke, as if he took pleasure in the violence. Was he clueless to how much he was hurting me, or was he doing it on purpose? Which would be worse? I can't even imagine how the detention center could allow him, of all the kids there, to get his hands on a book with that much violence in it.

He was a monster today—and I gave birth to that monster.

Even though he's my son, it becomes harder each day to love him. I go through the motions, but my heart is less involved.

My heart is with Ella. And she is gone.

MARCH 12, 2007: 3:00AM

My grief is a volcano. It lies dormant, but during dormancy the pressure builds. Cracks in the surface appear and small vents of sorrow, despair, and rage spew forth. When the pressure becomes too great, when I can no longer hold myself together, I erupt. Literally. Tears of molten pain pour from my eyes. My body is racked with sobs of longing and loss. Rage, the poisonous byproduct of murder, leeches the love out of my heart. Questions that will never be answered eat away at my thoughts and corrode my soul. The eruptions recede gradually—leaving me in a landscape devoid of all life, all love, all desire for a continued existence. Another layer of heaviness is laid upon me. You can't just shrug off the lava of primal despair and utter loss.

Today, the principal of the preschool pulled me aside and, very gently, suggested I not come back. He said I make the children uncomfortable; they are having nightmares. I've never talked to them about what happened to Ella, or about death. All we do is read and hug. I think I make the adults uncomfortable. Their capacity for being in the presence of so much grief, unspoken or not, was reached. Or maybe the kids really were weirded out that Ella's mom was there without her. Who knows? I don't know what's normal anymore.

All I see in my vista is pain. Everything else is gone. I am desolate and barren. I am alone with nothing but memories I cannot seem to access, a son I cannot seem to love, and a box that contains my daughter's ashes. I have a heart made to love but no one, nothing left to love. I have a child who brutally murdered his own sister. I know he needs help, but I'm losing all desire to help him. Instead, I want to see him hurt. I want to erase him from my thoughts, my memories, even my heart. Most of all, I want Ella back.

MARCH 13, 2007

Today I looked at my child for the first time convinced he murdered his little sister on purpose, in cold blood.

Paris sat two feet away from me and told me he had a dream last night in which he vividly remembered murdering Ella. He says when he woke up from the dream, he threw up.

"Why did you vomit?" I asked, thinking that maybe, finally, he'd show real remorse, not just defensiveness, boredom, smugness, or superiority.

He leaned forward, stared into my eyes as if hungry to see my reaction, and said, "I was upset because a small part of me felt pleasure in the act."

My son is a monster, and because he is a monster, I have lost my daughter.

I barely spoke a word after that. Something in me snapped. I cannot seem to feel anything, as if I'm dead now, too. He cried a bit, but it's an act. His tears were forced, fake. Crocodile tears.

I couldn't stop staring at him. I wouldn't hold his hand. I wanted to tell him I know he killed his sister on purpose; I know it in my gut. I'm finally acknowledging it is a more logical possibility than his demon story.

But I didn't say that to him. He will deny it. Or will he? What if I'm right? I don't know what to do if he looks at me and tells me, "Yes—I killed her on purpose." I will go insane. Everything I'm trying to hold on to will be lost.

No one was in the room but me. No one else heard what he said. That he "had a dream" in which he felt pleasure while he stabbed Ella Bella. It was not recorded. Juveniles have more privacy rights than adults, but right now I'm wishing they didn't.

The psychologist I hired doesn't think Paris is suffering from schizophrenia. Neither do I. Not anymore. I hoped for the longest time my boy was only capable of murder because of a mental illness he carries in his genes—his father, who left while I was pregnant, was diagnosed with schizophrenia when Paris was two, although he never displayed any signs until after he left us. Paris is smart enough to know this would be the perfect defense for him, that he "went crazy," but there is no evidence to support schizophrenia. And no one has been watched more closely than Paris the last six weeks.

I'll wait Paris out. I'll not speak freely to him, see what effect that has. Perhaps his true thoughts and feelings will expose themselves. I don't believe my son's story. He was not scared of a demon. I believe my instincts. I believe I gave birth to a monster.

I believe one of us will not make it through this ordeal.

I believe he did this to hurt me. Would he have killed Ella to hurt me? I would never have thought so before he did this. He had always been affectionate and loving with me. I thought we were close. But now, so much about Paris makes me suspicious: a combination of his behavior, his topics of conversation, his change in demeanor. I've heard from the authorities about their interactions with Paris and the terrible things he says to them, like how he'll kill their family members. He is playing at this "poor me, I am going crazy" defense, but the evidence against him is mounting and he's not pulling off "poor me" as well as he thinks. What I believe is his true nature—cold, calculating, drawn to violence—is seeping out of him in ways I do not understand yet.

My grief is overshadowed by rage. I'm tired of thinking about Paris. I want to mourn my daughter, my Ella. I don't want to be cut off from the feelings of love I have for her; I don't want them to be consumed by hate for my son. I want to forget Paris and walk away from him. I cannot. I'm bound to him the same as I am bound to my Ella. He is my son.

Reporters, women in the store, the neighbors, they all ask: Did you know?

Of course I didn't know. How could anyone know their child is capable of something like that until it happens?

But should I have known? That question hammers on my mind twenty-four hours a day.

If I survive this nightmare, it will be a miracle.

MARCH 18, 2007

It's Sunday. So many changes in the past five days.

On Wednesday, I showed Paris my anger for the first time. Before, I believed hallucinations made him do it, so I tried to protect him. But now . . . what do I believe?

I snapped at Paris over his obvious lies. I kept pushing him for answers, explanations. At one point, I said, "You said in your dream you felt pleasure. Is that real, Paris? Be honest."

Suddenly, he became angry, slapping the table. He shouted at me. "Shut up!"

It was the first time I'd seen any spontaneous, uncontrolled emotion from him since before the night he was arrested. I was taken aback when he flashed a look at me so dark and disturbed and hateful that I thought for the first time, *He could kill me. He wants to kill me.*

He stared silently at me the entire rest of the visit, stone-faced, his jaw clenched.

He has refused to see me since then.

I've learned so much more since that visit.

On Friday, I picked up my computer from the police. As I was leaving the building, one of the detectives stopped me on the front steps and asked if she could talk to me for a minute.

She confirmed Paris first hit Ella, then tried to strangle her. And then, the detective said, Paris stabbed Ella seventeen times.

Seventeen.

The officer also revealed Paris had been looking at "very disturbing" violent porn right before he went into the room to murder Ella.

I thanked her and walked away. My legs were rubbery. I almost fainted in the middle of the police department parking lot. I made it to my car, slid inside, and screamed at the top of my lungs, until I couldn't scream anymore. Cops walked by and just looked at me. They knew who I was. They left me alone.

I have no words left.

I am beyond grief.

I am dead inside.

MARCH 19, 2007: MORNING

The case against Paris continues to drag on. The detectives, the DA, and the defense attorneys are focused on getting autopsy reports back and interpreted, scheduling competency exams, asking me countless questions. Every ten days there is a review to determine if Paris should be released from custody while waiting for a trial or sentencing. Every ten days we all waive the right to the hearing. We know there is no way the judge is going to release Paris to anyone's custody since he has been deemed a danger to others. Even if I want him home, which I do not, the judge could not release him to me or anyone in the family because we are all his victims.

Paris still refuses to see me. He doesn't know how much I know now. But he knows I think he's lying, so he avoids me.

Yet, I show up every day at 5:30 just in case today is the day he lets me in. Every day the guards send me away.

I meet with his attorney tomorrow to get the visitation issue resolved. In one hand, I hold my rage because Paris is the one who gets to call the shots on this. In my other hand, I hold my despair because now I see neither of my children—Ella is gone, and Paris is not the child I raised. So much of who I was is gone. I can no longer mother either of my children. Emotionally, I swing all over the place: grief, rage, depression, anxiety, hopelessness, fear, doubt, hope, love, hate.

How could he have stabbed her seventeen times? I thought he loved her. How could I have been so blind? Why do I have to see so clearly now?

I'm falling apart. I'm shutting down, pushing people away. My core group of friends has dwindled to almost nothing. My mother and sister don't visit nearly as often. They leave me be, doing what I want them to do, I guess. I'm aware of how unhealthy this is yet do nothing to stop it. How can I? I want to spend my time alone. There is no one who can comprehend the nightmare of my existence—the pain and conflicting emotions. I know everyone in pain believes no can relate to them, but in my case, it is reality. According to the FBI, there are less than thirty-five cases a year of a sibling killing another sibling. Of those 35, most are not intentional or premeditated.

I no longer feel my Ella is with me. She is gone.

I am convinced Paris is evil.

I want so desperately to believe he's sick, but that's evaporating. He's only thirteen. He murdered his sister at thirteen. Stabbed her seventeen times. Fuck. Who does that? It's so alien to me, to think someone could do that. How do I love my son, knowing he stabbed my Ella seventeen times and *that part of him enjoyed it*?

How do I continue to do what's best for Paris?

If it were someone else who murdered my daughter, I wouldn't wonder how best to help them: I would want them dead. I might even kill them myself. If it were someone besides Paris, I wouldn't be paying their legal fees or worrying about what was going to happen to them. If it were anyone else but Paris, I wouldn't be torn between loving Ella's killer and hating him.

How do I grieve for my Ella when I'm collapsing in on myself? My heart has become a black hole. I am a living, breathing metaphor of the Big Bang theory. I know at some point I'm going to implode. When this happens, I'll either die or learn to live again.

MARCH 20, 2007: 2:35AM

Tonight I prayed for Ella to come to me in my dreams. And she did.

I was outside the same, white house from previous dreams. I held Ella in my arms, sitting in the same chair by the pool talking to her. Paris was somewhere; I could feel him. I was afraid he'd find us and hurt us.

Her weight and her smell were comforting, but Ella was very lethargic, sleepy, curled against me. Her wounds were healing. She was sore and tender. I lifted her shirt and traced the path of her stab wounds, traced the torn edges where the knife had gone in. She told me she hurt herself doing something, but she wasn't being honest. I told her I knew where the wounds came from. She didn't have to pretend. She held onto me and said nothing about Paris.

A man appeared behind me, standing on the steps of a cabin I hadn't noticed before. The door was rattling. I could not tell if the man was trying to get the door of the cabin open, or holding it shut.

I was terrified he'd open the door. I knew what was behind that door, contained in that cabin: Hell. My Hell. Something evil was in there, but the man looked at me while holding the door tightly closed and said, "Focus on her, be with her, don't think about this."

I hugged Ella; I knew it would be time for her to go soon. I asked her how to find her again. She whispered in my ear, just like she used to do, "You will always find me when you are here." At that, she disappeared.

I saw her! I held her! I talked to her!

I held my Ella. I saw her face. I spoke to her. I don't know who the man was, but he seemed so calm and serene and he kept the evil locked away.

I prayed to God before I went to sleep, first asking to guide my mouth while talking to Paris' attorney, so I would do no harm. I also asked God to tell Ella hello for me, to tell her I love her; I need to feel her. I prayed peace for Paris. I prayed to learn how to love again. I asked Ella to come see me in my sleep, when my defenses are down because when I'm awake my mind, my heart, and my soul are so heavy I cannot lift the burden of the bad to let any of the good in.

This is the second Ella dream I've been able to retain fully when I wake up. Strangely enough, when I woke, I was sleeping in exactly the same position Ella always slept in: on my back, with my right leg bent and my left leg straight. Both my arms were flung out wide. I never sleep on my back. Never.

I hope to see you again, Ella. Please stay close to your mama. Ella Bella, I love you.

MARCH 20, 2007: NOON

I'm exhausted but lighter in spirit. My dream of Ella last night gave me some joy today. I don't know how long it will last, but I'm grateful for even a moment of respite from the horror that has become my life.

It was so good to hold my Ella again. I told my mom about the dream. She said maybe it's Ella's way of letting me know she's okay. I want to think it's my little girl's way of telling me she was mostly unaware of what happened to her.

I called the detention center to check on Paris four times this morning. No one from that place ever returns my phone calls. If I get ahold of the supervisor, he gives me the runaround. I finally spoke to the probation supervisor. Paris still refuses to see me. They say when he's ready, they will let me know. It seems *he* is mad at *me. Fucking life.*

So much for a light spirit. After meeting with Paris's attorney, all light is gone.

I'm torn between helping my son and making sure he can't hurt another human being. I am torn between wanting to help him and wanting to hurt him. My gut tells me he did this to Ella, and me, on purpose, to eliminate her and watch me suffer.

The first psychologist found nothing wrong with Paris. It cost $15,000 dollars for him to come up with nothing. At one point he told me Paris might have a sleepwalking disorder. Are you fucking kidding me? Never, in thirteen years of being his mother, did I ever find him sleepwalking. I want to find out what is really going on with him, not just come up with some bullshit to get him out of trouble.

If I hire another psychologist who doesn't find anything wrong with him, I at least have the comfort of knowing I did everything I can do to help my son legally. But if there's nothing "wrong" with Paris, except that he likes to kill, and this doctor pulls a magic rabbit out of his hat to exonerate my son and he one day gets out to hurt or kill someone else—maybe me—I'll have that on my conscience. Or, I'll be dead.

His attorney made it quite clear to me today his job is to get Paris the lightest sentence possible. What that means is if no one can find anything clinically wrong with Paris, he'll then use my mistakes as a parent to argue there were mitigating circumstances which led Paris to do what he did. In effect, I will be the one on trial, not Paris. It would be made to be my fault Paris killed Ella.

I have no idea what to do, so for the time being I'll do nothing. I know at some point I'll have to decide whether or not to hire another psychologist.

For the time being, I need to remove myself from the equation. I am falling apart. I don't sleep—even if I take a sleeping pill. I'm high strung, under intense pressure, constantly feel on the verge of a nervous breakdown. I'm no longer whole and pieces of me are pulled in an infinite number of directions.

I smoke too much and my ability to function "normally" is nonexistent. I want all of this to go away. But it won't. I have no choice but to go through the hell my son turned my life into. I will never understand how my son was able to walk into where my Ella lay sleeping, hit her, then choke her, and finally stab her seventeen times—and now manages to keep himself together, sane and composed.

I am falling apart for the both of us.

MARCH 21, 2007

I made a small decision about my son.

After his attorney met with him this morning, my son says he will see me. Most likely, his attorney told him it would be a good idea because I won't agree to pay any more legal fees until I see him again. Not because Paris wants me in his life or because he needs me, but because he needs me to make sure he has money for his attorneys.

I will go see him tomorrow. I have not talked with him since I found out he didn't just stab Ella; he stabbed her seventeen times after he watched violent pornography. I won't yell at him. I won't accuse him of anything. I just want to see him, watch him like he watches me, and see if my instincts are right.

There is more he needs to tell me. He has successfully lied to me and deceived me for years about so many things. He was one person when he was with me, but another within himself.

I plan to make an appointment to speak to the District Attorney. I want to know my rights as the mother of Ella. I'm a victim also: my daughter was murdered. For the time being, my son and his interests are taken care of. It's time to focus on my daughter and me.

I'll do these two things, and then I'll think about the answers I get from the observations I make. Then I'll decide what to do about Paris—or decide what I'm willing to do *for* Paris.

I'll take myself out of his equation and focus on my life— what's left of it—and on Ella: my grief at losing her, my love for her, my memories of her—and then I'll attempt to discern what role I need to play in helping Paris, and in seeing justice is served.

Ella—I continue to love and miss you. Eternally.

MARCH 22, 2007:

Today I went to the juvenile detention center for the first time in a week to visit Paris. I was shaking like a leaf in the waiting room.

I didn't yell. I didn't accuse. I didn't say a word about the details the detective gave me. But I did stand my ground. I was able to stay calm.

I told him I knew what he did to my daughter. He asked what I knew, but I wouldn't tell him anything. I gave him nothing he can use to manipulate me. I left him in the dark.

I called his bluff. I know there's more than what the detective told me. I wanted him to be the one to admit to me the full extent of how he hurt Ella, and what made him do it.

"Somewhere in your mind, you know what you did. You will have to find a way to deal with it," I said, and his eyes were big. "You need to tell me the truth. Out of all the people in your life now, who do you think truly cares for you? Who else has your best interests at heart?"

He became emotional. He cried, yet I have the sense it's because he's scared of what's happening, or is going to happen, to him. Not emotional because of what he did to Ella, or what he has done to my life, but what might happen to him.

When I left the visit, I was confused as always. I begin to realize part of my dilemma is that I don't know how to stop being his mother. He is thirteen. Just a boy. My boy.

Being unable to stop being his mother sickens me, yet I understand it's because I *am* his mother, that somehow not being his mother goes against every feeling I have about being his mother.

What do I do? I seek and seek yet cannot seem to find a right or good answer to this question. To any question, for that matter. I need guidance. I don't possess the wisdom or the courage to make these decisions alone.

If you are there God, when you see my Ella, tell her I love her, that I am not forsaking her. I won't ever forget what she suffered. I won't ever forget I love her. Her life and its loss will not go unanswered for. I hold her in my heart every day. Every moment I'm awake and asleep I yearn to be with her. Every night when I go to bed, I'm desperate to see her, feel her, hold her in my dreams.

MARCH 25, 2007

In this one weekend, I've dealt with a visit from Paris's uncle, who at times was helpful and who, at other times, pushed me to the limits of decent behavior. I wanted to punch him in the face and throw him out of my house because of all his ridiculous insensitive comments, but the good Southerner in me prevailed. Even in the darkest time, good hospitality supersedes all.

Then, my mother called me upset because her current husband showed up late and drunk, when he was supposed to take my sister to the father–daughter dance.

Then, I tried to go thrift-store shopping with my best friend and ran into a mother and daughter who know Paris. They had no idea what to say to me, how to talk to me.

Then, there was a little girl who resembled Ella at visitation today. She was about two years old and kept asking where her Bubba was, just like Ella used to ask about Paris. I was overcome with grief, could not stop crying. I had to leave the room.

Finally, a very close friend called last night to tell me her sister was doing drugs. Then her husband called to let me know she was doing drugs too. She was high as a kite at Ella's memorial.

I am a sponge designed to absorb pain.

All I want to do is mourn my daughter and feel her in my heart. All these other issues—Paris, lawyers, doctors, friends, family—keep me from doing the one thing I want to do: hold the memory of my daughter close, cry for her, dream about her, love her, be with her.

God, grant me a reprieve. Bring my daughter to me. Grant me a reprieve. Bring my daughter to me. Grant me a reprieve. Bring my daughter to me. Grant me a reprieve. Bring my daughter to me. Grant me a reprieve. Bring my daughter to me. Grant me a reprieve. Bring my daughter to me. Grant me a reprieve. Bring my daughter to me. Grant me a reprieve. Bring my daughter to me. Grant me a reprieve. Bring my daughter to me.

MARCH 26, 2007

I meet with the DA in the morning. I want facts. I need them. It's time the people investigating my family tell me more about what they have learned. Tomorrow I go as a victim, not a suspect. It's time to let go of Paris a little and focus on my Ella.

I miss you, Ella. I love you, Ella. I'm about to begin to speak for you, my Ella. I'm going to start keeping my promise to you. I am going to create meaning from this. I'm going to do one thing each day that will bring me a little happiness. I'm going to live a good life for you, since you were robbed of the opportunity to live yours to the fullest. Maybe, in this way, I can bring a little bit of you back to me.

I love you, Ella. Mama loves you.

MARCH 27, 2007: LATER

I met with her. The DA.

I started by asking what my rights are as the mother of the victim. Not what I can do for Paris, but what can I do for Ella?

What does she need from me? Then I asked her to tell me what she knew about that night.

She didn't tell me everything, though she gave me details the detective hadn't shared. She gave me an overview. All this time, I've been answering the investigators' and attorney's questions, but I haven't asked them much. I wasn't ready for their answers. What more did I need to know? Ella is dead. Paris killed her. It wasn't until I discovered the way he killed her, that he stabbed her seventeen times, after first trying to choke her, that I realized I've been burying my head in the sand.

The DA didn't go over the autopsy report. She didn't have the investigators there to talk to me. She focused on what the Dallas FBI lab found on Paris's computer: pornography so distasteful it made her flinch to describe it. It wasn't Playboy bunny stuff. He was watching S&M, violent porn. Bondage. Sadism. She gave me titles and websites.

Paris searched for snuff films. Then he murdered his little sister.

He didn't find any, but what the fuck thirteen-year-old is Googling for snuff films? What the fuck thirteen-year-old even knows what a snuff film is?

The night he killed Ella he'd spent the hours leading up to it watching this hardcore pornography.

There's more the DA's not saying.

I can tell.

Just like I can tell this is a nightmare I won't, can't, wake up from.

MARCH 28, 2007

My visit with Paris today was a scene straight out of a horror movie.

I confronted him about the pornography on my laptop, how horrifically violent it is, how I know he'd searched for a snuff film. I pushed hard before he finally answered.

He said yes. He'd been looking the night he killed Ella, but it was so I would see it and get mad.

This is a theme I've heard from Paris before. The desire to make me mad, set me off, see me in pain. I asked him how anyone, especially me, was supposed to believe he didn't kill his sister for the same reason. Did he kill her to cause me pain?

His jaw clenched tighter and tighter. His eyes turned into black pits. His face was nothing but darkness. I was unnerved. I saw a glimpse, for the first time, of the person who would stab a little girl, his sister. Any little girl. Someone dark. Evil. Nothing but darkness. A primal look, nothing rational, no light.

The guard rapped on the window to call time. Paris opened his mouth. A millisecond before he said it, I knew the truth. Knowing did not stop the devastation of hearing it.

My son looked at me and said, "You're right. I *did* kill her."

Right before the guard walked him out, he peered intently into my eyes, said nothing, absorbing my agony.

For the first time in a long while, I saw something authentic on his face.

Pleasure.

MARCH 28, 2007: LATER

I believe him. My child. He killed his sister on purpose. To see me in pain. I believe he's a sick, twisted, monster of a boy. I believe he was angry with Ella for telling on him after sneaking out to the skate park the night before. I believe he was mad at me for making him apologize to the babysitter for lying to her about sneaking out, or because I chastised him for spending all his allowance.

I believe he looked at the pornography and grew sexually excited. I believe he killed his sister in a rage to hurt me. I believe he experienced sexual gratification from the act of murder. I believe he experiences gratification in proportion to every ounce of my pain and suffering. I believe he deserves to rot in jail. He doesn't deserve to be alive.

I believe he admitted this knowing there was no one in that room but me. No recording, no video. No one to witness his confession or his joy at hurting me.

I don't know what else to say. My child disgusts me.

MARCH 29, 2007

Another reporter found me and asked, like they always do, why did he do it? Did you know?

What they mean is: *How did you not know what he is?* And, *what did you do to him that turned him into a monster?*

My brain circles and circles and circles and circles over these questions. Why? *Why?*

Whyyyyyyyy??

I can come close to answering the how or what, but the answers don't provide any ease. Nor are they sufficient. My son *is* a monster.

How could I not know? I've gone over every second of Paris's life, from the second he was born. He was a sweet baby. He grew and cuddled and laughed. He was affectionate and he was loved. He was, is, so damn smart.

He did not pull the wings off flies or hurt the cat.

Later, when I asked him why, if he wanted to kill so badly, did he not kill one of our animals? His response to me was, "I would never kill one our animals. I love them."

Only in hindsight are there foreshadowings . . . but never enough to make me think, "Oh my God, Paris is a future killer." I assumed, like all kids, he was pushing boundaries and buttons.

The worst hindsight is probably the frogs. Paris was little, maybe three.

My mother owned a ranch in North Carolina. Her house was built into the side of a hill. There was a porch on the house; it must have been about thirty feet off the ground. When it rained, frogs came out like crazy; they were everywhere. One day, during a storm, I found Paris on the porch. He had fifteen or so frogs in a bucket and was dropping them off the porch, watching their bodies hit the ground thirty feet below.

I asked him, "Paris what are you doing?" He looked at me, told me he liked the sound the frogs made when they hit. Most of them were dead, but a few weren't so lucky. They were mangled on the ground, legs broken, barely breathing. I told Paris we had to put them out of their pain, end their suffering. He said he wouldn't do it. I had to kill the frogs myself.

There was the time he was twelve. I yelled at him for teasing his sister and aunt. He was supposed to be in time-out on the couch. Instead, he grabbed a knife from the kitchen and ran outside. When my mom and I caught up with him, he didn't threaten anyone; we had to grab his wrist to make him drop the knife. As soon as the knife fell from his hand, he collapsed to the ground, and I held him while he sobbed. I rocked him back and forth saying, "Paris, Paris, Paris, it's ok, Paris," soothing him like I did when he was a baby. It was terrifying to see him so out of control, so unhappy. By then, I knew he was dealing with depression, and justified anger, and so as a family we agreed he needed help.

I was worried he would hurt himself, not someone else. I took him to a psychiatric hospital. He was there for one week. They did nothing. There was no counseling. I was never given any assessments or diagnosis. I never once spoke to a doctor from the facility. When I requested he be discharged, no one said not to so I brought him home. I picked him up from the admissions office. I was provided with a list of counselors they suggested I follow up with. No one ever said the words suicidal/homicidal ideation to me.

Paris had friends at school. He is—was—well liked. No one thought he was weird, except for maybe the jocks. He was never cruel with Ella. He did older brother stuff, like occasionally steal her toys. He maybe poked her or teased her, sometimes to the point I was mad at him, but again nothing I haven't seen other older brothers do.

So what then have I done as a mother to make my kid a monster?

I know Paris was loved. I struggled with the feeling of being loved conditionally, so I thought, naively, that if I just let my children know they were loved unconditionally everything would be okay.

When I was young I had serious drug issues. When I was fifteen, there was a group who hung out and went to parties. We dropped acid, snorted coke, smoked pot, took pills, drank. By the time I was sixteen, being high on something started to become part of my routine, a needed thing. There wasn't any one drug I craved more than others. I just needed to be checked out.

When I was six years old, my father was executed in our living room; a murder my mom was charged with orchestrating but then acquitted of.

When I turned thirteen, my grandmother gave me a scrapbook filled with newspaper clippings about my mother's trial. She told me she knew my mother wouldn't talk to me about this part of her life. My grandmother knew I needed to know, because up until this point I believed my mom when she said she was innocent and had been framed. I read about some of the evidence presented at her trial. My mom admitted to the police she had discussed having my father killed before. Who talks about something like that? She would never voluntarily talk about my dad, so I started bombarding her with questions. All she said about him was that he cheated on her then asked her to break up with the women when he was done with them; he was a drunk; he was horrible; he never spent time with me; he was a criminal. Nothing good. Just bad. I started to think if my dad was so horrible then part of me must be horrible too, and that must be why I felt she didn't really like me or like being my mother. My mom likes to say I was the perfect child until I turned thirteen, then I went crazy.

My perspective is a little bit different. By the age of sixteen I tried heroin for the first time, and I knew I had found my drug, found the place I had been searching for, a place where no matter what I felt, I felt nothing. Things at home went from bad to worse. My mom was married to a piece of shit who has a thing for beating up women and old men. One day I packed my car with as much as it would carry, drove off, and moved in with my boyfriend. I did heroin every day. Some days I added cocaine, ecstasy, weed, mushrooms, whatever I could get my hands on. After a while the heroin didn't take me to the place where I felt nothing, but I was hooked. I had to keep shooting up to not get sick. I weighed ninety pounds, and almost lost an arm because of an abscess. I went home one day, begged my mom to put me in treatment. She said I was going through a phase and that I was weak. I remember telling her if she did not help me get help, she would be as culpable for my death as she was for my birth. I finally went to rehab and quit cold turkey.

After one brief relapse, I managed to stay clean for a year, but I was absolutely miserable. Without drugs to take the edge off of reality, life hurt. Then, during my sophomore year of college, I found out I was pregnant with Paris. I finally had something to live for, something to look forward to, something that brought joy, real joy, into my life.

I was two years clean when Paris was born, and I stayed off hard drugs for twelve years. I would have a drink or smoke pot, but it was nothing that impacted life in a negative way. I thought I was over being an addict.

When Paris was ten, I decided to start organizing and promoting concerts. There were late nights, the musicians, the shows … I fell. I relapsed, not on heroin. Cocaine. Occasionally meth. My business failed. I felt like a failure. My mom kept telling me that she told me my business was never going to work out. It snowballed. It wasn't an everyday thing, but at the end of my relapse, it was out of hand and ugly. Paris was angry with me. He had every right to be. It was a really hard time for us both.

I still can't believe I let myself go there, especially after what I already went through to kick my habit. As an adult, when I relapsed, it took me a couple of months to realize I couldn't control myself, but a few more months to manage to stop entirely. I didn't want to be high around my kids, and I didn't want to be disconnected from them. I was missing out on what was most important, their childhood. But I *was* high around my kids. I was not the best mother I could have been and I know I did damage.

By the time I got my shit together again, six months had passed and Paris resented me. He started to act out. He'd had to step up and take care of Ella on more than one occasion. Paris hated that we were struggling to make ends meet and so did I, but at least I was clean and there for my babies.

So, did my relapse turn Paris into a murderer? He was loved, even when I was at my lowest. And Ella loved him.

Oh my God. Ella. My little Ella. My little butterfly. She loved him so much.

How could he do that to her?

How?

MARCH 30, 2007

I spent most of the day alone. It's Friday night and I couldn't bear the silence of my house any longer. I went out to eat and have a couple of drinks, but now I'm home. Alone.

Nights like this are unbearable; nights where I need to be part of life again, only to realize I am so far removed from life it hurts. Going out for food and drinks, alone, will never replace the feeling of being with my children, my family. Those days are gone and nothing can ever fill the void that's left. Nothing erases the fact I come home to an empty house.

Did I do this? Cause this? I don't think so, but maybe? What if I did? I can't bear it.

Ella is dead. Paris is a murderer, her murderer. I am trying to pick up the billion shattered pieces of myself alone. Some days I have no pick-up left in me. Some days I can no longer exist. Some days all I know to do is get out of this house, eat, have a couple of drinks, and work the crossword puzzle at the bar, alone in a place full of people who have no idea what true evil, true despair, true grief, is.

MARCH 31, 2007

I spent the day with my mom and sister. I enjoyed my mom's company. I'm glad we are back on good terms. For now, though, being with my sister is too much. Being around her too long makes me miss Ella, because I see what I'm missing. When I see my mom with Little Sis, it reminds me I am not with Ella. When I hear Little Sis' laugh, it reminds me I will never hear Ella laugh again. I want to enjoy my little sister, but when has pain ever been enjoyable?

I am dead inside. Nothing inspires or motivates me. Most of the time, all I can do is sit alone to read or write. Even that grows difficult. I am immobilized—by grief, by powerlessness, by anger, by depression, by everything that has happened since February 4.

All I know to do is keep breathing. Some days that is difficult. Some days that feels impossible.

I'm going to church tomorrow. I am not looking for religion. I'm looking for a way to be with my daughter. I'm looking for spirituality and wisdom, the greater energy the minister spoke about in a sermon last week. I don't necessarily buy his dogma, but he is tapped into the spiritual world. He has a tell: true peace in his heart.

I must continue down the spiritual path. Something tells me it's the only way to go if I'm to live again, to be with my daughter again, feel whole again.

I don't know what else to do or who else to lean on. No human can truly understand. No human can show me a way to deal with this nightmare. I'm afraid I must wrestle with God in order to be anywhere other than where I am right now.

APRIL 3, 2007

The detectives told me they found sperm on my mattress. On Ella's body.

I did not think it possible to be broken any more.

I was wrong.

My shattered pieces are now ground to dust. The more this nightmare unfolds the less capable I am of writing. Words never convey what I feel. This problem is compounded by the fact the longer this nightmare persists the sharp numbness I feel becomes sharper while I become blunter, duller, less filled with the desire for life.

I'm now convinced evil exists. I see it more and more, every day, in my son. I saw it in him yesterday. He dropped his mask completely. For good. He no longer tries to hide his true self.

When I expressed what sorrow I feel when I see him, he laughed at me. I asked, "Why do you laugh? What could possibly be funny about anything right now?"

"You are all so fucking stupid."

He says he finds it amusing we thought he was so intelligent, so gifted, so creative. He's proud he was able to trick everyone. He told me he's come to realize he's a sadist because a boy in class was irritating him and all he could wonder is what it would feel like to stab his pencil into the artery in the boy's neck, to watch him bleed out, to die. All because he was irritated in class.

"Seriously. Fucking stupid. All of you."

At that moment, I felt such pity and compassion for my son because he could not see the truth.

"We are not the stupid ones, Paris. You are intelligent. You are gifted and creative, but you chose to waste that to become this person. There were a thousand other choices you could have made that night, and this is the choice *you* made."

"Did you kill your sister on purpose, Paris?"

He's already said he knows he killed her, not a demon. I wanted him to say it out loud; say he did it because he wanted to, that he was completely in control.

He didn't answer. I asked again.

Suddenly he threw his chest out and looked at me with this horrible look he sometimes gets. A smile, a smirk; not a smile of joy and happiness; a smile of hate. A poorly hidden grin that said, "Wouldn't you like to know? And by the way, I enjoy watching your pain."

He's lying about what happened. He killed my Ella because he wanted to. He has desired to hurt someone for a long time. He's been perverted for a long time. Somewhere in his head there's a connection between sex and violence. The night he killed Ella, he finally brought his sexual and morbid fantasies into reality. He killed my Ella intentionally. She died a horrible death because he's sick and evil and perverse.

He won't get away with it. I'll do my best to have him institutionalized; to make sure he receives mental help. I'll also do my best to make sure he's kept away from the public, unable to hurt another person. Ella's death will be answered for. He will be held accountable.

The death of my daughter, the decay of my son, opened my eyes to the existence of evil. At the same time, the existence of God has been made plain for me to see too. God has shown itself to me in dreams, in the people it has placed in my life, in the ability to get up and make it through every day, in the butterflies and the heat of sun on my legs.

I see the horror and beauty around me, inside me. I see life is nothing but a beautiful nightmare. A beautiful nightmare I will dream until I die.

APRIL 8, 2007

As time passes, as I find out more about the night Ella was murdered, I find it difficult to write about it. I find it difficult to do anything.

Now I know for sure Paris didn't do this as a spur of the moment decision. His actions were premeditated. Fucking premeditated.

I've seen the deposition of one the kids who hung out with Paris at the skate park. The boy told the detectives Paris had been talking about a pumpkin headed demon for months before the murder, something he'd read about in one of his books. This same witness could not have known about Paris's "hallucination," since it had not been made public.

Paris had been preparing, and practicing, his story, his explanation for his actions that night, for a long time.

It's time for me to let go of my son, for now, and keep my promise to Ella. I promised her I would live a life she would be proud of. I promised her I would find joy again. I don't expect this to be easy, but I made her a promise. I always try to keep my promises to my children.

Her birthday is coming. Her fifth birthday.

Life will never be the same without her.

APRIL 9, 2007

Another day and I wonder what to write. Another day I feel compelled to put something on paper.

When I visited Paris yesterday, I told him I would no longer allow him to lie to me, play with me, or get any satisfaction from manipulating me. He won't be able to do this if I'm not there. I told him I plan to visit less for the time being. He did not ask me to keep coming. He did not care.

I also told him I love him, very much. Murdering Ella hasn't stopped me from loving him. It has only made me question how to mother him.

APRIL 11, 2007

It's the night before Ella's fifth birthday. I'm not well. All day I've thought of what we would be doing today.

She would have been so excited tomorrow is her birthday. We would have picked up her cake. She would have asked what her presents were. We would have talked about her party. She wanted to celebrate at Chuck E. Cheese with her friends. At bedtime, we would have talked about the day she was born. I would have told her how scared I was to give birth at home. I would have told her how painful it was to birth her naturally, but how none of that mattered as soon as she was placed in my arms for the first time.

I would have told her to enjoy her last day of being four because she was never going to be four again.

Now I have to tell myself she will never be anything beyond four. She will never celebrate her birthday again. She doesn't get to close her eyes and make a wish when she blows out her candles. She doesn't get to eat whatever she wants all day long, go or not go to school, or open her gifts. Never again will she know the joy her birthday brought me.

Paris and Ella's birthdays were a special day for me because we all celebrated the day I was given the gift of finally knowing both of my children.

I bought Ella a cake and candles. I'm going to light them at 9:16 am—the time of her birth and the official start of her birthday. I'm going to sing her "Happy Birthday." I bought her a birthday card, so I can write her a message, seal it up, and keep it in a special place. I'll do it for Ella, to celebrate the life she had, to celebrate the joy of her birth, in the hope that wherever she is, she'll feel my love for her.

I'll do it for Ella because Ella would want to celebrate her birthday with love and joy, not the pain and grief I feel. Her birthday shouldn't be about loss. It should be about the day she was given the gift of life. It should be full of love and laughter and hope and joy because that's what the gift of Ella was. She was laughter. She was joy.

And somewhere she's about to turn five while remaining ageless. Somewhere she's still loving, still laughing, still hopeful, still joyful, and it's these qualities of her I'll try to hold on to, to remember about my Ella.

Happy birthday, Ella Bella. Your mama loves you very much.

APRIL 14, 2007

Today, for the first time, I truly begin to doubt my ability to live through all this.

In the visitation room yesterday, I asked Paris about the sperm found on the bed next to Ella. I told him I knew he told the cops the sperm was there because I was a whore; that it was not his, that it came from all the non-existent men he claimed I was having sex with.

"We both know it was you, Paris. I don't think you tried to have sex with her. I think killing her got you off. I think you orgasmed while you, because you, murdered your little sister."

He became enraged. His face completely changed from my Paris into the Paris who killed Ella. He slammed the table into me, pinning me against the concrete wall behind me. He cut off my air. I was in shock, paralyzed. I thought I was going to die there.

Then he pulled the table back, I caught my breath, and he slammed it into me again.

The table became his weapon. Despite what he did to Ella, there was still a part of me that believed he would not hurt me. That part of me is no longer naïve.

Finally the guards ran in to restrain him. He fought like a wild animal caught in trap. It took two grown men to restrain him. He kept screaming he was going to kill their kids if they didn't let him go. For the first time in my life I felt pure terror. I saw the person who killed Ella. As soon as the guards took him down and dragged him out of the room, I took off as fast as I could, running out of the detention center. I got in my car and tore out of the parking lot, driving while having a breakdown. I was in shock. I was terrified. And I felt like a fool.

He brutally murdered his own sister and I dared think he would never hurt me?!

I can find no reason to keep on living except that I don't want to die. But what's left to live for? My daughter is dead. My son is a cold-blooded sexual killer. And I'm alone.

What did any of us do to deserve this? Why did this happen to my family? My Ella? What is so wrong with my son for him to have done what he did, become who he is? Why do I even try to get through this? What for? I can never have Ella back. Paris will never be the same again. I will never be the Charity I was before.

What's the point?

APRIL 15, 2007

Paris told my mother at visitation tonight that the night he killed Ella he walked into the bedroom and began by hitting and strangling her . . . .

APRIL 17, 2007: 1:30AM

I'm doing my best to avoid the bed, because in twelve hours I find out exactly what my Ella suffered at the hands of her brother on the night of February 4. I need to know from someone other than Paris what he did. Paris only speaks half-truths, and those are delivered to hurt me. I need to know the truth from people who aren't trying to destroy me. I am scared to hear the truth.

I know it will destroy me. I'll hold in my heart every memory and detail from the day my daughter was born *and* the night she died. I will also hold in my heart the memory of who Paris was before he became the murderer of my Ella *and* what my son is now capable of.

How does a mother reconcile these two aspects of her child? How does she do this for both children at once? How does one heart hold all that? How does a mother live with this?

I'll soon have answers, but nothing will ever give me understanding. I'll soon have truth, but will it help me find peace?

APRIL 19, 2007

For two days now I've known Paris tortured Ella. Not just murdered. Tortured. He admitted this. The detectives and blood experts confirmed, and forensics verify, his stabs were slow and methodical, not frenzied, not an uncontrollable rage. Seventeen stabs wounds. Not all were deep. Most were shallow jabs and punctures. He told the detectives he stabbed her and pulled the knife out slowly; that it felt like stabbing a mattress or a marshmallow. Ella had also been hit very hard in the head and choked. She had defensive wounds.

She was fully awake to feel fear and terror; she was beaten; she was choked, tortured, stabbed, and murdered. Her chest, her abdomen, her legs, her back, all the places I have dreamed about, were covered in stab marks.

For two days I've known this and for two days I have been dead inside. I can't cry. I can't yell or rage. I can do nothing but be withered and numb. I get up. I eat. I meet with psychiatrists. I email. I function, but my mind is not connected to my body. My mind does not exist.

The DA and the experts answered all my questions—and now the shift is complete. There are no more *what-ifs*. Paris *is* broken. Extremely broken.

Everything I do is meaningless when faced with the reality that my beautiful Ella was beaten, choked, tortured, murdered, and died in pain and fear, without her mother, at the hands of my sick, disgusting, and pathetic son.

I exist only for two reasons right now: to make sure my son is locked away for as long as possible, and to find out the full truth about what happened to Ella.

APRIL 19, 2007: LATER

Today Paris was indicted for capital murder. I don't believe the full truth has surfaced. As much as I know, I am certain there is more. I'm not done with my son yet, but I want nothing to do with him directly. He'll answer for what he put my Ella through. I'll find as much of the truth as possible so there's no possibility he ever escapes retribution.

For two months he's lied to me. For two months he's played with me. For two months he's known exactly what he did to Ella. For two months he's experienced satisfaction from his cat and mouse game with me. For two months my existence has deteriorated into a nightmare. For two days I've been dead while still alive.

I wonder how long I can live this way. How long can I exist with no light in my soul, surrounded by darkness? The darkness is eating me piece by piece. There is no room for light when my thoughts are of nothing but pain, suffering, blood, torture, beatings, suffocation, sexual perversions, secrets, lies.

I am ceasing to exist.

What he did to Ella transcends words or explanations. It's abhorrent for me to imagine what my Ella felt that night. No one can begin to imagine the physical pain and the emotional terror she felt knowing it was her brother hurting her, terrorizing her, and ultimately stealing her life from her. At what moment did she know she was dying? Did she feel betrayed? Did she call for me and wonder why I wasn't there to stop her brother, to make her feel better like all the other times I did when she was in pain or scared? Did she know she was deeply loved by me, or were her last moments so filled with anguish she was completely consumed by the terror inflicted on her?

My son brutally took the life of my daughter, a child of four years old. He broke the law of Texas. He broke the law of family. He broke all moral and ethical laws. He broke the laws of love and respect and decency. He broke the law of nature. But above all he broke the law of God. The gift of life is a God-given gift; death is a natural progression of that gift. Ella's death is not a natural progression of the gift of her life. By taking it from her, Paris decided he had the authority and power of God to take it away.

"Thou shalt not kill." It doesn't get any clearer than that; it's black and white. There's no gray in what he did to Ella.

There's no reason, or illness, or tragic life story that excuses what he did—nothing but willful, cold-blooded murder, the taking of a life that was not his to take.

Whatever the outcome of this nightmare, I know he'll try to find an answer others find acceptable for what he did to Ella and his answer will be pitiful. Judgment comes in many forms and in many realms.

All I can do is hope that love, too, comes in many forms and in many realms. Hope that one day I will see my Ella again, and when I do, she will be whole and at peace.

APRIL 22, 2007: 6:00 AM

I just had a horrible dream about Paris. He, Ella, Ella's father, and I were at the old house here in Abilene. Ella and I were in the kitchen. Paris was upstairs. He came out of his room and was upset and agitated—he was mentally falling apart. He was talking nonsense while leaning over the railing of the stairs. I asked him what was wrong. He leaned too far, fell, and hit the floor in the living room. I ran over to him, held him in my arms, and asked him if he was okay. He wouldn't respond, so I said, "I need to take you to the doctor."

I meant I needed to take him to a mental institution. I knew nothing was broken, so I asked him to go upstairs and get dressed because he was in a towel. He said he couldn't get up, so I asked Ella's father to go get Paris some clothes. I again asked my son to get up, to go get dressed, and again he said he couldn't. I began to get irritated, so I asked him why. I was holding him, he looked at me, and he plunged a knife into my stomach.

I knew instantly everything he had staged it all just so he could kill me.

My eyes flew open and I was wide-awake.

APRIL 29, 2007

My Ella has been dead almost three months. It took ten minutes, hopefully less, to extinguish her life. How long will it take to extinguish mine? I wonder if my son wonders the same thing.

It grows harder to write. The words I use ... lonely, depressed, sad, angry, betrayed, grieving ... they all sound hollow, lacking, utterly not up to the task of describing my feelings, my state of mind, my existence. I feel so much, yet I feel numb. I am so full of pain I am hollow. My day begins and ends with the same thought: my family is gone, and I will never understand why.

MAY 22, 2007

I think this house is killing me. I can't sleep. I can't concentrate. I'm lightheaded. I have to get out of this house. All I think about here is what happened to Ella here.

JUNE 7, 2007

After thirty-eight days of praying to die, today I made the decision to live. I know for certain I'm not meant to die. Not yet, not now, not because of this. There is something I'm meant to achieve in this life, and I haven't achieved it yet. When I do, I'll find my Ella again.

And maybe save my son.

JUNE 10, 2007

I've discovered what it is that makes a woman beautiful. The shape of her physical being is beside the point. The shape of her soul is the only point worth being made. The quality of her heart has a way of shining through; transcending the physical to display the spiritual.

When I look at myself now, I no longer see a flat stomach or defined biceps. Instead, I see a woman who manages to survive despite having the odds stacked against me. I see past my features and see other qualities—feelings authentic and binding, not corporeal. Feelings - love, pain, grief, anger, empathy, longing. A woman's beauty should be measured by the sum of her experiences divided by her grace under stress.

Life is increasingly stripped bare. It's no wonder my emotions feel so pristine and raw. I have faced evil, been filled with love, and refrained from public bitterness when it is, by all means, my right to be bitter at the life I have lived—involuntarily and voluntarily. I have moments when I think all is lost, and moments when I can see the possibility of survival.

I think I'm all right, though. Something tells me even though I'm trying so hard, I will be okay even if I give up trying at all.

My beauty will shine through.

JUNE 11, 2007

I wonder if anyone besides me notices how quickly I'm deteriorating. Can other people tell when a soul is under siege? Can they smell my death wish when they're close to me? It seems to others I appear to be holding up admirably well. Privately I have gone insane. All the markers are there. I'm on the edge, about to implode. I taunt death. I find myself being reckless, tempting fate. I want to die, but I can't kill myself. That doesn't stop me from driving too fast, from drinking, smoking, eating too much.

I have the feeling I won't die no matter what I do or try. It's either my fate, or my punishment, to go on living the hell that is my life.

I am lost, abandoned. I have cut myself off from everything and most everyone. I don't want to connect with anyone. I want to stay lost in my thoughts because I know that is where I will find myself. I no longer know who I am or what the point of my life is. I wonder how long I can maintain the illusion of coping before the cracks become apparent to others. I'm damaged goods. I've lost it all.

It's yet to be seen how I will weather this. Right now, I could go either way. I could pull it together, or I could say, "Fuck it all" and go off the deep end.

I can't decide. I can't commit to living again—that feels sacrilegious, wrong, but I also can't commit to falling into the abyss. I'm resigned to being one of the walking dead. My body is stuck in the land of the living while my soul walks in the land of the dead looking for Ella. No matter how I break it down, I find no good reason to continue this pathetic existence, yet I hold tenaciously onto it.

It would so much easier to be dead.

JUNE 12, 2007

I checked out today. I've been in my own little world. I want to stay awhile. I possess no motivation—no drive—to be in public or to socialize. I want to tell everyone to leave me alone, fuck off, let me breathe unencumbered by social conventions.

I'm not doing so well right now, but I think I can pull it off okay. Or not. For all I know, I'm off my rocker. My perspective is warped after what Paris did to our family. I don't take good care of myself; I don't care enough to force myself to. I can't believe or accept the reality that this is my life now. My life is Ella. My kids. This is not a life.

Hiding is about all I can handle.

I miss Ella. I want her back. Or I want to follow her. I don't want to live in this world without her.

But then he would win.

The sun comes up, the sun goes down, and each day I still manage to breathe. Although not very well. I'm going back to bed, where I'll think some more. Always thinking.

JUNE 14, 2007: MORNING

The path leading to hell is not a straight and sudden drop; it's a vicious downward spiral traveled in slow motion. I have moments of peace, yet they remain too elusive to sustain for any notable length of time. These days my forte is sustaining and enduring ridiculous amounts of pain. I'm weighed down by it—literally. I am so heavy, so tired, I cannot sit up sometimes. I'm mentally wiped out. I barely have the energy to stay home and melt.

Funny how in a world as large as this one, populated by billions of people, I feel completely alone, in my own world, right here in my kitchen. This shadow existence—this is my world now.

Paris should have killed me that night.

I wish he killed me that night.

July 1, 2007

It's been almost five months since Paris tortured and killed Ella. I still breathe ... barely. My soul and emotions were thrust to places they will never come back from. I'm still not convinced I'm not slowly losing my mind while keeping up a damn good front for most, even myself.

The other night I went to dinner with friends. The entire experience was beyond awkward. When I wasn't crying, I was speaking randomly, uttering nonsense not at all related to whatever was being talked about, like someone having a conversation with their hallucinations.

I don't want to talk to anyone about how I *really* feel, how I *really* think. Not even to myself. I want to be deaf to myself.

All the thoughts and feelings happening inside me are chewing me up and spitting me out. For a bit I was sure I was losing my mind. I started antidepressants. The edges are off, but I'm not engaged. I exist in my own little world. No matter where I am, talking or quiet, alone or not, I'm always in a place no one else can grasp, a place I can't even find myself in.

Right now, I want to see Paris through these legal proceedings. He waived his right to a jury trial, but the judge can't render a sentence until the investigations are complete and the findings presented to him. Everyone is waiting on the full autopsy results and the DNA results from his semen on the bed.

After Paris is sentenced, I want to disappear for a while. I will buy an RV and take off on the road—solo. I crave isolation. I'm tired of drama, gossip, murder, pain, loss. I want quiet and solitude. No obligations. Peace of mind. At least for a while.

If I try to look too far into the future all I want is to die. The view is too bleak. If I focus on just one day, I can pretend I can make it through; pretend I am alive; pretend I have a purpose.

JULY 15, 2007

I went to see Paris.

I made the comment I couldn't believe this is our life now. He thought a minute and said the worst part is all the waiting.

I looked at him with disbelief and reminded him the worst part is Ella is dead, even worse she died horribly, and the absolute fucking soul crusher is she is forever gone to me while I live in this body. The part that really kicks me when I'm down is he doesn't realize what constitutes the worst parts of this situation. He only thinks about himself, while I think only of Ella and Paris, yet it does nothing to bring either of them back.

They're gone. What is done is done. I've lost it all. What more is there to say? I will never have Ella back no matter what I do, no matter how badly I hurt, or how much I wish for it. Ella, as I knew her, is gone from me for now.

I will never be able to forget what Paris did to Ella. His act of murder will always be between us. Bigger than that is the fact I will never be able to forget Paris is my son. I keep my promises. I love him. No matter what. I will always be his mother. No matter what.

No, the worst part is not the waiting.

AUGUST 29, 2007

It's has been a long time since I last wrote. This is because I'm not sure what to say. The last six months have been a hell I, many times, found almost unendurable. I exist in a void, yet the irony is, although I'm in a completely disconnected world of my own, all my pain is locked in here with me.

My pain has become my demon. At times I believe I'll crumble. At times I feel nothing at all. Always, somewhere in my mind, there is the thought life can be so much better than this. Life, I know, can feel good and be beautiful.

Just not for me. I had good and beautiful beyond compare in Paris and Ella. Now I have nothing but time. And pain. And thoughts. Lots and lots of thoughts.

How am I doing? I don't know. How am I supposed to be after the last six months? Like it or not, want it or not, I'm alive in some shape, form, fashion, but I don't know what the hell I'm doing anymore. I'm not sure I care anymore. I don't know if I'm shutting down or letting go or beginning to live again. Or am I simply going insane gradually, thought by thought, feeling by feeling, ounce by ounce?

What I am doing is waiting.

Waiting to die.

Waiting to be with Ella again.

OCTOBER 21, 2007

Paris was sentenced to forty years for killing Ella. I've been on the road for six weeks now. The last two and a half days I have been parked in New Orleans and done almost nothing. I took a cab to Circuit City so I could buy a camera. I want to walk next door to the St. Louis Cemetery Nos. 1 and 2 to take photos. They're the two oldest cemeteries in New Orleans.

I couldn't stop crying on the cab ride. We were stuck in traffic, on a bridge, and my tears would not stop. I wasn't sobbing. I was deeply mourning. I just could not stop my tears. The driver, a man in his sixties, kept looking at me in the rearview mirror, concern in his eyes. He finally asked me what was wrong, so I told him. He didn't change the way he looked at me like most people do after they hear my story. No pity or fear darkened his looks in the rearview. He just thought a minute and then told me that from now on I was going to be everyone's "well-it-could-always-be-worse girl." When I leave a room, everyone I come in contact with would feel hope because, if I can survive my life, they can survive theirs.

"That's great and all, but how the hell does that help me?"

"The ability to give people hope is a gift you will one day understand the value of. Trust me on that one."

Yesterday I promised myself I was going to do two things: buy a camera and walk next door to the cemetery. Once I got back to the RV I couldn't talk myself into completing the next step. I can't make myself walk to the cemetery literally across the street.

It takes me days to convince myself I still have what it takes to accomplish something as simple as walking less than a half mile to take pictures of tombs. I'm so depleted, so drained of any emotion that makes life appealing to me. Gone … all the joy, all the wonder, all the excitement. There's only one thing left in this life that matters to me, and he's the reason I'm in this hell in the first place. He cares nothing for me. He's a murderer. He's colored my world so black that even with the sun all around me I see nothing but black.

I spend all my time thinking. I'm enslaved by my thoughts except for when I sleep. Then I am locked in with my nightmares. I still don't know if I'm sane or have lost my mind. I don't think it matters. Sane or insane, my thoughts are simply one track: my children and all that has happened in the last eight months.

I exist in a world created by Paris' destruction. Life before February 4, 2007, does not exist. I don't know if I need to forget in order to remember or remember in order to forget. I know once I reach a certain place in my memories, my heart is torn in two and I can't breathe. My mind clamps down and pushes all that pain out of my way. I can't function when I think too much about all I've lost.

Sometimes I think the simple fact I'm alive is enough right now. If I want to sit in New Orleans doing nothing, it's my right. It amazes me I'm in one piece; I've lived in such torment since Ella died. Other times I think I'm alive for a reason and I'm wasting something—that I'm supposed to be doing so many other things than what I'm doing now. I just can't get the energy I need to do anything for more than fifteen minutes, much less follow through on something of an important nature. Shit, it takes me four hours to get in the shower after I wake up in the morning.

I can't be everybody's it-can-always-be-worse girl. Even Atlas shrugged.

I think I'll attempt to shower ... in the next fifteen minutes or so.

NOVEMBER 3, 2007

I'm now thirty-four years old. I live in my RV in Austin, Texas. My son is three months into a forty-year prison sentence. Ella and I have been dead ten months.

I smoke too many cigarettes. I drink a lot of wine. I can't function if I forget to take medication two days in a row. I barely function when I do. All I do is sit around, walk the dogs, eat, drink, smoke, shop, and think. Always thinking.

To some people it may look like I have a life, but I don't. I do things, but they mean nothing. I have money, but no family. No love. Nothing. I am lost. I am nothing. Everything I've done has meant nothing. My children are gone.

I have nothing but memories of a dead daughter and a murderer for a son.

I've begun the process of changing my life. I can't keep living in my RV trying to run away from Paris, from this horror, so I bought a house in San Antonio. I stopped taking antidepressants. I still smoke too many cigarettes. And drink too much wine. And eat too much. I quit talking to my mother. She has no idea how to help me, so she ends up hurting me more. She has no idea where I am. I've instructed everyone who knows where I am that where I live is confidential information. No one at the Texas Youth Commission knows where I am. Paris won't know where I am.

I will no longer be anyone other than who I am, flaws and all. I will keep my promise to Ella. Or at least begin to. If I have to live this life a bit longer, I will make it mine. I feel like a can of worms waiting to be opened. I don't know who I am yet, but I know Paris created a formidable adversary for the years to come. I love him. I'll do whatever it takes, feel whatever I have to feel, to try to save my son before my time is up. And if I can't save my family, then I will find ways to save others.

Grief has a way of making every second of every minute of every hour of every day the most acutely felt moment of pain you've ever experienced. It overwhelms your senses, thoughts, feelings, instincts. Everything is gone; you exist in a void. I had to make a choice: live or die. The only thing that keeps me alive is the rigid and stubborn belief that the only way to be with Ella again is to see this story through to the end as best I can.

In order to do so, I pay a high price.

I am meant to do something. Something big, maybe not, but something good. Of that I'm certain. I have become very certain I am, in my own way, insane. There's no good way to explain exactly what I mean by this. I exist in my own world. The landscape is increasingly bizarre and distorted. I try to remain open. I know I've been well guided thus far. I feel Ella more and more, especially when I listen to music. I hold fast to facts I know to be true despite all the evidence to the contrary:

1. Love is the only thing I have left.
2. I must stay open to life. I cannot shut down or shut people out. That only shuts me in.
3. I am not the crazy one. Or, more accurately stated, I'm the least crazy of those of us left.

Ella is with me. Whatever powers that be who pay close attention know I too pay attention now.

My only choice is to keep breathing. I've been burned before and always reemerged from the fire. I am a phoenix. This fire has been all-consuming, unlike any I've ever endured. I'm still engulfed in flames, but I feel my core begin to harden. When I come to be again it will be a version of me still unimaginable.

Or I will cease to exist at all. I can still go either way.

The only question left to ask now is, "How now, butterfly?"

NOVEMBER 22, 2007

Either Paris or I must be insane. I've never taken a life. No. I have. I'm wrong. I ended a pregnancy when I was fifteen. I was doing so many different drugs; I thought it was the best thing to do for the child. Actually, both children – the baby and me.

If taking a life is the litmus test for insanity, we are both insane.

Last year at Thanksgiving I baked pies. This year my son told me he decided over Chinese food to kill his sister and then planned how to do it while the sitter was driving them home from dinner.

Before I turned off the lights, Paris had a ritual he performed for Ella each night when she went to bed. He would stand in front of each window and door in the room, jibber-jabber magical words, and cast his spell to keep the monsters, demons, and ghouls at bay. Ella loved it. I loved him for soothing her.

This Thanksgiving, he told me she told him to cast no spells that night because if any monsters came, she would fight

them off herself. At that point I told him, "Shut up, Happy Thanksgiving, I love you, good-bye. I won't listen anymore."
Then I ran.

DECEMBER 29, 2007

Where is my meaning? I try so hard to love, so hard to remain positive and uplifting, so hard to make a message out of my meaningless life.

I'm tired though. So tired.

All I wanted in life was to love my kids, to have a loving family. Now all I want is to hear Ella laugh again. I want to feel her in bed next to me. I want to know the world is not a crazy place. I want to know that brothers don't brutally murder their sisters. I want to know if I kill myself I will smell my Ella again. This is more than one woman can take.

What happened to us? Where did love fail? Where did I fail?

JANUARY 2, 2008

Already it has been a strange and wonderful new year.

I feel alive—just a little bit. I spent half the night drinking and talking. I spent the other half having sex with Nic Leeman, the twenty-two-year old son of friends. I've spent the last day and a half agonizing over the act while perpetually horny.

Nic's mother was one of the first people I met when I settled down in San Antonio. One day she showed me a picture of him and lightening hit. I immediately wanted him.

For a change I feel something inside that doesn't hurt. Feeling sexual desire again reminds me I am more than a murdered child's mother; more than the mother of a murderer. I am still a woman; I am still attractive.

And that feels fucking great!

I thought I would be in deep shit for fucking the Leeman boy. I went over to their house tonight and spoke to his father.

I think he's okay with it, won't say anything if it happens again as long as it stays quiet.

I don't know why I keep thinking about it. It wasn't the best sex I've ever had. That was with —I've forgotten his name. Imagine that. I wonder why? I think because Nic's in my head, so everything else takes on that surreal fantasy feeling. What the hell am I talking about? My reality *is* a fucking surreal fantasy.

His father told me I looked beautiful. I couldn't help myself: I told him I feel great since having sex with his son. He's happy for me. Why can't I have a dad like that? Why are the Leemans becoming ingrained in my head, heart, pants? After tonight I truly love Nic's dad. He's put me at ease so many times the last couple of months. It won't be forgotten. I'm learning how to be more comfortable with women by being around Nic's mom, but there is still a sharp edge there.

Why am I so intrigued by Nic? Why am I obsessed with thoughts of sleeping with him again? Because I want to get laid, or because I want to be close to someone—be part of something bigger?

I can go one of two ways here. I can back off and wait to see if he wants me. Or I can go after what I want—whatever that may be. Right now, I want to touch him again—sober. I want to kiss him one time when we're alone to see if there's really anything there. If there is, it will be in the kiss.

I asked him what he thought when he met me. "UH-OH," was his response. I want to have an impact on somebody, to make someone feel things. I know in my heart I'm a hell of a woman who deserves to be loved, taken care of, made love to, be crazy over, lose your cool over, be stupid over, almost lose and win back in a big way. I am that kind of woman.

Damn ... why did I have sex with Nic and light this emotional dynamite? I hope I'm not completely delusional and that he's also thinking about me, trying to figure out what to make of our encounter, if more is wanted or not. Why is it so bewitching, this business of chemistry? It's odd really, how as soon as you see or touch some people, or look into their eyes, or fuck them, you feel a connection; with others you feel nothing at all.

I feel it with Nic.

Don't I?

Maybe I'm barking up the wrong tree, but at least I'm barking again. If it takes having sex with Nic twice to feel this way again, then so be it. Woof … woof ….

One kiss. That's all it would take to know if he's the one for me. I knew when I kissed Ella's father. I'll know the next time I kiss Nic whether we will stay what we are or turn into something unforgettable and heart-wrenching. I'm ready to get lost in someone. Not all the time. Not every day. But I need an escape route. An escape route made of warm flesh, soft sighs, chill of anticipation, and a little mystery. I promise it'll turn out good. I want to create nothing bad.

Ryan. I finally remembered the best-sex-ever name. Ryan Andrews. That was some good sex. We put Nic and me to shame. All Ryan had to do to turn me on was touch me. With Ryan I was free and uninhibited. Our sex was purely electric and chemical. Sex with him became an obsession. We were so good in bed. Words were unnecessary because all emotion was boiled down to raw, visceral, passionate, beautiful, wonderful sex. I loved it.

I'd love to reach that place with Nic.

I have a weird mind. Almost as weird as Paris', except mine is geared differently. I want to live. I want to love. I want to touch and listen and survive and smell and taste life for as long as I am alive and going through the motions of living. And then I want to be with my girl again. I will survive because she did not. I will keep my promise. I will live.

This, my girl, is what good sex, chemistry, mystery, lust, love, confusion, grief, and life are all about. Am I feeling everything enough for you? I'm not trying to make you sad. I only want to experience it all for you since it was all taken away from you. It feels awful and enticing all at the same time, doesn't it, girl?

What I would give to have Nic—in all his twenty-two-year-old glory—standing on my front porch right now.

What is it going to take to amaze me again? Make me have faith again? Feel happy again in my heart, my soul, my mind? Will it be a man? A song? A job? Another baby? What will it take to give me peace? And family. And sex. And life. And love. Most of all, love.

What will it take for me to love again? That's the big jackpot right there.

I'm sappy and need to let it go for now. What is done is done. What happens will happen, whether I want it to or not. Whether I plan for it or not. Whether it hurts me or not. This much, at least, I've learned.

JANUARY 4, 2008

Life hurts too much to live it. I'm tired of being alone, of being hurt, of being in pain. I know I'll stay this way. I'm too damaged to love again.

I'm pining for a boy. A boy who wants to sleep with me yet wants to have his girlfriend too. A boy who helped me feel alive again for a brief moment, and now contributes to my overall feeling of being dead.

I'm good enough to fuck.

I'm not good enough to know, hold, or comfort. He shows up at my house, but wants nothing to do with me outside these four walls.

I'm so tired of going to bed alone, waking up alone. Most of my time—alone ... alone ... alone. One would think I'd have the hang of being alone by now. It seems I'm meant to be that way. Alone I can learn to handle. It's feeling desperate that doesn't sit well with me.

I'm desperate to find meaning. I can't live without it. The string of my life is frazzled. Soon I will hang on my own rope. Hope does not spring eternal where I live.

It's maddening to have promised Ella I'll live again when all I want to do is quit. I can't let her down. I have to survive. Nic can't be the end of me; be the last push off the edge of this cliff I stand on. If my world were properly aligned, Nic would be in his proper place: a fling, a fantasy. My world isn't properly aligned, so the tiniest bit of pain hurts exponentially out of proportion.

All I ever wanted out of life were simple things: love, a family, someone warm next to me in bed. Instead I have murder, violence, demons, pain, pain, more pain.

How do I do this thing called life? How am I supposed to hold on despite this pain? Do other people feel this much pain?

Do we all walk around in quiet desperation?

JANUARY 5, 2008

I have to put an end to all things Nic. I need to go my own way for a bit, retreat into myself, live a little less boldly. Is that the right path to take, though? I thought I was supposed to live again. Instead, this situation made the hole I'm trying to claw my way out of deeper. Why do I have to feel anything? Ever? Why can't I just blow away never to hurt again? Turn into sea foam, a sprite, the wind, something?

Instead I become a sponge. I suck up pain and violence and try to convert it into usable good. And I'm fucking tired and fucking up everywhere I go.

Most days it's hard to make magic happen. Life is about creation except for when I'm with my son, who seems to be all about destruction. It takes a lot to create amid destruction while being beyond despair and grief.

I obsess over how many sleeping pills I have in my possession. I try to gauge how difficult suicide will make it to find Ella on the other side. What if I die and don't find her? I want my Ella back, but I can't leave Paris behind. Nor give him the satisfaction of thinking he's won.

It's no wonder I'm tired and feel beat down. I've been shred into millions of pieces this last year. I've been beaten the fuck up. Having sex with Nic was the knockout round. I am beaten. I am doomed. I feel it in my bones.

I won't last much longer. I retain possession of a body for which there is no soul, not even a spark of one, in the darkness.

JANUARY 6, 2008

I woke up in my own world of one again. For the most part Nic is gone from my mind. I exist alone with my thoughts. It won't kill me. I'm invincible, right? Nothing ever beats me.

Yeah. Right.

I thought I could have others in my life. Introduce them to the new me.

I was wrong.

My loneliness stretches far and wide and deep and cold. No matter what I do, my existence is in the void. There's nothing here. I feel permanently separated from the world around me. I'm invisible. I don't exist. I don't want to talk to anyone, yet I'm desperately lonely. I'm not happy, confident, sexy, beautiful, rich, nothing.

I'm a mother who lost everything.

Nothing makes sense anymore. Down is up. Up is down. All is hell. Fall to pieces. Cut the fall. Talk the drawl ... goodbye y'all.

JANUARY 14, 2008

Tomorrow I go to Giddings State School, Paris' new, almost forever home. Until now he has been in the classification unit; I've waited over a month to see him. When he is older he will start the Violent & Capital Offenders program at Giddings to (hopefully) process his shit.

Get help.

Get better. Hopefully.

I wonder how our visit will go. I have to steel myself, reign in my emotions, fortify my boundaries, to deal with a day of Paris. Fuck. I hate this world I live in.

There's one thing I'm no longer disillusioned about: You never know what the future may hold.

I'm just pissed I have a future. All I want is to be with Ella.

FEBRUARY 3, 2008

Tomorrow is the one-year anniversary of Ella's death. I'm not well, but it may be hard for others to see. I feel it. I'm stretched thin. Everything outside of my mind is muted; everything inside my mind is so fucking loud. My mind never stops, never shuts up. I go insane listening to myself knowing I have no ability to turn me off unless I die.

My regular days in hell pale in comparison to the special kind of hell anniversary days bring forth. Hell on steroids, meth, coke is as good as an analogy I can come up with.

I saw Paris yesterday. He gave me chills and left little room for doubt that he's a fledgling sociopath. He feels absolutely no empathy. He could care less about tomorrow; it's just another day for him except he gets more attention to feed his narcissism.

Sometimes I hate my son, yet I never seem to stop loving him. How is that?

FEBRUARY 4, 2008

Ella has been dead one year. An entire year I've spent in hell. I'm not sure how I survive this. I blindly move forward. I know nothing for sure anymore. I trust nothing. I'm scared of everything while simultaneously fearing nothing, except never seeing Ella again.

I hate what my life has become, but I know I'm doing the right thing. There *are* reasons for everything that happens in our lives; we just don't know them.

FEBRUARY 11, 2008

I've gone into total shutdown. The only activities I successfully engage in are drinking, smoking, and reaching out to organizations to try to get better treatment for Paris and other prisoners. I have no idea how this life will end, but I'll have accomplished something (hopefully) and been on one hell of a ride (definitely).

I've spoken less than twenty-five words in three days' time. I barely eat. I survive on caffeine, nicotine, Baileys, and love of my children. I rarely go out in public unless it's to see Paris (which has become harder to do), go to Giddings for his monthly reviews or the Youth Commission headquarters to raise hell, or to buy smokes and more alcohol.

I won't last long this way, so I've got to have as much impact as I possibly can before everything catches up to me.

I had a dream last night that I changed the Youth Commission for the better, but not until after Paris' release. A news conference about the changes was in progress, when Paris shows up, rushes the podium, and stabs me in the stomach on live TV. As I lay dying in his arms, I whispered that I would tell Ella he said hello. He began to stab me mercilessly, brutally, hundreds of times.

I awoke ready to work. No matter how I feel, no matter how poorly I take care of my body, or no matter how much my soul hurts, I *will* create meaning using this hell as my fertilizer. When life gives you shit, grow flowers for the butterflies to drink from.

FEBRUARY 29, 2008

Something has to give, soon, or I will die.

I spent the last twenty-four hours seriously contemplating suicide. I haven't told anyone. Well, I told my mom this morning, but that's the same as not telling anyone. I'm consumed with Ella, yet Ella is always out of my grasp. If I kill myself, will I find her, whatever the cost? She is where I am. I am with her already. I am not of this place anymore.

I drove to the drugstore to look at bottles of sleeping pills. I don't know how many it would take to kill me properly. If I'm going to risk the chance of seeing my Ella again, I want to make sure I get it right. No coming back to this life.

I can't kill myself tonight. My best friend comes to town tonight and I promised I would take her to get her birthday tattoo. I owe her this last gift. I will leave nothing for Paris, no note, no gifts, nothing. No matter what happens to me, Ella is in a good place. I've done my best to love. Paris is the ultimate loser and hater this go-round.

The most gruesome suicide I can come up with is to stab myself through the left wrist, leave my arm impaled on the table, take Xanax and drink Baileys until I bleed to death. Paris would appreciate the poetry, the metaphor, the message of that scene.

I probably won't do it. Most likely I'll continue to hang on to die the slow death of the disillusioned and sponge-hearted fool of life. I'm a coward. I want to be with Ella again.

MARCH 19, 2008

Today I'm ready to die. Maybe. I'm doing my best to "accidentally" overdose.

Maybe I don't want to die. I just want rest, peace, and an end to the exhaustion and depression. Nothing that comes from all this pain is worth going through it.

Paris has no concern for me. He had no reaction when I told him I wasn't coming back for a while. I never hear or feel Ella anymore. I am forever damaged. I don't know how to fix myself this time.

If I do overdose—Mom and Little Sis: I love you.

Nic: Get your shit together. Play your music. Forget about women for a while. Forget about partying. Play. You have a gift.

Rebecca: You're the best friend I've ever had. I'm sorry to hurt you.

Paris: I've always loved you despite the fact I know you're a psychopath.

APRIL 18, 2008

I continue to move through life as if I live in a padded room. My mind thinks so much my head hurts. I go through the motions of life, but my heart is straightjacketed, dead.

I'm working again, tending bar at the Cove part-time. It's just as fun to work there as it is to sit and drink there. I talk to lots of people, make some cash, kill some time. Stop thinking for a bit.

At the end of this life what will I have to show I existed? That's very egotistical of me, isn't it? Somewhere I'll have known I existed and somewhere I'll still exist. Maybe Nic will write a song about me.

APRIL 23, 2008

Another day in paradise. Passed out drunk on Tylenol PM to sleep the afternoon and night away only to wake up and repeat. I am not motivated to change the pattern. Sober or drunk I exist in a world where nothing will ever be pretty or good again. This world is so ugly, yet day after day I endure it. Why? How much longer must I?

How do I get my life back? Some joy? Some meaning? Where will it come from? Am I done being meaningful?

APRIL 24, 2008

Surreal seems to be the only adjective I can use to get a grasp on life. Last night I spent two hours having great sex with Nic. Then poof ... he's gone. Poof ... he's here. Poof ...

he's gone. But God, while it's happening, I love having sex with that boy. The rest of the time I wonder why I have sex with him. Ultimately there can be nothing that comes of it. He thinks he's in love with some young girl. I only want him because I know I can't have him. Works out for us except that my body loves his body. When I'm naked with him, all time and thought stops and pure raw primal sensation takes over where everything I do originates out of an instinctual place; no intellect is required of me. No intellect equals no pain.

I won't say Nic brings me joy or happiness. I'm not capable of feeling those emotions anymore. For moments too brief he brings me freedom from thought. He makes me smile and laugh. He makes me flexible. I know we both care a little more than either of us will admit to. We're both confused about who and what we are, alone and to one another. We do well in bed because both of us can stop thinking and indulge a bit.

Actually, I have no idea why Nic is fucking me. I just know he is. And I know he will again.

APRIL 29, 2008

It's Tuesday night. Last Friday afternoon, April 25, I swallowed forty-two sleeping pills, and drank a large bottle of Baileys. Instead of dying I took what may have been just a three-hour nap. Whatever it was, I had another visit from Ella.

I found myself in a place composed of soft light, a place that looks like what I imagine the inside of a womb would look like to a baby if someone shined a high-power light on a mother's stomach. Far in the distance, I saw a brighter spot of light. I knew with all my being that if I made it to that light, I would find peace. Rest. No more pain. I started walking toward that light. Next thing I know, Ella was directly in front of me. She was whole. She was wise. She was full of love for me. She was deeply sad.

"You can't go this way, Mama. If you go this way, you won't be with me again."

I dropped to my knees. I hugged her tight. I loved her so much it hurt.

"I know, Ella. I am sorry. I can't do this anymore. I am tired. I am so tired. Please don't be mad at me."

I hugged her again. I stood up and tried to walk around her. She got mad, very mad. She blocked my path, she stomped her foot, and said, "I told you if you go this way, you won't be with me again."

"I know, but I am so tired. I can't keep on like this anymore."

I walked around her, hating myself for not loving her enough.

She said, "Fine, if you aren't going to listen to me, I'll do this the hard way."

The next thing I knew she was back in front of me giving me a push there was no way she would have had the strength for in the physical world.

I fell out of my bed, crawled to the bathroom, puked until I cried from the pain of it, begged Ella to forgive me, and thanked her for saving me from myself. Now I know, for a fact, I have no choice but to be alive—for the time being.

Fuck. Fuck. Fuck.

If I can't die, I'll force myself to live. Since Friday, I go to bed alone. I cut back on the alcohol, but still smoke too much. I started eating better. Booked time with a personal trainer. Cleaned my house. Started to plan a party.

On Sunday, I went to visit Paris; then went a little more insane.

I wish life were over. I *am* dead, but all I want is to be with my Ella again, so I'll do it her way.

MAY 14, 2008

I'm here for a reason. I have too much love for there to be no reason to have it. I love too much, feel too much, soak up too much.

I'm going to India. I don't care how hot it is. I don't care how many terrorist bombs may explode. I have nothing to lose. My babies are gone. Paris drives me crazy. It's so hard to love the one who murdered your child.

Why can't I stop loving? I hurt so badly for people. I want so badly to ease the pain I see in people. Why can't I become bitter? I think I would hurt less if I could be bitter. People seem to shit on me all the time. My mom made an art form out of it. So did Ella's dad. Paris didn't hesitate to up the ante in the game. Nic certainly has.

Bigger and better. This is what you're meant for, Charity Lee.

There is a story told in many cultures which says a person dies two deaths. The first death is the death of the physical body. The second death occurs when no one else on earth remembers who you are; when your name is no longer spoken. I won't let Ella die her second death.

You *will* spread the love, Charity Lee.

JUNE 4, 2008

I like to take drives. It's so bright and busy in town I need get away. I have a glass of wine and head west with music. I know, wine and car. Not the smartest thing to do. I know. It's okay. I am safe. I've agreed to spread love and the universe has agreed to protect me, for now. I hurt and the universe knows how badly I need my escapes, my mental health drives. As I drive, I think and feel and purge and maybe, just maybe, gain a little strength or at least energy. I deflate and recharge at the same time.

I drive to continue to love and live and breathe.

I know without a doubt Ella still exists and is there for me to find, but I'm still afraid to die. For some reason I can't shake the feeling I'll die by Paris' hand. How do I stop this?

I love you, Ella. Doing my best to spread the love. I miss you, oh so much, beautiful girl. Love, hugs, and kisses for you and the universe.

JUNE 6, 2008

Today I decided I must always strive to impact those I come in contact with in a positive way, no matter how exhausting it is.

JULY 2, 2008

I'm done with Paris for a while. I'm so fucking angry with the boy. I hate him right now. When I saw him Sunday, all I could do was look at him and hate him. He wasn't my son at all. He is the sick fuck who murdered my Ella. I wanted to physically hurt him. I wanted to hit him, beat him, rant and rave at him. I wanted to inflict pain.

If not for Paris, Ella would be six years and three months old. She would have been tall and musical and graceful. She might have even lost some teeth. The fact I'll never be her tooth fairy made me want to inflict pain on him.

I don't know what I'm going to do with myself, but I must move forward if I want my life to change. I must live completely in the moment. The past is gone; the future is unpredictable and unknowable. I have nothing to lose. Whatever wisdom or experience I gain is extra padding for the room in my head.

Life is weird. It makes no sense. It really doesn't. We like to, need to, pretend it does. We need to pretend we matter. Maintaining a false sense of security is as instinctual as our sex drive and need for food. We must be more than somewhat delusional to survive life at all.

JULY 22, 2008

It's the day before I leave to volunteer at an orphanage in India. I'm freaking out. My emotions are all over the place. I went through Ella's clothes yesterday so I could take some of them with me to the orphanage. I've been on edge ever since. I miss her so much. I'm hoping I find her there.

JULY 23, 2008

I'm losing my mind in a plane somewhere over the ocean headed toward Paris, France.

Nic saw me off at the airport. He gave me a shallow hug and told me not to freak out. That's it. We share the same bed, often share the same space, and all he can handle is a perfunctory hug. He's unable to give me actual emotional support or show me affection in public. If he's the same when I get home, I'm done with him. I want to be taken care of. I need to be taken care of.

I've already been to the bathroom for one good cry and to ask myself, "What the hell are you doing?" I know what I'm doing. I'm looking for Ella. If I don't find her, what will happen to me?

I'm coming to find you, Ella. Give me a sign.

JULY 26, 2008

I couldn't do it. As I write, I'm somewhere over the Middle East feeling contradictory emotions while flying home. I'm ashamed of myself. I've seen worse living situations than what I saw at the orphanage. I've also endured worse suffering. All I could do was sit there and cry, surrounded by children who had nothing in life but still had more than I could give Ella. They were alive. This was too much for me, so I left and got on the first plane I could find to take me home.

I want to find Ella, plain and simple. Maybe I'm crazy. Maybe I'm not. Part of me believes I gave up too easy. Another part feels it's time to give her up, live my life. If she can come back, she can also find me. I know she still exists, but maybe it's not right of me to hold onto her so strongly. Maybe she needs her peace as much as I need mine. Maybe it's time I learned a little acceptance and keep on loving.

Which brings me to Nic. I have so missed the boy. I was in constant contact with him while I was in India. He talked me down from a lot of window ledges. I don't know where it came from, but he was there when I needed help. His presence in my life turned into something more than a booty call. I depend on him for support, advice, a shoulder to cry on, great sex. He's becoming more than a lover. We still won't kiss, and there is still a boundary in place that neither of us will cross. I think both of us want to, but we're waiting for the other to go first out of fear. So much of what we do, or don't do, is based on fear.

I need to kiss him, because whether I'm afraid or not, I want him in my life. I want to kiss him. I want to love him. I want to make love to him, not just fuck him. He's brought me back to life.

OCTOBER 26, 2008

Happy fucking birthday to me. The best gift would be to cease to exist. That would be the greatest gift of all since I can't have Ella back. I've become an angry, bitter, pain-consumed thirty-five-year-old woman. I don't like life, myself, or anybody else.

How I wish that were actually true. Unfortunately, I still feel love, but now love always feels like pain. Nothing new there, I guess. Love has always been painful for me. How to describe my state of existence these days?

I'm empty and black. I'm full of rage and love and infinite amounts of psychic pain. These feelings paralyze me. I've ceased acting sane. Life is brutal and raw and ugly. I have no hope of a good future because I believe nothing can take this pain away from me.

I am pain and pain is me.

OCTOBER 30, 2008

Nic, Rebecca, and I leave for Europe in one day. Nic and I can't get along at all. He drives me insane. I can't stop myself being totally fed up with his forgetfulness, laziness, lack of ambition, and motivation. Of course, these are all things I dislike in myself, but at least I have cause for being this way. What is his cause? How does he justify letting me support him? What is it about me he seems to think he's so attracted to?

I know what needs to happen. I'm too angry. I need to stop with Nic, go to Europe, come home, and then walk away and figure out what it is I'm to do.

NOVEMBER 4, 2008 – ELECTION DAY – AMSTERDAM

We've been in Amsterdam two days and already I know I'm as unhappy here as anywhere else. Wherever I go, I go with me. I'm at the point where I can't get along with anyone. I've been having issues with Nic and Rebecca all day. Different town, same shit.

Maybe I should embrace my rage, quit trying to keep it at bay, and push everyone out of my life. Evidently, I am "tactless, too blunt, say mean things, and don't know how to relate to people." I usually end up being right and I usually speak the truth, so is it my delivery or my message that people dislike? Whichever it is, all I seem to do is hurt people's feelings and create tension wherever I go. I'm not fit for human consumption.

I don't know how to engage in "normal" everyday life anymore. I don't know how to bullshit with people. Nothing about my life or mind is "normal." I'm constantly on the verge of a nervous breakdown. It's there every day, waiting, just beneath the surface of my skin. If you pay attention, it's written into every look on my face, every action of my life.

I read stories about people who lose the ones they love and soon after they follow them into death. They simply give up, lose the will to live, and die. I want to know how they do it. How do I make my heartbeat stop? How do I force my breath into its final exhale? How do I convince my brain to cease its functions? How do I coax my soul out of my body? How do I lie down and die?

I give up. I've been beaten. I beg and scream at the universe, "Just let me die! There's nothing left to live for." The universe laughs at me, then ignores me.

I'm stuck in Europe for two months whether I like it or not. I'm stuck here with two people, a lover and a friend. This trip is the embodiment of a fucking existential play by Sartre. Hell really is other people. I don't know what to say or do with these two right now. They left for a walk and have been gone over an hour. I can't say I blame them. I am interested to see the result of their walk. Will they have decided how to deal with me by the time they return? Will they have bonded in their joint care and concern for my obvious unwell being? Or will they go back to being just as obsequious and accommodating as usual?

I'm full of nothing but anger and derision and contempt for the entire world. It eats away at me. I try so hard to fight it, to be good, to think good, to act good. I'm fighting a losing battle.

They're back. They are sticking with obsequious and accommodating. I am sticking with rage.

NOVEMBER 20, 2008

This trip didn't go as planned. I would have been more surprised if it did. Nic took off in London. Everything wrong between us finally came to a head, culminating in him bashing his head into a glass table three times, knocking himself unconscious. Blood was everywhere which produced a full-blown panic attack for me. Instead of staying until January, Rebecca and I go home in eight days.

NOVEMBER 22, 2008

Rebecca and I spent the day traveling from Rotterdam to Paris. On the train Rebecca was sniffed three times by a drug-sniffing dog then questioned by the French police. Shitty drug dog. The weed was in my bag, not hers. Needless to say, we were both sweating bullets. The powers that be and Ella have been with us on this trip. So much has gone wrong, yet I am discovering parts of myself again.

It snowed in Utrecht, big, fat, fluffy snowflakes off a Christmas card kind of snow. I reveled in it, stood still and invited it to cover me from head to toe because I know Ella, even Paris, would have loved to have seen it. It was beautiful. It made the world soft and magical again for a moment.

I'm not so sure about my time in Paris. The name of the city alone: who can't I help but think of all the time? I'm trying to think of my week here as a good thing. While I'm in Paris I'll try to figure out how best to deal with my Paris, since I'll be trying to put my life back together when I get home. I need to know where he fits.

NOVEMBER 23, 2008

The possibilities in life are endless. Knowledge of this fact makes life both unbearable and worth living at the same time.

I thought today was Monday. Somewhere in all my travels I've lost a day. I was so tired last night I had an out-of-body experience (I hoped it was death, but obviously it wasn't) and then slept for twelve hours. I woke up somehow convinced it was Monday, but it is a Sunday in Paris for me. It's freezing cold and raining. Rebecca and I are doing laundry, smoking, and writing. Underneath the mundane routine of daily life, I'm deep in thought. Thought constantly weighs me down. I run thought marathons which never end. No matter how much I rest, I am tired.

Soon it will be time to attempt to rise from ashes yet again. I have an idea of what to do, but I'm not sure I have the will to do it. Not the will—the force, the energy.

It's still freezing and raining in Paris. We went out for a bit, braved the elements, found a café that has good food and a grocer. We'll survive, but neither of us is comfortable here. We've spent most of our time in the room. It's been good for introspection. It occurs to me it is a chance to rebuild strength to face life at home. We're both rebuilding our lives once we go stateside.

I must find a way to engage in the world in a somewhat healthy manner. With the way the economy is going, I need work, at least part-time. More importantly, I must begin to live again despite the condition of the world or the state of my soul. Life goes on whether we want it to or not.

So here I sit in a Parisian apartment six stories up with Ella metaphorically six feet down. Paris. It all comes down to Paris, ends in Paris. Paris would probably like to think he is the end all, be all. He would be wrong.

Twenty-one months ago I would never have thought I would be who I am, what I am, where I am, why I am, at this moment: the thirty-five-year-old mother of a sociopath, mother of a brutally murdered daughter, bearer of both life and death, survivor of all-encompassing, all-engulfing, all-enslaving pain, and grief that never stops.

Pain is always present, but I grow better at making it malleable, working with it, living with it. It's as real as any other companion. It has a life of its own. We're better friends now that we know each other so well. We're learning to coexist in this piece of work named Charity.

I find myself in an Indian restaurant in Paris, alone. I made the mistake of seeing my name in one of Rebecca's emails. Actually, the mistake was made before that when I decided to read her email after she left her screen open on a bathroom break. After reading my name, I read the entire paragraph pertaining to me. Evidently, I am not positive enough for her taste. She told her friend a direct result of being in Europe with me for the last month is she now requires a positive roommate.

I was in the kitchen doing dishes when she came out of the bathroom. The faucet started to come off its base, water spraying everywhere. I could not stop myself from laughing somewhat hysterically. If it's not one thing, it's another. She asked if I was okay.

I answered, "I'm doing my best to remain positive."

We haven't spoken much since. If she has something she wants to say, she needs to work up the balls to say it to my face, not behind my back. When she asked if we were going to the Louvre, I told her she was more than welcome to it. I've gone before. So today I'm on my own. I found an alley full of Indian restaurants.

I wonder what people think when they see me sitting here alone. Do I look sad? Troubled? Alive? I know I'm not the most positive being on the face of the planet. I also know I could be much worse after all that's happened these last twenty-one months. Rebecca is the last person I expected to think badly of me, though I guess nothing should surprise me anymore.

The last six months, in all these travels of mine, I've realized there are too many damn people in this world. The world is too impersonal. Peoples' worth is devalued. People are rude and less conscientious of others. One nationality thinks it's better than the rest when, in reality, people are all the same inside. It's only our culture (if you can call it that anymore) that's different from place to place. Emotions are universal.

NOVEMBER 28, 2008

Finally! I'm going home! I'm relieved to no longer be in Europe, glad to be flying home, nervous about what to do when I get there. Nic's waiting for me. My mom's expecting my call. She also helped me get out of India as fast as possible. She bought my return ticket. Paris is still my son and still the one who killed Ella. I have no job. I'm running out of money. The economy is collapsing. Part of me wants to go to Georgia and work things out with my mom. Part of me still wants Nic. Part of me still wants to disappear. I just don't know what to do.

Here's what I do know. I want to work with kids. They make me happy and that's a rare commodity in my world.

DECEMBER 3, 2008

If I ever wrote a book about my life it would be hard not to place myself in every character. I've played them all to varying degrees of success and a certain degree of failure. Hero and antihero; victim and martyr; tyrant and mouse; mother of life and death; harbinger and destroyer of hope. I am the bearer of both black and white, who is composed of nothing but grays.

If I ever wrote a book about my life where would it begin? There have been so many beginnings. Or would I start it with the end? The dilemma springs from the fact I know life both does and does not end. One of these days my body will cease to be, but everything that is me will continue to exist. There is no heaven where everlasting bliss is attained; however, there is a place to process, to rest. Knowledge is gained and lost; progression is made and lost; all feeling and consciousness continue to exist.

I want something beautiful to be the result of my life. All the good I've produced thus far has either turned to shit or been shat upon. If I knew what I wanted, I could turn shit into life again. I could grow tulips.

The love/nemesis of my life sucker-punched me. It makes sense if Paris understands me well enough to know my weakness, exactly how to try to destroy me, then I should understand him that well also. My son and I are locked in a cosmic struggle. He has taken it upon himself, for some reason beyond my grasp while stuck in this body, to challenge me to a duel, a spiritual game of chess. He is the yin to my yang. Ella is the dot that connects us and locks us in this battle.

To him she is nothing. To me she is everything. Both are everything for me. Thoughts of them color every aspect of my being, awake or asleep. The world continues to exist around me. I participate in that world, but what only Ella, Paris, and I know is that I simultaneously exist in my own painful world. What people see and experience of me is, and yet is not, truly me. I am real, but I hold back so much.

Why am I not crazy? No one I know has earned insanity better. My dad was murdered. My aunt shot herself. My uncle was murdered. My mom can be a fickle bitch. One day she is kind to me; the next she will not hesitate to stab me in the back if I don't play puppet on her strings. My son is a psychopath who murdered his sister. My daughter was stabbed to death by her brother.

Why? Why? Why? Why?

Maybe because I'm the one meant to make something good come out of all this. It would be hard to do that if I lost my mind in a non-functional way. Maybe part of the blessing is only losing my mind in a functional way.

DECEMBER 4, 2008

I've changed. I've become hard. I don't want to put up with anything I perceive to be unreal.

When I got out of bed this morning, I found Nic in my house. I don't want anyone popping into my house unannounced. He said he thought today was Ella's birthday. Evidently, he got the four and the twelve mixed up – 12/4 instead of 4/12. No matter how much I may want a relationship with Nic to work, it won't because he doesn't know how to move beyond codependence; I'm moving into a world of my own creation. My patience is gone. My desire to care is waning. Ultimately nothing will come of this. I won't have his children.

DECEMBER 5, 2008

I spent the last two days in hell, paralyzed. My sleep, smoke, drink, drive, and write coping style is back. I'm slipping back into blackness. How many times am I expected to wrestle my way out of it?

It's 9:30 in the morning and I can't bring myself to function because I'm stuck in my damn head. I hate being me. I hate being. Period.

I bought a gun not too long ago. I'm unable to shoot myself in the head. I haven't tried, but I envision it all the time. I know suicide isn't an option, but living is the only shitty alternative.

DECEMBER 8, 2008

I've made up my mind to move. I'm slowly, very slowly, putting this plan into action. If life is ever going to change, I must abruptly alter its course. Extreme desperation calls for extreme action. I don't know how, but somehow, I'm going to put a life together again. This time it's going to last. After all I've been through, I won't accept defeat. If I must take extreme measures to survive hell to live, I will.

I'll do what I need to do here and then I'll leave on a quest – a search for myself. I've forgotten who I am. Ella and Paris are both gone, for now. Dealing with Paris pushes me over the edge. I can no longer define myself as a mother. Nic is fading into memory. Obviously, I'm not cut out to be a good lover.

I don't know any more if I'm running away from my life or running on to the next lesson to be learned. I only know at times it becomes unbearable to sit still.

DECEMBER 10, 2008

I leave San Antonio tomorrow. I know I'll be back at least once, but I don't know if I'll be back to stay. I enjoyed Nic's company yesterday. I'm waiting for him to pick me up. I've made up my mind to end it with him nicely; I know we're at our end. No need to trample on his heart any more than I already have.

I have no idea what's ahead. Do I ever these days? My gut tells me I must get out of Texas, away from Paris. I can't heal if I'm living in an open wound.

So back to not knowing. Leave Texas, not sure where I need to end up. What if I'm doing the wrong thing, running away from Paris, Nic, and Texas? What if by running away I relive it again at some later point? All I know for certain is I must get away from Texas and Nic on my terms, see if it helps me figure out what I want out of this half-life I lead.

I know better than to stay here in Texas. Paris will kill me.

DECEMBER 24, 2008   CHRISTMAS EVE

A mere two weeks later - everything has changed. It's Christmas Eve. Two weeks ago, Nic and I agreed to marry; last night we agreed not to marry. I pointed a loaded gun at him to get him out of my house. I'm 98% certain I had no intention of shooting him. Someone heard the yelling and called the cops, but nothing came of it after I told them everything was fine. They did ask my how my TV ended up on the floor in pieces. It was obvious they did not believe whatever excuse I gave them, but they left.

Ella is still dead. I don't talk to my mother or Paris. I have nothing. I'm scared.

I scared myself, so from now on I'm keeping to myself. I have no daughter, no son, no mother, no lover, no friends. I have me.

DECEMBER 25, 2008.... CHRISTMAS DAY

A Christmas of nothing. This Christmas I have less than I did last Christmas. I am completely alone. I am still in shock. I pointed a loaded gun at Nic. I've truly gone mad. There is no turning back. Two choices here: either get my shit together or kill myself before I hurt someone. I have wanted to kill myself for a long time. The desire to do so is strong today, like April. I held the gun to my temple today. Sometimes my pains hurt so much I become convinced seeing Ella again is a dream and it doesn't matter how I die. But I can't bring myself to kill myself, so I suffer and everyone around me suffers.

I have only myself to blame for my loneliness. Paris started it, but I am the one finishing it. I've chosen to let the rage take me on.

JANUARY 2, 2009

It's Friday night. Nic and I are together again.

JANUARY 3, 2009

I think, I hope, I'm beginning to gather pieces of my destroyed life and create a new mosaic with them. Some part of me became stretched too thin the days following the gun incident. In that moment I was presented the opportunity to find out who I am and what I'm capable of. Thank God I wisely chose not to shoot; I was able to stop and think. I am who I thought I am. Pulling that gun, making that choice, brought Charity back.

Now all I need to accomplish is to hold onto her.

I'm going to turn this tide of rage around and live right, full of as much love as possible. It's my life now. All my strings are gone. Ella will always be. I know I'll hold her again one day.

I'll always miss her; I'll always think about her. Now is the time to live for her, as I promised.

I've have tried everything I know to destroy myself these last two years, trying to finish what Paris started. Despite all life has done to destroy me; I believe I'm learning a bit of what I'm supposed to learn.

JANUARY 4, 2009

I wrote Paris a postcard today. I told him I wasn't mad anymore. That, of course, doesn't mean I trust him, am naïve to what a threat he is, or want to talk to him.

JANUARY 14, 2009

My demons have clutched me close today, suffocating me. I panicked and bailed on a volunteer training session. I can get ready to go out, drive to these places, but can't go in. I panic. I get scared. I switch to autopilot and drive home.

I have an appointment with the shrink at 4:00 pm today. I'll force myself to go to that office no matter what; either that or I am fucked, because I can't control myself emotionally anymore. If I don't figure out how to interact with the world again, I'll have a very ugly and lonely life. I know because I'm already living it.

JANUARY 15, 2009

I went to the shrink, but the meds he prescribed are unavailable until tomorrow. Another day of hell for me. This shrink also told me I should disappear. How can I begin a life here if one day I have to disappear?

He told me to pretend Paris doesn't exist. How do I do that? Paris is my son, my enemy, the boy who killed Ella, and the boy who all but destroyed me. I can't pretend he does not exist. His assessment of me, our situation, was pronounced after talking with me for thirty minutes. I didn't book an appointment to diagnose my son. He shouldn't be diagnosing him either. It's unethical in his field to diagnose someone without having met them, talked with them, administered assessments to them for himself.

He is either some sort of genius or wildly incompetent.

I have my first session with a new therapist today. Let's hope it works out better; I'm beaten down. I'm placing my last hopes on a psychotropic medication and a woman I don't know who will listen to me rant. I hope I can manage work and school.

I got the job at the auto shop. I am going to do my best to succeed.

Life is truly hell.

JANUARY 20, 2009

I witnessed America claim her first African American President today. Obama had his day in the sun. Now let's hope he can spread the sun around. We could use some light. The economy is in recession. Unemployment is at a high point. The government is bailing out Wall Street and the auto industry. I've lost half my money.

Personally, things are getting better. I've been on medication for five days. I think it already helps; at least it has a placebo effect on my rage. My volcano rumbles but hasn't exploded. I feel calmer, more centered, a little more settled in my skin.

I started working again yesterday. I'm the secretary at Insley and Sons Automotive. I work Monday through Friday, 9–2. I like it. It smells like grease. The place is dusty and grimy. The guys who work there seem to be good people. The owner's girlfriend hangs out in the office all day. They grilled steaks at lunchtime, and we sat down to eat together. The work is easy. It reminds me of being a kid at my mom's shop, hanging out with the drivers and mechanics.

It reminds me of later in life, too, when I worked there, and life with Paris was still good. I think it'll be a wonderful job for easing back into work life.

This reincarnation of my personality has made me both phoenix and butterfly. I've been wrapped in pain and rage and anger and sorrow and grief for close to two years. I'm emerging from this chrysalis of hell. If I can survive the birthing process, I can regain my soul and build something beautiful with it. There will bad days, but I'm glad some good things are happening.

JANUARY 22, 2009

Life with Nic is at its end. I want to be better taken care of. I know ... I've said that before, but now, perhaps, it might actually be true. I'm waking up from my nightmare. Nic's barely engaged in his life. I can't blame him—he's young. He has suffered, but he doesn't seem to grow from his. He remains stagnant.

Let me not forget I'm the one who chose him. I haven't always been good to him. I should be grateful for the ways a year being with him helped to reawaken me, Charity.

Now that I'm emerging from my cocoon of pain, he may not be equipped to deal with the woman I've become or the woman I want to become. There's one essential difference between us that bothers me. In my heart I strive, with great pain, to be selfless. I don't always succeed. Most often I fail, yet I'm in a constant struggle to do the right thing, make someone happy, anticipate a need, to be at one and right with the universe. I agonize over every act of living I engage in and want nothing more complex than having someone ... wait . . . that isn't true. I don't want *someone*.

I want *me* back. I want to think less often about Nic, his issues, his limitations. I want to think about Paris as little as necessary in order to heal. I want to think more about Ella; how to turn all this black into pure good. I want to heal. I want to survive. I want to be loved and cherished for being fierce and fragile in my heart and soul.

I bought a bottle of red wine tonight and told the lady behind the counter it was good for my heart. She told me it was good for both of them. Smart woman, knowing about the second heart, the one either hidden in your soul or is your soul. It is the only one capable of containing both the joy and pain of life, all that is me.

Lately I've been dreaming about building hearts with little girls literally trapped inside them. I can't sleep through the night. More and more I feel I'm meant to face myself. Stop. Turn around. Look the phoenix in the eye. This is the last chance I may get in this body to learn what I came here to learn. I can feel it—the reason I'm here—floating in me. I can sense the gift of it but can't hold onto it long enough to see what it is.

My gut tells me my future is not Nic. My future will be about Paris and Ella, but hopefully in a manner which will heal pain, not cause it. I have to be ready for Paris when he gains his freedom. If I've fallen apart, he has won—and he'll be able to kill me. I won't let either happen. There's a battle between us. Good will prevail, but that doesn't mean good won't have a hard time of it.

I need to get used to being alone. I need to spend time getting to know this new Charity. I have a feeling that's coming anyway. May as well embrace it.

Kill it with kindness, right?

FEBRUARY 2, 2009

I have therapy every Monday. So far I like Dr. Zuelzer. She's capable of helping me through the great pain to come. She's old. She is—or seems to be—wise, though I don't believe the two always mutually coexist. She has a certain serenity that can come from either age or wisdom. I don't have any of the three yet. Age will come. Serenity and wisdom must be actively sought.

It's my quest. There are times I feel the key in me that will unlock this elusive wisdom contained in me; I feel it, but I can't turn it ... yet. I know about matters of the soul. I know these things because I've learned them somewhere, sometime before. I can't remember fully or properly when or where. The answers are in me, but they are not me. I can only be me if I find the key. It's this door to the soul I should be thinking about.

I'm beginning to understand that in order to find yourself, you must first lose yourself. Damn if I'm not lost, more lost than I've ever been. I hope one day I'll find myself and I'll be good—whole yet dented. Really alive instead of just pretending to be.

Being human is so hard. Being a severely traumatized one is nearly impossible. The pot at the end of the rainbow better be worth what it took to fucking traverse the thing.

Do you have any idea how hard it is to hold onto light?

FEBRUARY 3, 2009

Today is the day before the anniversary of when Ella died. Tomorrow, two years will have passed since I've held my children or been able to think of my life without pain.

I'm rereading Frankl's *Man's Search for Meaning*. I last read the book in college when Paris was a baby. All I underlined then still applies to my life today, except now I am more intimate with the concepts and contents of suffering. I sense I'm beginning to choose the right path to good. Unfortunately, it's the most painful path, too. Pain to hope.

I should go to bed while I have hope.

FEBRUARY 5, 2009

I read stories in the news about horrible things people do to one another. I hurt for every person of the story, the "bad" and the "good." Afterward, I read the general public's reaction to the horror unfolded before their eyes: hatred, anger, retribution, punishment. People *hope* other people will be put to death, exterminated, beat up, raped, commit suicide.

I read these reactions so sad for the world. Instead of attempting, as a rule, to do what's good, we use horrible situations to generate more horrors. Hate begets hate. Anger begets anger. Trauma begets trauma. Pain begets pain. Somewhere it has to end. How do I help others, and see for myself that love can survive suffering?

Yesterday was hell for me. I slept a lot. Drove a lot. Cried a lot. Hurt a lot. Asked *why* a lot. In the end, I accept I miss both my kids and I'm going to hurt.

But I woke up today, went to work and, by midday, believed, again, I do have a purpose. I'm living up to what life expects of me, slowly but surely. I will falter and make mistakes. I'm severely damaged but grow stronger for it spiritually.

Cosmic irony. It's a bitch when you see it for what it is.

Today I gave Nic the opportunity to walk away with courage. He chose not to take it. I flat out told him he would be unable to find himself with me. He argued. I told him we don't want the same kind of life. He agrees yet refuses to muster the courage to face the test he thinks he wants to pass: losing me, getting out of his comfort zone, walking into the forest of himself.

I'll give him a couple of days to take matters into his own hands. If not—I will.

I think.

FEBRUARY 6, 2009

I didn't give him a couple of days. I woke Nic up this morning and told him it was time he went his own way. I'm not yet, but I know I will be, sad. I'll miss him and get lonely. These emotions I will live with; I'll put them on top of the pile I already live with. It's time to be on my own. Time to face my demons.

How now, butterfly? What now? Where do you go from here? It's time to get better. Therapy. Check. Medication. Check. Willingness to walk through hell to catch a glimpse of heaven.

Check.

FEBRUARY 9, 2009

One of these days I'll be a hunted woman.
Today I'm a severely haunted one.

FEBRUARY 10, 2009

I went to my first Parents of Murdered Children meeting last night. It did not go as well as I'd hoped. I began to feel anxious about going as soon as I left work. I started to have a full-blown panic attack and still had two hours before the meeting began. I tried to stay calm. I went for a drive with a margarita. I went to the meeting. I had to ask to introduce myself. I bared my soul, then debated with the meeting leader about how punitively Paris should be treated once an adult. Evidently Parents of Murdered Children supports the lock-them-up-and-throw-away-the-key mentality. They have letter writing committees whose sole purpose is to write letters to the parole board speaking against the release of everyone who committed a violent crime. Then another lady cut in to talk about a memorial she wanted people to attend, completely attempting to shut me down when I challenged their beliefs about perpetrators of crime.

Next came a ten-minute discussion about the newsletter. It hurt to be shut down and it upset me their focus is incarceration rather than help. Another panic attack set in. I stood up during the newsletter talk, stomped off loudly, despite my fluttering heart and increasing inability to breathe.

The leader of the group called today to apologize. She gave my number to some of the other group members; asked me to come back in March. I'll go. I need to get to know them before I'm shown why I shouldn't lean on them.

It's time to start putting the pieces of my soul back together, time to do it well, because this nightmare will never change. I'll always live with all I've done, or could have done, as a mother. I'll always live with the knowledge my son is most likely a psychopath. It will always constrict my heart when I am reminded somehow of every moment of pain and fear and betrayal Ella felt at her death.

I'm awakening to the full reality of the task ahead, what it will take to put Charity back together, again, and turn this hell into something good, helpful, that will honor the love my children taught me. I know I can do this. I always thought I was a tough girl, a survivor. Now I know I have it in me to be a strong, wise, loving woman.

In order to be her, I willingly undertake this spiritual and psychological quest. It's time to strip myself raw, look into a mirror, decide who Charity truly is, and say hello. Abraham wrestled with an angel. I wrestle with my demons, and the angel, inside me. I hope the angel wins.

FEBRUARY 16, 2009

I spent my first full day alone. I didn't drink but I didn't manage to quit smoking. I'll try again tomorrow.

I did accomplish good things today. I went to therapy. I reached out to new people and sent postcards to old friends. I talked to Rebecca; can't wait to see her in Seattle later this week.

The phoenix is forming in the ashes. Birth and death are such painful process. We come into and leave this world in pain. In between, there are moments of peace, love, light.

Something new develops in me. I grow curious about, and excited to know, the woman I am asking myself to become, prodded to become, meant to become.

I do not know *the* answer, but I begin now to get a handle on what I must do for meaning. It's enough, for now, to know I'm curious to find out who I can be if I follow universal prompts - wherever they may lead.

FEBRUARY 23, 2009

I have a photo of me holding Ella taken when she was around ten months old; she had just finished nursing. I am lying down, and Ella is sitting up, smiling. Paris must have taken the photo. I look happy. I look calm. I look peaceful. I look fulfilled.

What happened to me? Even before Ella died, and Paris revealed himself, I lost that look. I want that look back. If I don't get it back, I'll die.

So here I go, into the abyss, willingly. I hope—

I was about to say I hope *I'm* right, but this trip into the abyss isn't my idea. I trust the signs and messages the powers that be have sent me the last two years. They must be working. I'm still alive and doing better than anyone would expect under these circumstances. I don't look forward to delving further into my pain, but I do look forward to the insight, strength, and fulfillment I know I will wrestle forth from it. Time to see if this phoenix can fly.

Tomorrow I am at Giddings to meet with Paris and Dr. Robinson, one of his psychiatrists. I feel prepared. I want to see Paris with my own eyes, listen to him with my own ears. I want to talk about his good memories of Ella. I want them for myself. I want to see his reaction to them.

It is time; I have to see him. The mother in me wants, needs, to see him. All signs point to it being time for a visit.

It's hard to explain. Certain thoughts and ideas come to me, such calm and serene thoughts, too focused to be my thoughts, showing me how to navigate the waters around Paris. My other side navigation system – signs.

I know when I tell people about my signs, many write me off as, at best, "not quite all right, yet." I'm sane when I talk about these things. I believe with my whole heart a greater consciousness guides us if we choose to look and follow, no matter how difficult the path may present, no matter how breathtaking or heartbreaking the sight.

FEBRUARY 25, 2009

Depression and exhaustion have me in their grip today. I spent two hours or so with Paris and Dr. Robinson at Giddings yesterday. I held my son. I shared pictures and good stories of Ella with him. It was the first time he's seen photos of her since he killed her. I let him have two. He broke down, for real, when he saw them. He went back and forth between the boy who killed Ella and the Paris I thought I knew from before. When I walked away from him, and left him stuck in the same spot, I felt sadness and pity for my child.

Our lives are so fucked up.

MARCH 6, 2009

My new car was wrecked this week. A woman slammed into the passenger side going sixty-five miles an hour. I didn't get upset, stressed, or panicky. How ironic is it I can handle myself well in an intense emergency that could involve death, barely skip a heartbeat, yet I cycle through multiple panic attacks before I can walk into a grocery store?

Life is full of irony.

I believe I have faced death head-on, no longer live in fear of it, so I can begin to live life again. I don't want to die anymore. I try not to actively seek death. As Paris said, "We all die eventually."

When I die, Ella will be there, I will be there, and we will both go on. Death is another birth.

To prepare for therapy I looked back in my journals. I can see I had new meaning for my life the moment I woke up from my faint the night of Ella's death. My new meaning became the need to regain meaning. No matter what lengths I have gone to, no matter the level of depravity I have sunk to, it has always been the will to live, to love, and survive. That has been my meaning.

MARCH 7, 2009

I woke up at 9:30 this morning and have not stopped writing and typing since. The day has gone by. I've worked my way through two months of journals and two packs of cigarettes.

I need to stop and come back to this world for a bit. I stopped at the day I met the DA and detectives to find out exactly what Paris did to Ella. I had to stop typing; I broke down into tears of guilt. I still feel I should have been there to save Ella, even though I know there was no way I could have known what Paris planned to do that night. Who the hell ever thinks her son is going to murder his sister?

MARCH 8, 2009

Up for a little dream interpretation? I spent twelve hours yesterday either typing about the first three months after Ella's death or writing in this journal about it. I went to bed last night warily hopeful I would dream again about my kids, especially Ella, since she's who I spent the day focused on, as always.

Instead, I dreamt about Nic leaving me in a particularly cruel way. He had started up with some girl who was really blond and really boring, who told me I had my chance and blew it because I'm crazy. I told the girl because of his love for me he would never really be able to love her. But he still left me.

I woke up sobbing, scared, feeling the physical constricting heaviness that grips me when I look into an abyss I must enter soon. What the fuck is Nic in my life for? To wake me up? Yes. To restore my faith in good guys? Yes. All done. What now, life? I need some clearer signs, because I'm not understanding the ones I've been given so far.

I'm good, most of the time, at somehow knowing what to do with people in a manner that follows love's rules. With men, I lose that ability. I can be loving towards them, but I can't live in peace with them, any of them, and I've had all kinds of men over the years. I can only stand to be around Nic for a few days at a time and then I retreat again to this world. After a couple of days of that, I get panicky; think I need him. I carry huge amounts of guilt around for being so wishy-washy, but I am wishy-washy when it comes to Nic, so at least I'm being human honestly, albeit with my usual sense of bluntness.

All I know to do with this life is to go with the flow and be who I am from day to day. There's a rhyme and reason for the life I've lived, a reason I am who I am at this very moment. I'm able to handle my resurrection again because I know I'm doing, and I am, who I am meant to be—most of the time. In a nutshell: even though everything is still wrong in my life, I'm finally on my way to being right again.

I know things now I only grasped at before my family imploded. I know how to love better even though it fills me with fear to do so. I'm intimate with rage and disgust and violence and all the horrid things people do to one another. I can too easily put myself in each part played out in tragedies, imagine the mindset of all in the scene, and I feel great sadness and pain for all involved. Each time I read or hear the story of someone else's pain, I absorb a little more pain, swallow down a little more of life's sadness, and send up a plea for comfort and peace for everyone in pain to Ella and the powers that be. I always make a point of asking her to comfort the children I read about who have died horrible deaths. Maybe that's why I haven't felt her as much lately: she's very busy if she goes to all of them.

Ultimately, I stand alone in this world of mine—well, not totally alone. Ella and Paris are there. The world I primarily live in is the one in my head, my heart, my soul. My world is secret to all but me, Ella, the powers that be. My world is deeper, more complex, gut wrenching than the one in these pages, but it's becoming a peaceful place for me in spite of the pain that created it. It's my eye of the hurricane; it's where I hear Ella and get my signs and signals, my messages. When I can take my world no longer, I come back to the world in these pages to process my thoughts, and then go out into "the real world" to act on what I've learned, hopefully in a way that makes the world a better place and me a more loving and wisely evolved soul.

I want grace, both in style and bearing, and to attain as a state. One is man-made, and the other a gift inherent in life if you seek it. We all find ways to cope. They run the gamut for me. I know some are better than others, but who am I to say any of them were wrong? I'm alive today and attempting to create the woman named Charity. I find my name so ironic. It pretty much sums up the type of human I'm meant to be, want to be.

A couple of days ago my inner mind, that one that seems to hatch all kinds of idea and plans, hatched this plan that led to me inviting my mother to be in town for Ella's birthday. Now my outer mind, the one that makes me second guess everything, wonders "What the fuck?" My outer mind takes those ideas and plans, begins to play out scenarios and possible outcomes my inner mind ignores, which leaves my inner mind, once the plan or idea has been enacted, to retreat to absorb the experiences to add the final product to the mosaic of my motivation and being.

God, I am crazy.

MARCH 10, 2009

Yesterday I began PTSD therapy. Fuck me. The session was recorded. I closed my eyes and talked my way through memories of my traumatic events. We started with the moment I learned Ella was dead. I talked for ten minutes, all in the present tense, but it felt like an eternity, almost like I was back there in time. The physical reactions I experienced were right here back with me. The emotional pain – right here back with me. The frantic but dulled thoughts – right here back with me.

There were also feelings I haven't thought about since that night.

I forgot until yesterday how frantic I was to see, be with, both my children that night. At that moment, I wanted Paris as desperately as I wanted Ella. After that first twenty-four hours, I haven't ever felt that again.

Here's the clincher: I'm supposed to listen to that recording twice a day until my next session. Yet. I listened to it. I'm sure in time I'll understand why reliving this moment over and over, going through this pain over and over, is helpful. That time is not now. I'm exhausted. This is the third time in two days I've willingly transported myself into my abyss. My outer mind is screaming very loudly, "Run, run, duck, fucking hide, take deep mental cover—batten down." My inner mind says, "Way to go, you're finally taking your pain out of Paris' hands and putting it in yours, turning around to face yourself, not because you have to survive, but because you want to live."

How about that? Am I figuring out how to sit in the saddle again?

What I'm beginning to pick up on is I might be able to have a little more inner peace if I turn around and hug my pain. It's not going anywhere; might as well become friends with it. As it teaches me what it knows, pain will spend less and less time with me but, like all good friends, pain will always come back for a visit.

MARCH 11, 2009

This is the normal daily routine for me now. Wake up. Quick soul check to see where it is: heaven—hell—purgatory. Begin day, try to remember to keep up the constant inner dialogue that convinces me of the need to keep going as best as possible, the need to hope for the best, the need to pour the contents of my fucking heart into everything I do, and the need to find hope again so I can do these things. Think. Cry. Panic. Think some more. Feel an iota of joy if lucky. Remain obsessively focused on the evolution of my soul and the karmic scales that dictate my conscience and ethics. Try to cuddle up and play with the dog. Remember it's supposed to feel great. Walk the talk daily. Bed. Exhausted yet addicted to insomnia.

I am scared, yet hopeful, of dreams. I don't want to go to bed and miss a moment awake now that I'm starting to make a new beginning. I feel like a kid in that regard. Once my head hits the pillow, I want to avoid all the thinking I do. There's never a truly restful moment. All thoughts, all actions, all feelings, all I see and hear and say eventually leads me right back to Ella and Paris. I'm still consumed by them, but now that negative energy is being harnessed to suit my purpose—as taught to me by life—and that is to do good; counterbalance Paris' bad juju; honor my Ella, make her proud of me—love—love—love.

I don't always want to admit it, but I'm beginning to respect myself after remembering all I've lived through these last two years. I've become a woman of character and wisdom—even if I can't follow that wisdom every day. I've acquired knowledge of my soul the hard way. I have honor and most often have performed gracefully under intense pressure. When I do fuck up, I fuck up big, but I've learned how to sincerely apologize. Most of all I begin to admire how, no matter how bad life is, no matter how badly I mess up, no matter how bad my last decision—I haven't given up. I'm living. I'm learning, willingly. I have a long way to go, but I know I can go the distance now no matter what.

I don't always like myself these days. Some days I hate myself, and this life, enough to fall into the abyss. Some days respect is worth more than like.

MARCH 19, 2009

Therapy exhausts me. Talking myself into the past and reliving the day my world imploded has me bone wearily, achingly, hopelessly tired. Every time I talk about the moment I saw Ella dead for the first time I remember more: how she looked—how I felt—the body bag—the blood on her face—my wailing and uncontrollable kissing of her—fighting off the hands trying to hold me up or pull me away or comfort me.

This session was exponentially taxing. I remembered more details at one time today than I have since that night. As a result, I'm in my own world. I'm in a suspended state of pain and awe, love and hate, all twisted round each other. Piaget taught that all of our learning is based on schema, constructs—levels built one upon the other—like Lego blocks. You look back at your past experiences, yours and other's reactions to those experiences, and the consequences of those experiences and reactions, and assimilate as you go. You draw upon your past experience and construct new schema like you build ever evolving and complicated creations from Legos. My past certainly schooled my schema and made me a survivor, but my Legos were ambushed, kicked over by a closet bully, and my levels made meaningless.

After that much damage, deconstruction was the only choice. Deconstruction is the only choice. It's so obvious nothing about my life or my soul will ever be the same again. I'm altered in a no-going-back way. I'm filled with the overwhelming compulsion to redeem both of my children. Good *will* come from Ella's death. I'll protect my son and continue to follow both my instinct and my heart.

I miss my children so much. At this moment, I sit on my front porch in the middle of a storybook view of color and cloud and birds. My flowers surround me—headphones on—cold beer is sipped—words are flowing. How many days did I spend sitting outside, writing, listening to music, and watching my kids play, swim, run, jump, explore, skateboard, dance? How many hours? Minutes? Seconds? Breaths? Heartbeats, laughs, smiles, hugs, kisses? Not nearly enough and never again.

I have to relive my nightmare to get my memory of the good days back. I hope that alone will make it worth the pain I'm in and that I will emerge from this pain the most beautiful of the phoenixes I've ever been. Despite my life I'm still moved to tears at the knowledge of how much love I have in me. This nightmare has broken me open; all that love can pour free. The volcano is erupting. Life and death. Destruction and creation. Chaos and balance. Love and hate. I am all of them. They are all me. I am connected to life, connected to an undercurrent of energy, in a way I cannot explain. When I write I feel the rhythm of it under everything I say—a unifying buzz. I live in world upon world upon world and I try to reconcile them all, bind them to one another, by writing.

I don't know where I'm meant to go from here, or how I'm meant to do it, but I will take the journey to get there. I don't know how to convey the soul-splitting experience of being Charity Lee. But I will write the words that do.

MARCH 20, 2009

People are beginning to notice I'm finding my voice. Many who care for me tell me I'm a role model, my writing is profound, my way of speaking engaging. I'm a growing force to reckon with. I thank God I'm a good force and not the one I gave birth to because I'm facing my inner demons and turning them into angels.

As I go back and listen to the therapy session recordings and reread my old journals, I can't believe this life is mine. I've lived in a surreal fucking world since my father was murdered. I am both in awe and fear of myself. I want to know what I'm going to do next. What door will open in front of me? Where is my soul, my heart, to go next? Both have been on such an unbelievable journey already. It's still a miracle I am who I am however inevitable it is/was meant to be.

My earliest memories are feelings and thoughts, not events. From an early age, my thoughts and feelings made my head burst. I've always been a thinker and a feeler, not a container for events. It is why I started to journal. I can't remember a time when life has not been intense. The only three times I truly had inner peace in the face of the intensity of both thought and feeling were when I was pregnant with Paris, then Ella, then the beginning of 2007—a month before Paris changed my life to one of hyper-intensity and functional insanity.

Paris miscalculated when he chose to release his inner monster by killing Ella. He thought he would destroy, obliterate, erase me. Almost, Paris. Almost. But I'm waking up. I'm unleashing myself. I'm gearing up. I'm proud of myself. For the first time in my life, I love everything about myself—the ugly and the good.

MARCH 23, 2009

Nothing is ever simple anymore. Nothing is ever easy anymore.

I helped a little girl today. When I arrived at therapy, she was in the lobby, with her mom, crying. I had to try to comfort her, the both of them, if I could. Her foot was injured, so I asked her about it. She said she injured it skiing. A minute or so went by and I leaned over and said, "It looks like you're having a bad day."

"Yes," she said.

We talked a little more and I told her Ella's breath advice—in with the good, out with the bad, a couple of funny ditties—and she said she was feeling better: still sad, but a little bit lighter for a moment.

Dr. Z came to get me. As I walked away, her mom told me it was good to talk to me, that I had made a difference in their day. The girl's name was Madison: the same as Ella's best girlfriend. Imagine that?

I saw Madison again on my way out. I looked like hell because I had just relived hell. She looked at me. She gave me lots of shy smiles in the lobby, and she gave me another in the checkout area. I said, "See, you're not the only one who has to cry sometimes," and tapped her on the nose.

It means so much to hear I helped someone feel better today.

MARCH 31, 2009

As soon as I arrived at work today Paris called. He was crying, told me he got into a fight, put in security, and wants me to visit this weekend. He said he had a "breakdown" and wants to talk to me, to apologize. I also got a call from one of the attorneys about a letter he wrote my mom. I think he's up to something. Most likely he's worried about screwing up his ability to get out of jail. I think he's going to rehearse his first little "breakdown" on me and see how I react.

How should I react? I will, of course, call him out for whatever emotion he fakes. Or should I? Maybe he learns from my criticism, but is that a good thing? Perhaps it just helps him learn what areas of emotional affect he is lacking. Should I just listen to what he has to say and keep my thoughts to myself? If he asks me my opinion, just tell him I need time to think?

One thing we both have is plenty of time.

In his last letter to me, Paris wrote about nights we drove from my mom's house. He would put Ella's toy phone up to her ear like a pillow so the button would stay pushed. She loved it. She would go to sleep with phone noises ringing in her ear. He wrote about wondering whether he did so out of love for her or just to shut up her "incessant bitching." He was nine when he engineered her phone pillow; I thought he was the best big brother a sister could ask for. I was so wrong about him. Next time I'm wrong about him I could die. Or someone else could. Life never seems to work out the way I want. I'm not so sure that matters anymore. I think, I hope, what matters is I try to make the best of life and do what I can to live honestly and ethically. Notice I said nothing about sanely. In fact, I think it best to start with the assumption that life is orderly chaos. That way you're ready to live in between order and chaos, or at least attempt to.

I still have moments when I think, "Soon I'll wake up next to Ella with Paris telling me it's time to wake up and this will all have been a bad dream." How old will I live to be? When I envision my future self, I see myself alone, but I can't see myself to know if I'm old or not. What am I saying? I'm already old. I don't know if my body will keep up with my soul. I don't see how it can. I feel ready to burst at the seams as it is and I'm only thirty-five. What a fucking intense thirty-five years it's been.

Where do I go with all this pain now? I challenge myself to a duel. I'm the last of my demons.

APRIL 1, 2009

Externally, I'm maintaining. Internally, I hear the voices of panic and fear chiming in loud and clear. There's nothing I can do in a day to remove myself from my nightmares. It will take time. Resilience. There's the constant hum of profound loss underneath everything I do. Since the night Paris killed Ella I have not been able to see any issue clearly while at the same time seeing the world far too clearly. I reel from all I see.

I make a good show of it, but I have no idea what the hell I'm doing. I live my life based on intuition, grief, rage, dreams, and very intense thought. I hate being isolated and obsessed with the need to talk to no one but myself in these pages, but it's all I can do. The only activities I know I can do with any certainty right now are write, struggle with therapy, rise up to deal with Paris when needed, go to work (although barely at times—what a battle most mornings), and think and emote on stellar dimensions.

Where am I headed? What's going to happen with me, Ms. Jekyll and Existential Void Hyde, now? I'm good—have an evolved character—strive to change the world in any way I can. I also drink too much, smoke too much, spend too much time alone, and struggle to accept I am the mother of both a murdered child and the mother of a murderer. Two years later, I'm still in shock at my life.

What now, Charity Lee? You have to visit Paris this weekend—try to figure out what he's up to and how to handle it. My mother's coming for Ella's birthday, Ella's seventh birthday, so that means a joint visit with my son and my mother.

It's time to change, time to shed this heavy skin. It's wearing me down. It makes my soul dull. No matter how much I shed, I'll never lose the curse of deep thought. That much is evident. It's time to face my life in the nude, time to be raw and open. All these vices of mine are like a coating of aloe. They keep the sting away but do little to heal my third-degree soul burns. I have to figure out how to let go of my demons and embrace life again.

APRIL 7, 2009

I watched Ella's memorial service last night hoping it would help fill in some of my memory gaps. It brought back some memories, but more than anything it brought back grief. At the end of the service there's a shot of Ella lying dead in the funeral home. I knew it was there. I knew it was coming. I thought I was prepared.

Seeing Ella lying there dead again hit me like a bolt of lightning. I was right back to how I felt the ten days she lay there. I began to cry uncontrollably; my body trembled, twitched for about an hour. My sobs escaped my mouth no matter how hard I tried to hold them back. Full-blown return to ground zero.

Today I'm fragile at best. My body hurts and aches, especially my shoulders. I'm emotionally sensitive; my thoughts are in a frenzy. Organic pain, anxiety, grief, and sadness are my composition today. I still have the trembles. I'm not holding together well.

APRIL 8, 2009

I've survived, again, seeing Ella. In proportion to the amount of suffering I navigate, I grow stronger and wiser. Of course, I also grow more isolated and eccentric in the same proportion. Pros and cons, yin and yang. Nothing can ever be all good or all bad. It just is what it is.

Strangely enough I feel more like an adult now than ever. I'm beginning to fit into this new Charity. I feel more attractive. I feel wiser and curvier. I feel mature, totally mature for the first time. I've been all things to all people—daughter, mother, sister, friend, enemy, lover, saint, sinner, adored and hated, inspiring and destructive to all those around me. Now it's time to call upon myself to be all things to me—become Charity upon the loss of her children—reborn.

APRIL 9, 2009

I keep picturing myself as some sort of mutant Buddhist monk. I spend most of my time in contemplation of my soul, writing, tending to my flowers, painting furniture—reading, reading, reading, think some more. I take brief forays into the world with my begging bowl to gather the scraps I need to nourish my soul: volunteer training, school stuff, dealing with my son. Most of my time is spent processing input from the different levels of my mind, voices within and from without. Not hallucinations. Intuition. Knowledge of the next thing to do and how to do it best (hopefully). Dreams. Signs.

I'm a soul who, at base, loves to learn. I'm also a soul who, for a reason outside my understanding or concern, can integrate all I've experienced, all I've felt, all I have knowledge of, into something tragic yet inspiring—bringing creation out of destruction, making what is horrible, ugly, and bloody look beautiful again.

Right now I feel a sense of centeredness within my soul. I'm on track, on the right path—I'm beginning to fulfill my new purpose. I still have faith in good. I'm discovering vats of untapped faith in myself. Another intense and unpredictable phase has begun in my life. Then again, it's not really a phase; it's just my life—intense and unpredictable.

My mom will be here in the morning. Ella's birthday is Sunday—Easter Sunday, this year. To honor Ella, I will get along with my mother this visit. I will even try to enjoy her foray into my world.

APRIL 11, 2009

I am now truly one hundred percent alone. Mom arrived yesterday. After a joint visit with Paris, she is gone. Tomorrow is Ella's seventh birthday.

I felt sorry for myself awhile. I've cried a lot since my mom left. We went to see Paris together. On the way home we started to argue about him, who he was, and by default, who I was. I got really angry. She left. Just as she always does when confronted.

Everyone finds me too intense or angry to be around. Maybe I am. Not one single "friend" I've made since coming here has reached out to me since I broke up with Nic. Of course, they never did before, either. My own mother doesn't like me, and my son hates me enough to kill Ella.

So ... to recap: I have a sociopathic son who is a killer, a mother who doesn't like me and hates being a mother, a murdered baby, and no friends in this town. I live amidst ceaseless and demanding pain and anger. I make a lot of mistakes. Yet, at this point, in spite of the cards in my hand—all the pain, all the tears—I know I'm doing the right things for myself and in regard to my children. Something beautiful will come from the loss of my family and, ultimately, of myself. I'm not fighting the pain anymore. I'm embracing it. I will get a master's degree, write down all my thoughts, and share all my words.

I have a nagging fear I'm burying myself in writing and school like my mother did with work. I think there's one huge difference, though. She went to work to lose herself and her pain, and to make money. I'm going to work to find myself and help other people. I don't want a completely solitary life, but I can't settle for one that feels just okay, but not *right*, for me.

The knowledge of what to do next manifests in my mind at key times. Ever since Ella died, I'm able to visit a place within myself I call the "observation room." I zone out. Get still. Preternaturally calm. Stare into space. See nothing around me, but I sit and watch the actual process of a thought leading to an emotion or an emotion leading to thought. I'm watching a complex interweaving of memory, emotion, education, instinct, intellect, and higher consciousness take place. To scramble the puzzle up and make it harder to solve, life throws in lots of external signs and wisdom of its own into my heap—a lifeline, so to speak. When I snap to, another baby step in my evolution has been achieved. Poof! Another piece of the puzzle is found, but it seems questions always lead to more questions.

After tonight's journey to the observation room, I decided to let go of being worried what others think of me and my story. Like it or not, it's my story. It has made me who I am. As far as myself—I know I'm flawed. I also know I'm good—a really, really good soul—and I'll do whatever it takes to dig that soul out of all this spiritual destruction. Death is birth, after all.

There's nothing to stop my soul from evolving. Not even death. I'll continue to exist and learn and love and hurt no matter where my soul is. I've tried to stop myself in so many different ways. Everything I've experienced, good and bad, has taught me something and ultimately led to growth.

All battles, no matter how noble their original cause, end only in blood, pain, loss, and suffering. I'm not fighting anymore. I lay down. Although vipers still exist, I don't want to play the role of mouse anymore. I will be the phoenix, the dove, the butterfly.

I know what to do, for the time being, with my son. I'll follow my own heart, conscience, and instinct with him. I won't treat him unfairly. In spite of all he's done, and all he could become, he's my son. I love him. I want to be wrong about him. If I am, I am. If I'm not, he'll be treated humanely, and people will be kept safe.

When it comes to my mom, only time will tell. For now, our relationship is on hold. I want a much different life than hers, so I'm going to live it. As for me—I'm doing what I need to do and have to do. I'm on the right path, no matter how lonely or painful.

APRIL 12, 2009

Today is Ella's seventh birthday.

I'm inside myself staying out of my thoughts. One thought is to take four boxes of sleeping pills this time. It seems three simply doesn't work. One thought is I'm on the right path through this hell. Another thought is I can't move, do anything—it's all too heavy today. I know for a fact on days like today, I am both sane and insane, on point, but out of key.

The Charity of my youth is back: the one who's introspective, always feels alone because of her weird life circumstances, the observer, the thinker, trying to make some sense of life. The only difference is my thoughts are more sophisticated and my feelings more encompassing than at eight or ten or twelve.

I think I may be a freak of some sort. I have such a hard time finding any place or people I fit with for any extended time. I don't know if I'm an outsider because of who I am or what has happened in my life. Is it possible to even split the two? I am who I am because of everything I've lived. I've lived all I've lived because of who I am.

I read *The Lovely Bones* again over the last couple of days. One line says, "She has learned not to talk, it changed nothing. Time was the only thing that mattered."

The fact I am drawn to those words is further proof I need to shut up for a bit and process word-by-word—written and read. Words are going to walk with me in and out of hell. Words will save me and hurt me. Words will help me maintain. Words will see me through and bring me down. Ultimately the only thing I have left is my voice and my character—my soul and my love for my children.

Did I mention it's Easter Sunday? Life, resurrection, salvation, all the good stuff. I wonder how many holidays I'll be alone before I find friends or family of my own? A month? A year? A lifetime? Does it even matter anymore? Cars are parked all over the neighborhood because families are having big Easter Sunday meals. I've eaten a piece of bread and choked down some of Ella's chocolate birthday cake.

What's going to happen to me? Nobody's coming to save me. No one has any answers for me. Obviously most people I know care about me very little. I know Nic loved me—he just doesn't really know how to. I know Rebecca loves me, but she's far away and living her own life. I keep waiting for Nic to come and get his motorcycle. It's the last of him here. There's no point in seeing him; I can't go back no matter the pain.

I'm in pain today. Everything I love is gone. Please tell me good things are coming my way. Please tell me I'm going to get healthy, move on, make new friends, fall in love again, work well, and make good. Please tell me I'll live again without constant pain and anger and fear. I'm so tired, so alone; I don't know how I continue to exist, if I truly even exist at all to anyone but myself.

I'm a total hypocrite.

I vandalized Nic's bike this morning—very coldly and methodically—could not, did not, want to stop myself. Today there is no love, no empathy, no desire to keep breathing or trying to make meaning out of all this pain and bullshit. I'm drowning in it; it stinks. No one stays near me.

I was so desperate not to give up on life last night I texted Nic—told him it was Ella's birthday and I was alone because my mom left. Nothing. I waited and passed out asleep, hating myself for giving in to the desperation and loneliness I've brought upon myself. For giving him any sort of power over me.

I woke up this morning and the first thing I thought is, *Another day all alone in the world.* Immediately engulfed in the reality of my life—I'm so completely alone, it's a foray into insanity—I decided it was me or the bike. I wanted/needed to destroy something/all things that keep me focused on the past with Nic. I needed an outlet for all this rage and fury and pain and supreme loneliness, so I pushed the bike over, cut a bunch of wires, broke all the lights, broke a mirror off—little things that will mean a big fix.

Stalkerish and crazy of me, I know, but now I know I have reached the end of the road with Nic. I don't care what he thinks anymore. All I need to do is get through this hell intact. No more indulging in anger. It's time to learn to live calmly with it if I can.

It's very difficult for me to believe I'm not insane. My therapist says I'm not. She says I am troubled and remarkable. Does she know just how troubled I am? Do I know how remarkable I am? There is a very fine line between sanity and insanity; it's a line I cross unpredictably, consistently.

Suicide has been heavy in my thoughts lately. I won't do it. It takes all I am on days like this not to disintegrate again, fade to black, let it all go and cease to be—even remember why I hold on in the first place. Where will I find the strength and character to do all I need to do? Therapy. Masters. Domestic violence work. Friends. Heal. Live outside myself again.

APRIL 14, 2009

Another day physically alone. Eight days with no word out of anyone in San Antonio. No word will come. I don't exist to anyone associated with Nic anymore. It's been a painful and traumatic process pulling myself out of the grave. It doesn't matter if others understand either my method or my madness.

I found a picture of myself around the age of six or seven yesterday. It was taken after my dad was murdered. I put it next to Ella's picture on my desk. We look a lot alike in all but one regard: Ella looks happy. You can see it in her eyes. I already look thoughtful and resolute, gaze and chin firmly set. Was I born that way or made that way?

"Liberty is the right to choose. Freedom is the result of the right choice." I have no idea who said that.

"Work on your own salvation. Do not depend on others." Buddha.

APRIL 15, 2009

Solitary confinement might be needed but it is killing me. My friend Sam came and took my gun from me. I'm not doing well. I want to die. I don't care if I survive. I don't want to be one who beats the odds. I'm tired and I want to quit and I want to die. I want to go to the store and buy sleeping pills. I want to go inside and go to bed, never to wake up. I want an end to this pain. I am tired, worn out, see no point in my continued existence. I am unloved. I have no one to stand by my side. My own son hates me enough to want me dead and to have killed Ella.

I don't know how to keep myself alive.

APRIL 16, 2009

I broke down last night - drank a whole bottle of Bailey's, took twenty-four sleeping pills, texted Nic. I'm rather ashamed of myself. I don't know how to keep getting on this horse. My energy is sapped. I'm alone, completely alone. I don't know how to live anymore. I can only fake it so long before all the raw pain gets me again.

I woke up both disappointed and relieved I was awake, alive. I can't shake or loosen my hold on this body. My pain is too big for it, yet it seems to always accommodate more. I want to see my solitary confinement as a place to grow, a place to create peace—and it is—yet solitary confinement is still solitary confinement.

It's been ten days since I broke up with Nic. I haven't quit smoking. I haven't quit drinking. I don't walk the dog. I sit and I cry and I hurt. I try mini-suicides. I want out of this haze, but I'm the only one in here groping for a way out. There's no one else lost with me. There are no hands on the outside reaching in to help me get me out. It's up to me to save myself. But how can I? What's my motivation? Do I really want to get out? Since when has life cared about what I want?

Last night, I couldn't remember why I'm still alive. Today, now, I can remember I'm alive for Ella. I'm alive to learn. I'm alive to help someone. I'm alive to love someone. I'm alive because I'm alive. It's not death I fear or how I'll die. What I fear is that my soul won't be in the right place to see Ella again. If I give up trying, I'll never see Ella. I'm this life and this life is mine. I have to learn to live it again. I have to figure out how to let go of anger.

I feel unloved and unlovable. These days alone are putting me through the wringer. I'm sure other people must think about me from time to time, yet none of them reach out. It seems I'm am always the one reaching. Of course, I push away too.

Is it so hard to be my friend? Is it because I am too human, wear my heart on my sleeve, have strong opinions—what? Either people can't really see how much pain I am in, or they see it and it scares them because they feel helpless in the face of this ugly reality. If it's the first, I'm fumbling in doubt as to how they can't see the pain in me. I feel it ooze through my pores and watch it contaminate everything it touches. I feel it course through my blood carrying poison to all parts of me. It's etched into the new lines on my face, the haunted look in my eyes, the fragile pieces of my psyche which are somehow still holding together. If it's the second, is their fear so great they can't even wonder how much more helpless *I* feel in the face of all this?

No matter how much good work I do in criminal justice— no matter how many people I help or love—Ella is and always will be dead. Paris is and always will be dangerous, and will, one day, have to become dead in my mind. I'll have to calmly walk away and hide. I'll always be walking backwards away from Paris—always backwards. Truly dead kids don't, won't, can't try to kill you. Even if Paris doesn't kill me, living with the thought of it, I think, will be worse than my actual death if he gets me. Although, if he gets me, I'm sure that won't be so pleasant either.

Maybe the reason I'm still alive has something to do with my writing? Live through it all, write it down, because one day the words will mean something to someone other than me. I'd always planned to leave my journals to Paris and Ella upon my death with a note telling them to read them if they wanted to, with the hope they'd come to know their mom as more than just a mom, but a woman—a human.

Ella knows all this about me now, and most likely a whole lot more than I do at this point. Paris can't know because he's at the other end of the human scale—still human, but a less evolved soul. He'll never understand me on the same level I grasp him.

Who knows what will happen to my words now when I die?

This is the hardest life I've lived. This is the most painful life I've lived. I know I'll lose other people, but it won't register like this loss. If I can continue to navigate this life and death, I can do anything. I have to, but I still ride the fence on whether

I want to. When a *have to* squeezes out a *want to* you have follow through. Wanting can expand your heart with so much wanting that you shatter.

I want Ella—still—every day. I want to hold her, hear her voice, listen to her sing, smell her, touch her. I'd give ... I was going to say I'd give my soul away just to touch Ella. I wouldn't, though. I may touch her, but only once. To stay with Ella, I have to find my soul, heal it, and let it fly again. Then, when I die, I'll be able to rest for a bit in her company.

I don't think we're as different dead as we are alive. In fact, I cannot—do not—believe we lose anything but our body when we die. We don't really die. We lose the use of our body as a teaching aide, but we still learn and think and exist as ourselves—me but more aware that I am me and more aware of my purpose.

Every definition of the word *die* implies a form of diminishment—failure—or expiration: you're used up, no good. Why? Why is death seen so negatively? We ultimately have no control over it—no matter what lengths we go to convince ourselves. We all die. We're not diminished by it. We aren't a failure for dying.

We don't expire. I'm not a carton of milk. I'm energy. I can't be destroyed—just transformed. I won't run out of energy one day. I'll always be just energy. Carbon-based starburst by-product am I—a child of the stars and heavens.

Fuck it. There are so many purposes behind purposes—worlds upon worlds, infinite space and time—the whole purpose is probably awareness of that fact.

It is what it is.

APRIL 20, 2009

I am sick of dreaming of Nic. All the things I wish I could say to him, to help him understand, are what I dream of. I dream of babies and yearning and to be touched again. The last thing I heard myself say in my dream was, "I don't want you back, but I miss you." Then I woke up.

The first functional—the only functional—thing I've accomplished so far is to have the damn motorcycle towed to his apartment. I'm tired of looking at the thing. It was a gift from me, and it's shitty and ungrateful of him to leave it here. So I paid to have it towed. I've paid for everything else, so this is no surprise. Anyway, the last connection is gone. It's a sign of progress and acceptance on my part—getting the bike out of here. I'm not waiting on him to come get it anymore. My fantasy of him fighting for me is over. I'm sick of having him in my head, and I want another life to start. The majority of my time spent with Nic was in fantasy land—I tried to overlook how different we were and pretend we could be something we aren't.

I find it intriguing that over-saturation of emotion is both overwhelming yet also necessary for desensitization. In order to truly grant to yourself acceptance of yourself, you must first strive to fully understand what you're accepting. At the point you realize you'll never understand it all—you accept. My life will revolve around my own world. I'll keep dealing with Paris. My career will deal somehow with criminal justice. I will go public with my thoughts. My writing will never cease. Mourning progresses and regresses.

Life goes on—and on—and on—and on—and on....

In therapy today, I began to see how vague and black those days after Ella's death were. I remember hearing footsteps in the hall and getting warm and peaceful in the middle of a full-blown panic-induced existential crisis. I cried out to her over and over to come lie down with me. "I can't sleep without you, Ella. I need you—I'm tired, Ella." And she did. I slept peacefully that night and was very, very warm when I woke up. I knew she still existed. She still does.

I remember picking up her box of ashes. Everyone at the funeral home handled me with the utmost care and hush-hush tones. I walked into the office and saw the box, there, on a desk—centered. A plain white cardboard box with heavy-duty super-strong tape. I knew it was Ella, but it still hadn't registered. The funeral director handed her to me. I took Ella in my arms, in this hard-little cardboard box, and I began to silently cry.

All I could think was how similar this was to the first time I held Ella in my arms. Someone handed her to me and I held her and she was alive. Now she was handed to me for the last time and I was holding her, but this time she was in a box—dead. Someone wrote "Ella Smith" on top of the box. I scratched it out and corrected it with "Bennett." Ella never knew herself as Ella Smith. She was always, always will be a Bennett.

I remember countless hours spent curled around that box, sleeping with that box, watching TV with the box in my lap or by my side. Countless hours spent talking to Ella, sobbing on my knees wherever I fell to them, pleading for Ella's forgiveness for not knowing, not being there, failing her.

I remember putting her in the urn. I put my hand in her ashes—ran her through my fingers, felt the small remnants of her bones. How could this be the same warm body I used to hold? I remember the panic attack when I realized I did not know how to clean my hands when I was done feeling her for the final time. I could not just wash her off. I looked outside and saw the dew on the grass shining, sparkling like diamonds thrown about, and knew exactly what to do. I walked outside, dropped to my knees, and ran my hands through the grass, giving her back to nature.

I still ask Ella to come lie down with me, and most of the time she does. I still talk to her all the time, silently and out loud. She even has the ability to answer me from time to time. She comes to me in dreams. She is a voice inside my head guiding me to what I hope is the next right step to take. She gives me goosebumps when she is near to me. Ella still exists. Of this, I am certain and, because I am certain of this, I know I too will exist past all this. Blessing and curse as usual.

At times I wonder if I'm not able to experience the world anymore, or is the world unable to experience me? I understand why others find me so hard to comprehend. Lots of lonely days ahead I'm afraid, Charity, my girl. Test after test after test. The problem is, when you truly believe this is not a pass or fail test, it makes it hard to know what to study. From another perspective, it gives you the freedom to learn all you can about everything—not just in books (although never discount them as meaningless), but life, the good and the bad.

After all I've weathered the last two years, I'm now reconciled to the idea that nothing is impossible; life is unpredictable, but navigable. I still get lost and it's still Ella or Paris who steer me back on track.

Tonight, I'd like a night full of good dreams of Ella, no dreams of Nic, no dreams of blood or wounding, stabbing, dying in fear. Peace; all I want is some peace.

Here's to hope.

APRIL 23, 2009

The downside of hope is depression. Depression eats all hope inside you. I quit my job. I can't function in the "real" world when my depression starts chewing. I fear words are beginning to leave me. I'm so entranced in my world, talking to only myself, I'm beginning to forget how to deal with and engage in the daily world—how to talk to people, how to desire talking to people. Most of my time is spent with my mouth shut. My pen moves. How to talk to people? My fingers type. My eyes read. My heart aches but my mouth is mostly mute. How to talk to people?

I received a letter from my son today. I was scared when I saw it—wondered what new roller coaster ride it would send my mind on. All he wants is for me to send his box of books to my mom so he can have them again later. That's it. Oh—PS—thanks for visiting.

I'm relieved and disappointed and sad. Relieved there was nothing gruesome or morbid about the letter. Disappointed there's nothing personal either except Paris' wants—Paris' needs—I'm an afterthought. Sad because in my mind it's further proof that Paris is a sick, callous, remorseless, and very dangerous killer. Will he develop into a serial killer, or will he be stopped? Those two questions actually have nothing to do with one another, do they? Most likely he will, and most likely he won't be until it's too late. It already is. Ella is dead.

My therapist decided I can have a break from the PTSD sessions. I'm obviously exhausted and in pain, even more so now that I'm alone. It's time to decrease the pressure for a bit. The therapy has helped with the memories of losing Ella. I'll have to go through the same process for, about, Paris. I let fear of him stop me from fully living—anger at him stop me from fully living. By fully living I don't mean jetting off to sky dive every weekend or safari in Africa, nor do I mean work, work, work. Fully living means knowing I have a purpose and am fulfilling it.

I think I have a purpose, yet it could also be a finely constructed mirage of denial so I won't realize I'm insane. If it's a purpose, and not a mirage, I'm not sure I'm fulfilling it. I've seen enough of life to know the only purpose we may have in life is the mirage. Our specialty, though—well it would appear my specialty anyway—is to deflect all the desperation at not knowing into fuel for the search. Turn shit into tulips.

I read an article which stated the deepest cuts a killer makes are the ones that give him the most pleasure. Does this mean what he found most pleasurable about killing Ella were the final fatal stabs? Which of the death by 10,000 cuts he inflicts on me are the most pleasurable to him?

I would love to stop all this, be able to walk away, say that's it—no more Paris, no more serial killers, no more research, push it all away. But I can't. No more than Paris could keep himself from killing Ella can I stop what it is he started. This is my world. It will change but, at its core, it will always come back to this as long as Paris is alive—especially if he's free. If I walk away, I'll always be looking over my shoulder. I have to parry with the dragon while I plan my campaign.

I want to be wrong. I want to visit Paris in a mental institution in la-la land, spending his time painting, because his guilt finally got to him. I don't want a seemingly well-adjusted psychopath son chomping at the bit to get out of prison. Once upon a time I wanted to see him graduate from art school.

APRIL 26, 2009

I see the horrible disgusting side of life. I see the beautiful side of life. I'm quite sure I see too much and feel too deeply. My entire being is composed of the knowledge of both how beautiful and sacred life can be—is—and how many ways there are for us as humans to make it ugly, violent, degrading, twisted, and meaningless. The knowledge of good and evil.

Paris shoved the fucking apple down my throat and forced me to gag it down. Too bad he didn't eat some too. In order to do what he has done; he can truly have no spot of Eden in his soul.

APRIL 27, 2009

I have been reading *Demian* by Hesse. Dualism. Following your inner voice, no matter what it leads to—good or evil—so long as you find your true self. When I first started reading it, it reminded me of Paris. As I keep reading, I see me in it too, and what I see of Paris in it is always in opposition to what I see of me in it: dualism. Paris and I are two halves of the whole. I was happy to be a third with Ella, but he had other things in mind.

I was listening to a commentary about killers on NPR. Being discussed was the issue of appearance related to criminals. If someone who looks like Paris—or Ted Kennedy or Ted Bundy—kills someone, people seem to have such a hard time believing someone who looks that "normal" could do such things as stab their sister to death, let a girl drown, kill and kill and kill. People fear these killers more because they do seem normal and functional. They remind them too much of themselves. They start to look around and wonder who near them may actually be crazy. Or dangerous.

What they don't know, or won't accept, is that we're all crazy. And dangerous.

In the long run, who is crazier? The person who has their eyes open to the world, or those who want to keep theirs shut and pretend there is only one world and it's wholly good. Why do so many people, including myself, try to hide from their suffering when it's the only way to find your joy again? If you never allow yourself to fall into your loss, you will never float up into your joy.

Again, dualism.

Today, at this moment, my duality is at peace with itself. Today I know I'm becoming the voice I hear in my head—the vision I see of the Charity to be. Today I know I'll bring into the light the woman I've always wanted to be. I just didn't get here the way I thought I would.

APRIL 30, 2009

Maybe it's my lot in life to feel alone—to be alone. Today, Dr. Zuelzer asked me to describe the young Charity. I remember her being serious. I don't remember any friends other than adults before the third grade. My friendships were always contentious. I was the odd girl of the popular clique. I was shy. I thought a lot.

I look at a picture of my six-year-old self and see a young girl who has already seen much. Her jaw is set to withstand. I don't look happy, but I don't look sad. There is something about my eyes though. I look older than I should. I don't remember when the picture was taken. It was sometime before or after my dad was murdered. Does it make a difference? I already knew before my dad died I didn't lead a "normal" life.

I had favorite hiding spots—one pre-murder and one post-murder. Pre-murder, my favorite place to escape was in the garage sitting in the passenger seat of my dad's Rolls Royce. I would get in the car and sit in the dark. I was a very small child; I could never see anything in my mom's car. The Rolls, though, it had big plush leather seats—so fat they had the little buttons that push down into the leather. I could see all around me sitting in that seat. More importantly though, it was quiet and dark. I could think. I would sit there in the dark, smelling all the leather—and think until my mom found me.

Post-murder, it was the huge magnolia tree in my grandparent's front yard that called to me. I stayed with them the summer my mom was in jail, on trial. I would climb to the top with a book, sit up there and read for hours. Mamasam was always in her own world, so I got to be in mine until Papa came home. I enjoyed spending time in his world too: the gardens, the yard, practical activities like errand running. I always knew Papa loved me—no matter how gruff. He was the rock in many ways. He's the only man to have survived with a woman of our family as long as he did.

Post-murder, I don't remember being truly happy again until I found out I was pregnant with Paris. My mom changed, built a wall around herself to survive; life was chaotic and dysfunctional. Looking back I can now see the dysfunction was always there. After my father's death, it was no longer background noise in my life. It became the soundtrack.

It seems my family can do nothing small, nothing average. Too much murder, too much money, too much mayhem.

I look forward to seeing my family when I die. I would have liked to know my father. My mom wouldn't talk of him after he died, and all I knew about him really was the bad stuff. I'd like to know all of him. I'd like to know if he loved me—is proud of me despite my life, how I lived it, how I lost it. I would want to tell Mamasam and Papasam how sorry I am for not realizing how much they meant to me until they were gone. My actual memories of all we did when I was young may be fuzzy, but there's no mistaking the tone of what I feel for them: only good feelings, none of the anger or bitterness that comes when I look back on memories of my mom and Paris.

I like to think everyone is with Ella—my dad and my grandparents. I like to think my dad's parents are there. I don't remember them, but I do remember my mom telling me how heartbroken Old Man Bennett was when my dad died. He loved my dad. I hope they're at peace together. I like to think they're all around me, that they help me all they can, root for me. I like to think one day I can come home to family again.

I was wrong about needing to fight with myself, my demons. I don't need to fight anymore. I've fought my entire life. I'm just going to sit with them, converse with them, find out why they're demons now when I know they started as angels. My demons and I will come to a truce. I won't neglect them if they won't hold me back. Two years and eighty-five days of hell has made even my demons tired. Even they are ready to negotiate.

The six-year-old me knew, on some level, there was more to life than what I saw. The six-year-old me could never have imagined how much more she was going to see, feel, and think. If she had known—she would have gone insane. The thirty-five-year-old me is the same in all regards but for the sanity. Most of the time I feel I am the truly sane person in the room, and almost everyone around me has gone crazy, because they don't see what I see – the totality of life.

Why are people scared to turn around to face themselves? Or, better question, because I scare myself too, is why do we consistently give in to that fear? Why am I weird if I think everything we do has cosmic implications, that my daughter still exists and guides me, yet others are sane in believing they drink God's blood, that only the pope can talk to God, that Allah condones the violence done by the Taliban, that Elvis is now a minor Hindu god.

From this point on, I place my faith in what I know to be true. I follow my own heart and well-honed, earned instincts. I live the way I want to live; look the way I want to look. I will tattoo my family story across my body. Color my heart whatever color I want. I speak with honesty, bluntness, and no shame, as strangely as I want. I have fought for and earned the right to be me.

This is something else the six-year-old and I have in common. We both know we're different, but not unique; we both think and feel our way through the world; we're both aware not all is as it seems; and we're both determined to be ourselves.

We both hope we know who that is.

So much for peace. Further proof of how unstable my life and I are: I go inside thinking I'm at peace and end up deciding to write my son and send him pictures of when he was young. He needs to know I haven't forgotten who he is now, but I do remember who he was. I remember when I look at all those pictures.

I remember who he was—who I was. How the hell did either of us get to where we are now? How can that beautiful, loved, and outwardly happy, gifted child turn into a sexually motivated killer? How did that serious, introspective girl career out of control only to get grounded again when she gave birth to a psychopath?

I cried, then cried some more for both of us. I always knew we were growing up together, and one day our paths would diverge. I never would have imagined just how much. I could never foresee a day I would love and hate my lifesaving and love-teaching Paris Lee.

It will never make sense, yet I sense it all does.

It gives me hope none of what happened was in vain, yet pains my heart we must suffer to evolve. The more pleasure something gives us, the more pain it exponentially causes. We are all bound to this universal truth, so bound we will do painful things to others to keep our own pleasure close and our pain at bay.

False fronts—again.

Do you know I think all the time of all the various ways Paris could kill me? In all the scenarios, I just want to make sure I tell him I love him and that Ella and I will be waiting on him. It's the truth, but to hear it at that moment would infuriate him. If Paris ever gets me, I don't think there will be much mercy shown or much of me left. If Paris gets me, I know I will feel everything Ella felt and more. He will take more time with me because finally he will have the real object of his rage at hand rather than a symbol of it.

What the hell kind of life is this that I even think these things? That I kiss Ella's urn instead of her nose? That I refuse to hold my son's hands after all the time I spent holding his hands when he was in NICU with jaundice? When I hug him now, I think how strong he is, how easily he could kill me; instead of being in awe of my child's transformation, I live in fear of my child's transformation.

Wonder what he makes of mine? I am sure he did not expect me to survive. Wonder if it makes him mad I'm not as easy to destroy as he thought I would be? Metaphorical death didn't work. Yanking the carpet out from under me only fucked me up more. The only way to really beat me now is to make me disappear.

If Paris kills me one day, I'm going to haunt him, lovingly.

MAY 1, 2009

When it comes to alcohol and cigarettes, I have lost all respect for myself. They're killing me and sustaining me. I coughed up blood again. It shocks me, yet here I sit and smoke. The very second I stub one out, I put another to my lips. I still want to die. I still hope I'll just cease to breathe. Slow suicide will not allow me to see Ella again, so why can't I stop all these self-destructive tendencies of mine? That's easy. They keep the pain at bay. The pain of being alone. The pain of having no one but a therapist to talk to. The pain of being a mother. All of it—pain.

I can't leave my house. Going out into the world shows me what I miss about not having my kids. Going out also shows me the abused kids, the hungry ones, the ones who hurt others, the ones who have been hurt. I'm no good in the world most people think of as real. I do all right in this bizarre and tortured world in my head, yet I can't reconcile the two—they're too polarized to be co-mingled.

My first session of domestic violence training is tomorrow. I'm scared. Now I'm always scared walking into a new situation. I wonder at what point contact with the world will send me reeling. I know it'll be hard to see these women and children in pain, in fear, hurt. I know exactly how fear and pain feel at the moment of impact. It's just the beginning of the feeling. I'll cry with them, I'm sure. I wonder if that's allowed. To cry with them. To hold them if they want it.

MAY 1, 2009

I'm cheating and doing May 1 twice because I have a new journal and I want it to start officially on the first. Blank pages of paper fascinate me. A journal is nothing but a bunch of bound wood pulp, yet once it's full of words, it's a totem for your life. It contains wisdom you forgot you knew.

I'm getting the hang of this solitary lifestyle. I'm beginning to enjoy certain aspects of this life. I have to take that back. I'm learning how to function in pain—manage it better. It hasn't decreased or gone away. I haven't felt life is good again.

In seventeen stabs of a knife, my entire world was taken away along with Ella's. I have to rebuild with worse than nothing—my materials are all so odious. At the rate I'm going, it'll be a very old woman who maybe, one day, finds a way to enjoy life again. I'm afraid no matter how much good I may do, I will feel empty forever.

I spoke with a friend at TYC today. She told me about a woman whose thirteen-year-old daughter was murdered by a twelve-year-old neighbor. While incarcerated at Giddings, he said he was going to kill the girl's mother for keeping him locked up. He gets out soon, so the mother is leaving Texas. I would like to correspond with her. It's not often one can talk to another person whose daughter has been murdered *and* believes the killer wants her dead. She believes it enough to leave the state, her home.

Where will I end up when I leave Texas? Should I tell anyone where I am? I can't tell anyone where I'm going once Paris is out. If he really wants to hurt or kill me, he would hurt or kill those who know me, unless I was notified beforehand, then I could warn the cops. God knows where I'll end up. I just want to be safe and useful.

I can always use the last of my money to disappear to a friendly third-world country or island. That's actually not a bad idea. I can still be me. I don't think Paris would be able to get a passport, so I could be safe somewhere else. Of course, there are sick people all over this world of ours. Wouldn't it be cosmic poetic irony if I was fleeing one violent death only to meet another?

So here I am; both in limbo and out. Life is constantly in a state of flux, so I guess true limbo isn't possible. No matter what you do, you're living. It's possible, though, to be in a state of suspended animation. There's still life in me—I'm animated—it's just happening on a different level of consciousness right now. In lay terms, I begin to feel the need to leave my cocoon shortly. See where the wind takes me.

MAY 2, 2009

My mind is ablaze today. I have all these next steps I've been working on and more of them are clicking into place. I've made up my mind it's time to find and consult an attorney concerning testing for Paris and to have representation familiar with all the information at his hearing. I won't give up this fight easily—if ever at all. I know, in my heart, despite all the anger and loss and pain Paris has brought to me, I'm still guided by my love for him—not my hate.

I also want legal advice on retaining ownership of my story. I've come to believe I'm meant to go public with my story, become a vocal advocate for both exceptionally violent offenders and their victims. But how do I do that?

Every issue we face in life has to do with one thing—how do we reconcile our duality? Find harmony? My children were the price I paid to find my soul—to let my starburst shine forth. If I fail to rise to the occasion and fulfill my journey, I will have made both their lives meaningless. If mine isn't meaningful, theirs was for naught.

I don't know why I didn't realize this until just now, but if Paris does get out soon, I may not have much time left to live. Five years? Ten years? I should start enjoying this world more and work harder to leave it a better place than I found it.

For the most part, I approve of who I am. I know both who I am and who I'm trying in every conceivable and inconceivable way to become. I still have mommy issues. I always will, since I'll always have a mother. I'll always have the influence, directly or indirectly, of having been born of a mother. What I no longer have issue with is approval ratings. I also no longer have issues with being who others want me to be at the expense of myself.

Today was my first day of FACT training. FACT is the Family Assistance Crisis Team, a group within the San Antonio Police Department that helps victims of domestic violence. It's not pretty or glossy or easy, but it's what I know, what I've seen, felt, and feel. Today, from 9 am to 4 pm, I felt I was in a country, a town, I grew up in. I know the language and the lay of the land. I know all the characters. I've never been physically abused by a man. I've been given my fair share of emotional abuse and dished out my fair share too. I've never been sexually abused either. My older half-brother tried to convince me to lick his penis once when I was five. I told him no way and told my mom.

She did nothing. Or nothing happened. He never did it again. She told me when I was an adult that she had told my dad and he didn't believe it, so she let it go. I think my brother was thirteen or fourteen at the time. I've been in situations with men that I've found awkward, ethically or emotionally wrong, but never had anything done to me against my will, without my consent.

I've been with my fair share of lovers, but I think they knew this was the one area not to go with me. One boyfriend told me I wasn't the type of woman who gave off the vulnerable vibe, so guys knew I wouldn't stand for it and would fight back. I dumped him quickly. That he spent that much time thinking through vulnerable versus invulnerable characteristics in chicks, I found mildly disturbing.

Sometimes I think because I'm the product of criminals, murderers, manipulators, narcissists, and emotional chess players, I have a radar now for people and their intentions— their more hidden motivations. People let you know, in oh so many ways, who and what they are. Most of us are so caught up in thinking only of our own lives, we don't pay close enough attention to other's needs, wants, dreams, and nightmares.

We should.

Irony of all irony, though? If I have this radar, why didn't it go off for the one person in close range who was hiding so many fantasies and nightmares? Why did I have no idea who Paris is?

For most of my life I've felt I see, maybe not clearly, more of people than even they may be willing to see for themselves. The night Paris killed Ella that vision came sharply into focus. Some may say my view of people is clouded by all I've seen, that I'm bound to see through the scanner darkly. I find that to be bullshit. For the first time in my life, I've begun to see things clearly.

We are all good and bad. None of us is more important or valuable than another. Some are less capable or gifted in some things than others, but are no less an expression of life. There are no real differences among humans except for those generated by us to control our own fears. Underneath our color, our culture, our gender, our class, we are, in the end, the same.

We are human. We hurt. We love and want to be loved. We are able to perform acts of heroism and hedonism. The only thing different is the expression of these thoughts, beliefs, feelings due to aforementioned man-made constructs (or woman-made, let's not get all PC). There are gods of the earth for farmers. There are gods of the hunt for hunters. One is supposedly better than the other because of what? The only reason one is a hunter and one is a farmer is because of where they originated and what the people who created them had to do to survive. Do you think the hunter god or the farmer god cares? It's all the same God, after all—just as we're the same kind of human, you know, just human.

I am tired of all the animosity in the world. I want to be a factor in helping somebody else find peace. My hope is the more peace I create, the more peace I will feel. A lot of people have questioned if the FACT work is good for me, since I still struggle so hard with my own experience of violence. It's a misconception to think one must be at peace in order to create peace. It helps, and is certainly recommended, but it's not necessary.

I'm in such pain myself how could I not want to comfort someone else in pain? I know how they feel. I'm not afraid to sit with someone while they're in pain. I wish more had done—did—it with me. I don't expect these women to be ready to walk out and change their entire lives right away. I just want them to know there's someone who understands, doesn't judge, has been plunged into hell too, and that they are cared for, even if only by me.

I like these days, the ones where I feel as though I've attained a millimeter of progress up the Mt. Everest of my life. I'm to the point where my soul is acclimating to less warmth, life, breath, and light. Now begins the rest of the ascent.

The only reason I cling to this damn mountain is to see what the view from the uppermost part of my soul looks like. To know what it feels like. There will be other hills in life to climb, but this is my Mt. Everest. I know this in my bones. Even losing Paris to death won't compare to losing him to murder. The only thing harder than this would be if I had more children and Paris killed them too.

I won't dwell on this, though. It's pointless. If I had to choose between another child and Paris, I would stop him. If he ever comes near me or mine again with death as his goal, he will have to settle for me or no one. It will be him or me. If there were absolutely no other choice, I would kill him. I created him; I would destroy him if I had to.

If it ever comes to that, please let me stop him but not kill him. I don't want to have to decide to kill my own child, my first born, my only son, child of my heart, child who gave me my heart.

Don't let life be that cruel.

MAY 3, 2009

I have a parade of tiny butterfly women superglued to my mantel. I went to clean the mantle this morning and, apparently, a spider smaller than an iota has chosen a butterfly as his home. It actually jumped at me and was clearly willing to do whatever it could to defend itself. It wouldn't back down. I blew on it and that just made it want to defend itself even more. I hate spiders, but I have to admit I admire this one.

Is it instinct or courage that made that tiny spider stand his ground with me? Am I operating out of instinct or courage? I don't feel courageous—ever. I just feel I'm doing what I have to do. I have a minimum of choice in the matter. I'm proud of myself for enduring, but find it nothing to boast about. It's not as if I wanted to survive.

"To practice the way singleheartedly is, in itself, enlightenment. There is no gap between practice and enlightenment or zazen or daily life."—Dogen.

MAY 6, 2009

I've been putting all the personal letters between Paris and myself and Paris and my mother in chronological order. I just finished rereading them. There's no way my son has a conscience. I know I'm not wrong. There's no change in the letters from the first one to the last one. They're all about what Paris wants—what Paris thinks the problem, my problems, are. No remorse. No anger. No destruction of his soul because he is the destroyer.

I have to go public. I know in my heart of hearts Paris could kill again. I will do anything to stop that from happening. What if I'm next? I can't face that situation. If Paris ever did try to kill me, and succeeded, what's the point of anything?

MAY 8, 2009

I saw Nic tonight and now I'm in a tailspin. At first, I didn't think he was at the Cove, and then, I just knew he was there; I felt him. I walked in anyway. I saw him and I couldn't stop. I should have stopped. I should not have gone inside. I couldn't stop hugging him. He dragged me off so we could talk. He couldn't stop crying. I miss him. I don't miss all the rest. I miss *him*.

What are you doing, Charity Lee? You were doing better, and then you see Nic, and all hell breaks loose. He kissed me. I kissed him back. This isn't just some sexual thing that occurs between us. I *know* he does something for me.

I don't know that I even care what anyone says or thinks anymore. If I can have someone who loves me, why can't I be "dysfunctional" in this one aspect of my life? For the most part I'm damn "functional" in the rest of my life, despite everything that's happened. Why can't I have one area of my life I don't know how to function in?

What am I doing?

I miss him. I'm no good for him. He isn't good for me. None of that matters right now. I don't care what his parents think. I don't care what my mother or my therapist or my friends have to say. I just want to talk to Nic. Touch Nic. Smell Nic. Tuck myself in next to Nic.

Even as I write this, I know what a fool I must sound. I don't care anymore. Whomever believes life makes sense is a fool, so that could possibly make me a very wise woman.

What does he mean to me? Represent to me? That's what I have to figure out. Why do I always have to figure everything out?

I really thought it was over until the moment I saw him and remembered why it was so good to see him again—I really thought I would never see him again. I didn't want it to end the way it did. I was so happy to see him I cried, not at all what I intended. As soon as I touched him, I could no longer hold up the façade of strong, independent, with it, inspiring Charity. I just wanted to tuck into Nic.

I'm beginning to suspect life really is this difficult for most of us. The only difference is in how we choose to deal with the realization that life is no fucking bed of roses. I don't know, or think I care anymore, if I am dealt all this shit because I can handle it, or if I can handle it *because* of all the shit I have been dealt. I don't think it matters.

No matter if he comes back or not, wake up in as much peace as possible, Charity Lee. Cut yourself some slack every now and again, woman.

MAY 10, 2009

Happy Mother's Day, Charity Lee.

Believe it or not, it's been a good day for me. I didn't get depressed or even in a funk. I went to see Paris. It was sad. He looks like my Paris, my boy. I can still see my son, yet everything that comes out of his mouth isn't anything I ever thought my Paris would say. He talks about gang divisions, tells stories about dogs getting stabbed, and how he really doesn't care if I come back to visit or not.

I loved him today, but the connection is gone.

Nic's still here. I've given up trying to figure out why, but I do know some things need figuring out. Why can't I commit to anyone? Why do I find it so difficult to believe someone can love me and want to make a life with me?

Why do I think I know what's best? I know what's good and not good for me, but I want so badly to help others find the good in themselves, I lose sight of the fact they have to flesh out their own lives. I'm here to help and support, not guide.

I just want a peaceful life and to make the world, my world, a better place.

MAY 12, 2009

I feel I've finally made it to the turning point of this tragedy. I accept that Ella is dead physically. I know she exists spiritually and is with me when she chooses. I know Paris is sick and dangerous. My son is a sociopath, plain and simple. And I still love him, plain and simple. I know I have a purpose for existing: do as much good as possible and spread the love. I know I love Nic. I'm tired of going from one relationship to another. I want one to work, to last. I want to know how magical it feels to have lived an entire life with someone. I know I love Ella as much today as the day I came to know she existed. And I know I can now start to keep my promise to her. I can live this life. I want a good life again.

MAY 14, 2009

I reread Paris' Hare checklist interview answers. At one point he states he didn't think it was wrong to kill Ella because "we're all going to die anyway."

It reads exactly like every study I've read about serial and/ or sexual killers. What law of nature did I once break to bring into being such a destroyer of life and love as him? How can someone truly have no regard for anyone other than themselves and their own desires?

When Nic got to the house today, he opened his mail and read he's due in court for having no insurance on his motorcycle when he was hit. It went all downhill from there. I'm embarrassed even to write about it.

He began to rant, throw a tantrum like a child, said they can all go fuck themselves. I pointed out he's the one who chose to drive the bike without insurance. It went further downhill. He huffed and he puffed. I let him know, very bluntly, how immature he was behaving; I won't live around all his ranting and raving, so he could leave and chill. I also mentioned I think he sabotages himself on purpose out of extreme fear and dependency on his mother.

I said all I feel. It wasn't rosy.

He asked me if I wanted him anymore, so I had to say no. I love Nic. I want him to have a good life. He's too scared to face his demons. He's in victim mode.

He said he'll kill himself if I show my face. I reminded him we both play a role in our relationship problems, so he pulled his knife and, superficially, cut his wrist in the front yard, saying it will be my fault if he kills himself.

I don't want a violent life.

When the knife came out, fear came out – my fear. I don't think Nic would hurt me, but knives, stabbing, cuttings, blood all send me into primal panic mode. How callous and insensitive of him. He knows me. He knew, somewhere in his mind, what effect that knife and threatening to cut himself would have, fear, only he thought I would pacify him instead of telling him to go to therapy.

I've dealt with Paris and I've dealt with myself. I know what real suicide looks like. I know when someone is trying to manipulate me.

The only violence I'll accept in my life is what I encounter in my line of work. I won't tolerate it from myself. I won't have a lover who brandishes knives and threatens suicide and blames all his bullshit on me. I already have Paris to play that card.

Even though none of this afternoon went as expected, I'm at peace. I'm not responsible if Nic chooses to harm himself or accidentally harms another.

I have my life back. I'm going to live it and live it well. I'll go to school, work with battered women, write, read, meet new people. Become a mad scientist with the good heart. I'm done with bullshit. Life will always throw obstacles in my path, but there's a certain grace with which I'd like to handle those obstacles now.

I have full faith there are others out there who want to live as vividly as I do. I hope I'll know them when I see them. I suppose if they're vivid, I will.

MAY 15, 2009

I hope Nic is okay, but he most likely isn't and will continue being mental. I keep seeing him on my sidewalk with the knife to his wrist yelling it will be my fault if he kills himself. I can't stop myself from thinking, *Self-centered, mother-whipped fucker. How dare he pull a knife out around me?* At that moment, he doomed himself, and I learned I'm committed to creating a life which reflects I cannot, and will not, condone violence in my life.

I want to peacefully and patiently fulfill my promise to Ella to live life well for her and to help as many as I can to find some way to cope with life in ways which will bring them peace and knowledge. I want to give others comfort and confidence in themselves. I want to help them remember they're valuable just because they exist.

I think I'm finally a grown-up now. I love like a child, but that's the last bit of child in me. Not that I ever really was a child. I was small and I was young, but always pensive beyond my biological years. Years only delineate for us how aged the body is, not our soul. My soul feels old and that's hard to reconcile to daily life. My body just feels tired.

I'm poised and ready at the starting line, but the flag has yet to be waved. I need to start. I have so many daunting tasks ahead of me through which I'm striving to magically create heaven out of hell. I'm starting graduate-level work focused on what I've personally experienced. It will soon be time to go public with my experience. I have Paris to deal with for at least two and a half more years. I have no family and my friends are far away.

It has to be a miracle I survive at all. I'm like a spiritual Duracell Bunny. I just keep going and going and going eternally.

As I begin to rummage through the attributes I desire in myself, I realize I've achieved many of them already: strong, fierce, loyal, wise, loving, intuitive, sincere, emotional, complex.

I want to be a force of nature: a wind of change and a warm breeze that comforts. I still crave the company of others who try to be themselves in beneficial ways. I want a soulmate. I want dear and intimate friends. I want to love a child of my own again.

I want ... I want ... I want ... .

After all I've experienced and survived in the last two and a half years, wanting is not selfish of me; it's almost unimaginable I would ever want again, because getting what you want means you can lose all you have, and losing it devastates. To want is tantamount to courting my demons.

I attended a restorative justice seminar the other day. One of the speakers said the only way to survive the effects of devastating evil is faith and support. I lean heavily on the faith component. I have faith if I'm attempting to do what life expects of me with love, then life will love me back. I have faith life gives me all I need to rise to any challenge, as long as I'm open to learn. I also have faith if I turn my back on love, I turn my back on life.

Luckily for me, I was born with a curious nature. I know in my bones this curiosity has been a key component of my ability to weather hell. I always want to know more of the story, and my life, when I take a step back from it, is a very engaging story. It's hard for me not to be both repelled by it and engrossed in it. When I look at my life, I'm looking at a car wreck and a beloved at the same time.

What does life have in store for me still? As long as Paris is alive, it'll include a dimension of hell and real potential for danger. Knowing what I know of life now, I expect it'll still surprise me and give me a little bit of heaven again too.

At a loss for words today, not because of pain, but because of joy. Today was no special day. I worked in my Mad Scientist Lab AKA my office, ate lunch at the Cove, talked with some pals there, went to therapy, the grocery store, and talked to an attorney I think can help in the legal fights to have Paris assessed further. Nothing different about this day but me.

I have survived. I have meaning in my life again. I can hear life talk to me and I feel it take care of me. I see beauty again. Enhanced beauty. I have an appreciation of life I've never had before, even when I had my children safe in my arms.

I met a neighbor today. Her name is Fran and she's very old. We talked for a bit. Well she did most of the talking. I listened and listened more. I think she enjoyed having someone to talk to who did listen. If I see her out for a walk again, I will ask if she would like company from time to time on her walks. It could be nice. It would be safer for her and, if I'm right, she would enjoy conversation. I've always enjoyed talking to older people. They have such interesting stories and a perspective only gained after a lifetime of living. There's so much to learn from our elders. It's sad that being old excludes one so in our culture. We worship youth in America and neglect the old.

As Fran walked off, the last thing she said was, "Hang in there!" That was her good-bye. I like that as a good-bye. As far as I know, she knows nothing of me, but she's old enough to have learned we would all rather be encouraged instead of informed of a loss.

Fran was a messenger. Life does talk to me. I know these epiphanies I experience are conveyed to me via my thoughts and feelings, but it's a transmission from my soul, which I am now aware is life, God, love, whatever.

Today Dr. Zuelzer said she thinks I should become an attorney after getting the Master's in Policy. The attorney I spoke to today concerning Paris told me I sound like an attorney. I've thought about becoming an attorney before. I'm beginning to think I really could do it. I was scared before that I wasn't smart enough, that it would take too much time away from the kids, and ultimately, I had no real reason to be interested in that level of commitment in any area of the law except maybe estate planning.

Things are different now. There are things I'm still afraid of, but I won't let fear ruin my life or hold me back anymore. I've walked, crawled, and dragged my way out of hell. I can walk through fear. I have faith now in my intelligence on all levels: spiritual, emotional, mental. I am a foolishly wise woman. I know next to nothing about some things and a lot of something about other things. No doubt I am tenacious. Law school wouldn't take time from my kids anymore. In my heart, everything I do from now on will be about them. I have every reason to be interested in the legal field now—there's no getting away from it.

If I became an attorney, I could then become a politician or a judge or someone who can influence the system, shake things up a bit. I could spend a few years suing agencies for policy change, represent families of incarcerated youth (not the youth) either pro bono, or start my own nonprofit clinic. Then, who knows? I could be a force of nature with all the gifts I've been given. I would have a background in education, a Master's in Policy, a law degree, and a license. And a heart forged from pain into a diamond.

The more I think about it, the more I like the idea. It would be such a good position to effect change at the levels it really matters - law, politics, and the pocketbook. Isn't it sad our society's level of human decency and love is so welded to money, power, and control?

I am going to change my last name. No more Bennett. Being a Bennett has brought me nothing but pain. Rebecca asked me today if I would change my first name when I changed my last. No. No. And no. I love my name and, for the first time in my life, I feel it fits me. Or I fit it. I've wanted that most of my life. Charity is love. That's who I want to be.

I just watched, ten feet from where I'm sitting, my cat, Thomas, toy with a little snake until it was dead. All the while,

I'm turning beetles over when they land on their back, so they don't die in frustration. It's obvious Thomas feels such pleasure torturing and tormenting that snake. It's his nature.

I'm not going to be tormented anymore. It's no longer in my nature. I won't be tormented and left to die. My nature is to put up a hell of a fight.

MAY 19, 2009

I have a meeting at Giddings tomorrow with the Assistant Superintendent. I've been putting my complaint together about some of the books Paris received from his grandmothers today. They both continue to send Paris books on serial killers and murderers. Obviously I don't agree with this. I've been reading old emails, old complaints, and old so-called solutions—also TYC policy. I'm back ready to fight again. Whatever battle or experience comes my way, I'll find a way to deal with it lovingly and morally, to the best of my ability. Putting together this complaint is further encouragement that I could be a lawyer. I'm very analytical and know how to put together a good argument based on fact and enough emotion to remind people this is our life, not some charitable project I'm working on.

This is my son I'm fighting for, not some ideal or punishment or policy change. While TYC continues to assert they are providing Paris appropriate treatment, I disagree. I want to do everything possible to have him correctly diagnosed and, based on as much scientific evidence as possible, let the court decide what justice is. Dispensing justice is not mine to do. Thank God. My job is to look for more truth and insight where my son is concerned.

My soul is covered in a layer of fuzz. The phoenix is on the rise. What will be my next pinnacle? My next point of destruction? Is it possible to be this utterly destroyed once, twice, three times, more? After surviving once, do you grow more accepting of destruction and learn to cope, or are you traumatized all over again? Or are you so desensitized from years of seeing the world as a violent place, you just cry and go on until the next chapter begins?

I still can't quite believe this is my life now. I remember what it felt like to be my kids' mom: to have them close, to feel their bodies and know they were safe, to talk and listen to them, to smell them, to hold them, to love them. Every moment, I still know how it feels to miss them.

Both of them.

I am still their mother. Gone are the holding, knowing they are safe, smelling them parts. Left are the talking, listening, trying to understand, and loving them parts.

I talk to Ella all I can, and I'm grateful when I feel her with me, however she comes to me. I will never not miss or think of her every day. I will never stop loving her. All I do is for her.

I try to understand Paris. I've become a lay expert on juvenile psychopathy research, testing, and diagnosis. I've become a lay expert on both juvenile and adult sexual predators and sexual serial killers. You know, just in case. I'm versed in the basics of juvenile law and TYC policy. I'm mastering the art of complaint writing and getting my voice heard. I'm learning how to be political. Everything I do is also for my son.

I'm in this world because of his actions. Embracing it is the only way I can survive it. May as well light up this dark world as much as I can.

Good luck tomorrow, woman. Flex your fuzzy feathers a bit; get warmed up.

MAY 20, 2009

I am done with my meeting, but not the issues. I flexed my feathers, informed the staff I am back and ready to take it to any level necessary to facilitate a change.

My mind is in a whirlwind. I'm not sure for what purpose life is using me. I just have to keep going where it leads. I have so many thoughts about how to approach the issue of

TYC again. I'm convinced there's a way to bring the maximum potential for positive change for all parties involved.

Today I realized I'm glad I'm taking the Death Penalty seminar. I'll need to be familiar with all of this should Paris ever decide to kill again. I'm opposed to it. State-sanctioned murder is still murder. I'm going to look into groups opposing it and size up their reasoning and activities.

I've come out of hiding and am poised to get reacquainted with the world of TYC and more prepared to meet the world at large. All it will take to achieve my goals is one step after another. I've been wearing Ella's diamond earrings. One represents perseverance—a diamond can withstand anything. The other is my constant reminder to let the carbon-based starburst I am to always shine bright.

MAY 21, 2009

TYC has agreed to stop books, magazines, shoes, and such sent to Paris from anyone but me after I read them some of the passages out of *The Girl Who Played Go*, one in particular in which a young girl was raped with a red hot fireplace poker, and showed them the pictures in *The Watchmen* comics, one of which depicts a woman being raped, then murdered. His father was removed from the mail list and barred from visiting due to a court order from years ago suspending visitation until certain criteria were met. No one person can send Paris more than $25 per month. It was agreed I would email the grandmothers the new rules. So I did.

His paternal grandmother has said nothing so far. My mom said she wouldn't be talking to me, but her attorney would be. Bring it. I'm on the high road concerning this issue, ethically, morally, and legally.

At some point I'm going to begin to press for input in regard to Paris' recitation of the past. What is the use of the Capital Offenders program and the role it plays if the victim's own account isn't considered, especially if the victim is willing to participate? I'll go so far as to enact my role in group with him if need be. Anything to prove the doctors, and myself, either right or wrong. It's a thought I've been pondering, getting Paris and I together. It could be valuable to all involved, for many different reasons, but at what cost?

Is it worth it to go that route? Paris won't change and would enjoy my pain. It would be excruciatingly painful for me to be vulnerable with Paris, but I would do it to show him, no mistaking it, for who he is.

I just Raided a cockroach and it's lying here dead in front of me. I feel guilt. Sorry, God. I can't live with a cockroach. I just can't. Forgive me.

Back to today. Now my plate is full again. I will be working on my master's, working with my battered women and kids, taking on TYC (again), battling with my mother (again), and building an entirely new group of friends, all the while attempting to maintain a level of peace and act kindly with love.

Damn. That's a lot, but you know what? I can do it. I'm prepared. I know who I am, what I'm capable of, and I know I can do all those things. This is why I survive this hell, to do what I do. It all feels right; it all fits together, somehow. It will become more apparent as time goes on. I have faith I'm connecting the right dots.

I know my heart when it comes to Paris. I trust my gut (not to mention all the psychiatrists) when it comes to Paris. I look at him now and know who he is, at least in a basic sense. No one but Paris knows how far his fantasies have taken him away from the boy I thought I knew. I love him anyway. I want to do everything possible to make sure a fair determination is made in regard to Paris' pathology.

I won't give up. I also won't give in. I won't stop trying to rock the boat until someone sees an entire ship is sinking.

Wow. My mom is really pulling out all the emotional manipulation tricks she knows. What she doesn't realize is they don't work on me anymore. I received an email this morning in which I was called a thief, a bad mother, a monster. She says I'm scared if I look in the mirror I'll see Paris, and she all but blamed me for Ella's death.

My mother has no idea who I am. I'm done with her. Let her do what she will. I'll defend myself if I'm put in a position where I need to. I'm not my son. I'm not sick. I'm not out for revenge or absolution. I will no longer allow my own mother to add to my self-doubt. I don't agree with her interpretation of who I am. She doesn't know me, this woman I am now.

I'm no longer afraid of her. I no longer need her approval and no longer value her opinion concerning my actions. She offers no comfort, no faith, no respect, no love, no friendship. She tries to threaten me, knock my ego around a bit, bully me with lawyers.

How sad for my family. I can't control Paris or my mom. Neither can I control what they decide to do to me except I can choose to not take it anymore. I'm solid again. My fuzz is beginning to turn into the strongest, most beautiful feathers I've ever seen. Soon, I fly again. Then I'll soar and instill as much color into the world of darkness I come from as I can. No matter what my mom says to me, does to me, or thinks of me, the only thing that will stop me from trying to make the world a better place is death.

Then I'll hug my daughter, kiss my daughter, tell her I love her, and hope I kept my promise to her to live well and love well for her.

Now I have something else to look forward to: I have a meeting set up with Will Harrell. I've been conversing with him all day about Paris, school plans, career plans, etc. Will is currently the ombudsman over TYC. Before that he was the director of the Texas ACLU. He's moving to TYC to be director of specialized services. He was named by *Texas Monthly* as one of thirty most likely people to influence the future of Texas.

Since meeting him for the first time, I have admired and respected him. I always wanted to speak at length with him. I'd like to know how he got to the position he is in, how his life has become what it is, and how he manages to carry such an enormous and taxing workload. I could use some ideas in that department. I also think it will help with my efforts at TYC for them to see we are in contact and encourage them to allow me to help them.

On the personal side, I feel it would be good to know him. He seems like a friend you can have a good conversation with no matter the topic, or at least, on the topics I now know. Common world. I admire and understand his altruism and how much he's sacrificed to do what he does. He slept at Giddings, in solitary confinement, on Christmas Eve to get a feel for it.

These are characteristics I want and need in friends.

MAY 25, 2009

Today is Memorial Day, a day to honor those who have died in battle. It's a military tribute, but, of course, for me it's about Ella.

She died in a different kind of battle but a battle, nonetheless. Now I'm embattled. I seem to have more enemies than friends right now. My mom is too worried about her own power waning, her ability to control slipping away, so she accuses me of seeking power and control. Her animosity towards me and her need to maintain her image of herself as a selfless woman warp her interactions with Paris.

Now his paternal grandparents have emailed me their opinions. They also see me as seeking control and say if I'm looking for someone to blame, I should look in a mirror. His grandfather said I never allowed him to be a grandfather to Paris. Their words, animosity, and anger don't sting as much as what my mom hurls at me. It does nag my already over-nagged mind, so I have to take a few moments and sort it all out.

First of all, this comes from people who sent Paris a book that contained scenes of a woman being tortured by being beaten to a pulp and then had a hot poker shoved up her ass. She was later publicly executed. This was only one page. Seventy-five percent of the book is murder, rape, torture, sex, and obsession with death.

JUNE 1, 2009

I should know by now not to challenge the universe. On the other hand, how can I not?

Due to the completely inappropriate material sent by both grandmothers, neither one is allowed to send anything other than letters to Paris. I'm now an orphan because of books. Books and murder have defined my entire existence.

In the last week my mom first said she wouldn't talk to me, but her attorney would. The next day she emailed to let me know she was tired of my "barking;" she's going to "bite back" this time. We are not dogs.

She accuses me of assuming no blame in either Ella's death or Paris' creation. She's blind and deaf. She says I'm out to prove Paris a monster to absolve myself of any responsibility for his actions. I'm trying to find out the truth. Paris is the one proving himself a "monster" as of February 4, 2007.

According to her, I've exposed him to sexually explicit behavior and stolen all his money. She makes no mention of the fact she is the one who dissolved his trust, illegally. She makes no mention of how much of it has been spent on lawyers, psychiatrists, guardians ad litem, testing. No mention of how this has consumed all of me. All I do is work on something that somehow relates to Paris and Ella. Money and time well spent, in my opinion. She has hired an attorney in Texas. If I continue to "bully" her, she's going to have said attorney sue me, on Paris' behalf, for mismanagement of his funds.

Don't ya just love her?

I'm done with being her black sheep, her deranged, narcissistic, unbalanced, irresponsible, rage-filled and fear-controlled daughter. I know she's wrong about me. It hurts like hell my own mother regards me as a rabid dog. It hurts like hell she is not interested in mothering me, but in defeating me.

After I drove four hours to see him, Paris refused to see me. On my way home, once I was far enough away where I couldn't turn around to go back, he called to attack my character and motives. I hung up on him. He called back and left a message along the same lines. He told me not to contact him, but then outlined all the ways I could.

I don't have to see him, or talk to him, to love him or continue along the path I'm on. I'm tired of listening to my mom and my son tell me what I am motivated by. They say it's hate. The need for control. I'm tired of being told I need to take an honest look at myself to see the evil inside of me. I am tired of them mistaking their mirrors for mine.

JUNE 7, 2009

I'm experiencing a mild sense of panic concerning the enormity of the task I've taken on, but I know I'll accomplish it piece by piece, moment by moment. I've never felt as driven. I've become a woman unlike one I ever imagined and I really, really admire her. I've come into my own. I'm unleashing Charity from the abyss. We've become friends, the abyss and I.

I meet P. Cummings tomorrow. I hope my intuition is right and I've finally found the right attorney to help me take this fight to the next level. Things have to change at TYC. I'm tired of being patted on the head only to have them break all the promises they make. I'm tired of watching the buck being passed. I'm seizing the buck and holding it hostage until negotiations result in real change. The main issue I'm focusing on, at this point, is assessment and diagnostic practices at TYC.

I feel like an actor must feel the moment before walking on stage, well practiced, well researched, well contemplated, but still scared of being unable to express or convey the quality of the character. Only I'm no actor and this is no stage. I'm real. Paris is real. Ella is real, and really dead. And this *is* my life.

All I have left to convey is character.

JUNE 17, 2009

It seems as though life has come full circle since February 4, 2007. I barely have time to write anymore due to school. And that's as small as the circle gets.

This time I am not with my kids, but everything I do is still unquestionably inspired by my love of them. I go to Ms. Cummings' office tomorrow to get started on the Paris polygraph fight. Her sister, a pathologist, is going to write a report on Ella's wounds, and we will use that report to argue and assert my way toward getting those tests done. Paris can always refuse to take the tests, but if he's as smart as he likes to think he is, he'll realize all his lies and all my work have him pinned in a corner. The DNA is there for the sex angle, and if he chooses not to take the polygraph, he looks guiltier. If he takes the polygraph, and fails, he looks guiltier. Guilty of deceit—scared of being exposed.

When Paris is cornered, he's dangerous. When I'm cornered, I'm creative. I know what I'm doing with Paris. I can feel what direction to take to make it come about. Not make it *all* come about—I don't have that power. I know how I need to present this to the world, and I know it's a puzzle I'm still putting together. I know I'm not crazy. Or delusional, or full of uncontrollable rage. I'm not out for revenge, nor do I have ulterior motives. All I want is to be a seeker of truth and bearer of love and compassion.

I'm also full circle as I'm, once again, prepared to create my world as I see fit, create me as I see fit. I feel there's nothing I can't achieve since walking through this hell. I'm grateful I can still create beauty. Two years ago, I thought it impossible to create something out of nothing, meaning out of despair. Now I know I'm creating something out of the meaning that has always been there for me: love. My kids taught me about love so well I can't give up my faith in it.

Paris is refusing to see or talk to me since I had the books and such taken away. I drove down there a couple of weeks ago. He knew I was coming because I sent him a letter ahead of time. He refused the visit.

I won't lie, because of how much I still love him, it hurts when it's so obvious he doesn't feel love for me. But it doesn't hurt as badly as it used to. I accept who my son is. I accept this is my life until he turns eighteen. I know both the limit and scope of his "feeling" toward me. What if all I'm accomplishing is making him "feel" justified in hating me even more? What if I'm writing my own death sentence by pursuing the truth about my children's last moments together?

The first moment they had together, Ella was about ten minutes old. Paris came into the bedroom after I gave birth and I gave Ella to him to hold. He had her in his arms and I could tell, as soon as he looked at her, he fell in love. I wasn't there for their last moment together. I can imagine it—vividly—while not being able to get my head around it at all. I've imagined hundreds—actually, no. I have imagined two scenarios over and over and over. Paris' version and my version. His version doesn't fit with facts. Today his caseworker told me she believes Ella caught Paris doing something. Would he have killed me, or at least tried to, if I'd been the one to catch him at whatever he was doing?

If that turns out to be the case, I desperately hope I'm making the most of the life forfeited, living well for Ella, loving those like Paris because I want what happened to Ella to change these kids for the better. Through our loss, for them.

It's ironic, possibly healthy, possibly not, I choose to live in the moment now; to live more fully and consciously. This is no accident. If I live too much in the past, I'm overwhelmed. If I think too far into the future, I'm overwhelmed. I've learned my limits in all three worlds—past, present, future—and I'm much better at balancing my visits to each of them.

This life is not, at all, what I thought it would be. It's been more than I ever thought I could bear. I've done things and seen things I never thought I would do or see. I've felt things I never knew were possible to feel. I've been destroyed on the whim of my son, yet I'm more alive than ever before. All because of the love I have for my kids, no matter where that love has taken me.

I'm human. I have my doubts about what I can accomplish, but after facing my worst fear, I can overcome any fear.

JULY 1, 2009

Since talking with Dr. Ferrera last year, I've had time to contemplate the possible futures I face with Paris. The conclusion I have come to is I truly *will* have to get away from my son one day. This is not based on fear, but rather evolution.

In time I will have to let go of Paris, but not what he's taught me, good and bad. He was the first to teach me of both selfless love and selfish hate. There's nothing I can do to help or change him. He is what he is; he does not want to change. I believe what I saw from him February 4, 2007. I believe Dr. Coons, Dr. Ferrera, and Dr. Dietz.

If I don't let go one day, I'll grow old in the world Paris thrust me, one of his creation, not mine; a world full of manipulators and game players; one big chess game with everyone trying to come out on top as the winner. I'll forever live in a criminally tinted world, just by being the mother of a psychopath and the mother of a murdered child.

I want to live a different world one day, so I need to put together a different plan. And a backup. Always have a backup.

I love you, Ella. I'm going to follow my heart and instincts, and life's prompts, no matter how insane or scary it may seem to me at the time.

JULY 9, 2009

Damn. I don't even know where to begin or what to say. So much has happened there are too many thoughts and feelings jumbled in my head right now; they're tumbling all over one another in a vain effort to make some sense of themselves.

I met a thirteen-year old girl while working with FACT on the Fourth of July. She'd been raped by her stepfather then beaten by her mother with a broom and coffee table for "trying to take her man." I spent the entire night with her, talking to her, holding her, walking her through the process of getting a rape kit. My heart hurt, but it felt completely at home with her. I want to work with people who've been hurt, betrayed, and forcibly thrust into their own surreal worlds.

My name is Charity and that's who I want to be in this world: love. Love complimented by wisdom and strength.

JULY 13, 2009

I threw the glove down at TYC's feet today. I was able to get the new clinical director and the prison social worker to admit, in a room with twelve witnesses, that TYC does no psychological testing. I got them all to admit they'd seen no remorse in Paris, at all, ever. I know what I'm doing. I'm on the right track, even though it all feels so wrong.

Since I woke up today, I feel something shifting, uncoiling, inside me. My dreams have been nightmares. My soul has disassociated itself from my body a lot today. I'm having epiphanies about my future and plotting my present. My life is mine. I choose to give it to others no matter what anyone may think of me.

I live myself better than I write myself, yet if I couldn't write myself, I would not live myself.

JULY 15, 2009

I'm throwing myself into my son's cause for the last time. I don't go back to school until January. In the meantime, I'll give my first-born child all I've got. I'll get the testing completed. I know I'm not wrong about my son. No matter who stops talking to me, who thinks I'm crazy, who thinks I'm weird, I'll follow through on this one last act of love and go on with my life.

After this, I'll stop wondering if he will kill again and stop fearing he will find me. If he does, I'll deal with it. I'm tired of being scared. I'm tired of living in limbo. I'll no longer agree to be anyone's black sheep. I want to live. I want to love. I want to help as many others as I can.

My son and I are both anomalies. I'm the progenitor of a psychopath; the entirety of what I feel is all the love and pain he's incapable of feeling. There's cosmic irony in that.

"Oh, my friend, it's not what they take away from you that counts. It's what you do with what you have left."—Hubert Humphrey

JULY 17, 2009

Curiosity is my savior. I hang on, no matter what, just to see and experience whatever's in store for me next. Even in the deepest darkest pit of abysmal pain there was one atom in me amazed at the capacity, range, and depth the experience of being human encompasses.

Curiosity is my fuel. My motivation to heal is fueled by it, to which is added an inability to stop loving. Whatever the hell that means. I live in so many different worlds and each has its own definition of love that's so diametrically opposed to one another it's hard to discern love from insanity sometimes.

If Paris and Ella were with me, and we lived in a world that doesn't yet exist for the three of us, we would be out in the rain right now. Sun showers. No lightning. Warm water and beautiful moments full of light with my babies. One of these lifetimes this will be resolved, and we'll have moments together again. Next go-round, I won't forget as much as I did in this one.

It is written. So it shall be.

AUGUST 5, 2009

Today, I seem unable to tell the difference between love and pain. They've merged into one and the same. To experience one is to dive into the other.

When I was ten years old I wrote what I considered to be my first grown-up poem. For the first time, I figured out how to phrase my more mature thoughts.

There are those who hate,
And there are those who love.
Those who hate know why,
Those who love ask why.
But in their separation,
The two are always one.

I've always known, on some level, this is the lesson it's been my task to learn this lifetime. I must have badly needed to learn it considering what it's taken to get me here. Wherever here is.

I awoke this morning to my phone ringing—Dr. Ferrera calling me back to discuss Paris. I wanted to make sure my emotions weren't clouding my memories of our conversation last year. They aren't. I'm correct in remembering all we discussed and have been doing right by my son; although it seems to be my lot in life for everyone whom I love to believe I'm always in the wrong. I'm the black sheep. How's that for fucking irony? So be it.

Dr. Ferrera reaffirmed Paris is in "no small dose" a psychopath and most likely to be violent again due to the addition of the sexual component of his psychopathy. He advised me, again, to hire a security/risk management firm to plan for the future.

Good morning, Charity, time to wake up. In today's news … Charity awoke to the utterly crushing last blow to whatever hope she had left about saving her son. Essentially there is nothing to save in him. He is what he is.

It's not only Ferrera's reaffirmation of the diagnosis or my own bleak future I needed to be able to know the truth. Two weeks ago, I saw it myself clearer than ever before. Paris tried for thirty long minutes to cry; he couldn't. My son cannot cry. He says he wants to be able to cry, but he just can't.

I looked across a plastic table at my Paris and told him he didn't have to try to cry for me anymore. I know who he is, and I love and fight for him anyway. Why not relax and be himself while he has the chance, just talk with his mom?

So he did. We had quite a pleasant visit for us. He told me he's bisexual and has been for a while. Of course, my mother has known for quite a while, but he says he didn't tell me out of fear of how I would react. I told my fifteen-year-old creative and beautiful son to stop with the bullshit. He knows as well as I do I wouldn't blink at that news. After hearing my son murdered his own sister, I've learned to accept anything Paris can throw at me.

After experiencing everything Paris has done, and watching him turn into someone I don't know at all yet know better than I want to, I've turned into something just as rare as a psychopath: the mother of one.

There are others out there. Surely they're as diverse as their offspring. That would be an interesting support group. Life is strange in so many ways, who knows? I wonder how many of us there are and how many there are of those who don't know their child is a psychopath. Of those, I wonder how many died, before they knew; how many were killed by their own psychopath.

I'm not alone in thinking thoughts such as these and feeling the emotional nuclear fallout of them. At this moment in time, though, I'm alone in dealing with all this waste. Physically, I am alone. Spiritually I have my other group of loved ones. Emotionally and psychologically I have me.

Paris thinks I'm trying to keep him locked up forever because I can't let go of my rage, that I can't see him as anything other than a psychopath. I told him he's both right and wrong. I'm not trying to keep him locked up because I hate him, am mad at him, or want revenge. I love him. I'm learning to deal with my anger in much better ways. I've never truly wanted revenge. He's my son. I don't ever want to see him suffer inhumanely for what he did to Ella. Sure, I've felt it, but I haven't let it dictate any decision I've made about him.

I think he should be locked up because every day that passes shows I'm not wrong in my opinion of him. I love him as much as I ever have. I have had to adjust how I express and deal with that love.

I'm not loving and mothering a "normal" child. There's every reason for me to assume I'll never get to act "normal" again and most often I'll be misconstrued and misunderstood.

It was a good visit for us. No raised voices. No evil looks. A truce of sorts.

But, just to remind me it's still a chess game to him, he let me know at the end of our visit he was worried about who I was becoming because my mother told him about the incident of pointing a gun at my twenty-five-year-old lover's head. No eye blink needed. I know how not to break stride around him. I know he likes to see me stumble.

I found it sad. I responded, "Both you and Mama seem to spend so much of your limited time together talking about me instead of talking to me. It would seem to me two people as intelligent and compatible as yourselves would have more interesting topics to discuss since it's already been decided, and agreed upon by you both, I'm the weak link in this chain. Why not move on?"

Before he could respond I hugged him and told him I'll let him know when I plan to visit again.

I feel sure of my perceptions and interpretations of him on a level I never seem to know how to convey the complexity of in words. There is no uncertainty. We can all attain this level of certainty if only we give in and listen and pay attention to what life is saying to us. Life can be a guided tour rather than incessantly being lost. To some that may sound insane or at least a little weird. To me it is divine affirmation from within.

I come to understand the story of the Fates much better now. Perspective always changes; life is woven as you go. I wonder what happens to all the cut strings. Either I can't remember or the story never addressed that issue. I'll have to reread it. If an answer isn't found, I should write my own tale of the fate of a cut string—a new myth—because honestly, merrily, merrily, merrily, life is but a dream and a nightmare boat ride, any way you look at it.

AUGUST 9, 2009

I worked all weekend at different substations. Four people: an eighteen-year-old girl with a black, bloody eye and a two-week-old baby; a twenty-year-old named Destiny with two little girls, aged four and two, pregnant again, with the same man beating her since she was sixteen; a forty-three-year-old woman with a very large swollen black eye; and a male sex offender who is abused by his wife of thirty-seven years—she spits on him.

This is my world. I am comfortable here. The people I speak with seem calmer, less scared than when I first met them, at least at that moment. Who knows what their future holds?

I've been letting it all go today by driving a lot. I had a lot to get done today, but all I could do was drive. Writing and driving. Two things I must do when the need arises. I drive. I think. I write.

AUGUST 10, 2009

Another day under my belt. I'm grateful my days begin at all and that they always pass as time always moves on.

I just left Paris' monthly review. I'm a wreck before I arrive at Giddings. Today I felt rather tense and hot and wound tight except while driving. There I can relax. I couldn't eat a thing. I would have vomited.

I'm beginning to sound like a broken record, even to myself, but what the hell?! Why is this my life? Jesus fucking Christ already. Living in an alternate mentality is very taxing and hard to comprehend.

Paris refused to see me ... again. Instead of feeling a sting, I feel annoyance.

As our kids grow up, we adjust our parenting based on their age and developmental level. From two to three, three to four, five to ten they're always changing, so we do too, albeit somewhat slower than they do. Paris changed from being thirteen to being a psychopath. That isn't covered in any parenting manual I'm aware of.

AUGUST 31, 2009

Should have known better to think life could not get worse. I found out today that my mother—my own damn mother—is suing me for allegedly stealing Paris' money.

It's not enough my first beloved killed my second beloved. It's not enough I've made it this far instead of dying. It's not enough I was almost destroyed by my son. It won't be enough for either Paris or my mother until I am destroyed. I won't give them that. My mother had my childhood. My son had my love and my life. None of that seems to matter to either one, so I'll have it all back now. They can have the money. They can have one another.

I'm devastated. I thought I knew all the shit and curves life can throw at you. I was wrong. I'm no longer the daughter of Kyla. I'm no longer the mother of Paris and I'll never be the mother I want to be of Ella. I'm no one's lover, no one's rock, no one's love.

I am Charity. Period.

And while I'm proud I've found myself; I can't help but cry uncontrollably. I'm Charity and I'm nothing, and I don't know quite how to navigate between the two. I'm crazy and I'm not. I'm sane and I'm not. I'm content, yet I'm mired in pain. I cry, but I don't know how much of my existence stems from pain or joy. I can't have anything but faith life will continue to take care of me as long as I take care of my life. Cliché, I know.

The only word left to express who I am now, all I have gone through, all that is left is … Charity. Love me, like me, hate me, try to destroy me, want to kill me, take all the money, and all my faith in the world. You'll still never get what it is you're after. I'm none of these things but Charity. I'll allow no one to take me away from me ever again. I'll show everyone, including myself, none of these material things are truly the things we are made of or meant for.

I'm fervently hoping someone will finally stick it to my mom. I know it's wrong and unspiritual, but I'm so over being fucked by that woman. She's so rich, so used to winning, she needs to be put in her place. This is all selfish fantasy.

For one moment, it would seem retributive if at least one of them could be made to hurt as badly as I do. But they're different. What I really want is what's best for Paris, society, and me. I want peace. I want to breathe. To sleep the whole night through with no nightmares to haunt me or visions that cause me pain. To calm myself—to find a life again, to love again, to care again, to live again without this fear and pain obscuring my vision all the time.

How ironic is it I spent the last week on a road trip driving through land that made it so clear how inconsequential I truly am, only to come home to have it made abundantly clear that nothing about my role in this life is inconsequential in the least? It's just one very tiny, very important, bit of it all.

How I evolve, what I learn from all this bullshit, means nothing; it means everything.

Not only is my mom suing me, she's also launched a full-frontal assault on my character. She can have as much fucking money as she wants. I don't give a rat's ass. Neither she, nor Paris, will ever get what they both want: power over me, the ability to make me feel fear.

This time she can kiss my mother-fucking, grief-deranged, bad-ass, mom ass. She has no one but herself to blame for my ability to fight back. I learned how to fight from the best.

- Bad-ass black dress for court: $250
- Cash needed to get my mother off my back: more than I care to mention.
- Look on my mom's face when she's proven 100% wrong about me and has her life of questionable finances brought into the light: FUCKING PRICELESS

The year before Ella died, I almost had to file for bankruptcy despite the fact I had plenty of money in my trust. A car was repossessed. Credit card debt was due. We moved out of the house I had built for us to settle in because I could no longer afford the upkeep on a 3500 square foot house with a swimming pool. We moved into a two-bedroom rental house not all of our possessions would fit in. I worked two jobs: waitress and graduate assistant. I began my first semester in graduate school.

Our lives were on their way to completely changing. I know my high-stress level affected both of my kids. Now, not even three years after Ella died, she's grabbing for money and control. She and my son are in league. She dares to impugn my parenting of Paris after Ella's death, two and a half years she has been mostly absent from, yet still a huge problem when she did interact with us.

All I have left to say is, "Fuck that."

I am as angry as I sound. I won't roll over for anyone. Two and a half years ago, Paris bitch-slapped me. Historically, a bitch slap would have been the slap of a glove across your enemy's face. A challenge to a duel. They both want one so badly, I'm going to give them one. You don't grow up with a narcissistic borderline mother and give birth to a narcissistic sexually deviant psychopathic son, and still have the ability to breathe, much less write whole sentences, without learning all their weak spots.

My weak spot is I don't want to be ugly and vicious. I want to fight, I want to believe the evidence will speak for itself, but I don't want to become like them. That weakness is what they count on to beat me. What they did not count on is that I learned how to turn my weakness into a strength.

If I have to speak to her, I may have a hard time—no, I won't. I'm not who she says I am. I don't have to prove it to her anymore, but since she's painted a picture that isn't me at all, I'll prove it in spades and walk away with a clear conscience.

This is my final hurrah in my role as her daughter and his mother. After this I'm no one but Charity. Mother of Ella and Paris. Faith healed.

SEPTEMBER 10, 2009

Life goes on as difficult as always.

Last week I dove into a major depression. I wasn't as bad as when I lost Ella, but it was bad. I lost all motivation to fight my mother and her ridiculous allegations. I continuously bemoaned the fact that this is my life.

Tonight is a good night to write. I'm sad but not depressed. It's pouring down rain, which is in and of itself a fucking miracle in Texas, as is all of life. Despite all the atmospherics, I'm still at a loss for words to describe this double-whammy world I now live in. I do it to help myself acclimate, to stay grounded in my reality.

I am Charity. I am thirty-five. I am the mother of two children. I am learning what I'm meant to learn in this life; maybe not the details, or how to make it all work, but the basic concepts.

Love. Give. Live. Be real.

I know things, but honestly, I hurt so bad it makes it so hard to act on what I know. Where do I stand right now? I'm not engaged in the world at this moment, yet I feel more connected to it than I imagine a lot do. I feel so connected it suffocates me, yet disengaged enough to continue to participate in it. Honestly, I am tired of participating. Really, really tired of participating.

I wouldn't mind, at all, ceasing to be for a bit so I could be with my daughter. I care almost nothing for what happens to this body anymore. I want this body to die with my soul in the clear, ready to learn from its mistakes. I'm ready to hold my daughter again, but if I can't yet I'm committed to be a soul driven by integrity, honor, love, humaneness.

Of course, I don't always act this way. Of course, there are times I need people to carry me. All the people I know (other than my mom and son) are justified in their love and hatred for me because at least they've dealt with me. My mom hasn't dealt with me. She's manipulated me. Lied to me. Used me. Blamed me. Judged me. Shamed me. Abandoned me. And now she's screwing me over.

The last two and a half years have forged me. This last thing my mother is doing to me begins to cool the molten self I became upon the loss of my satellites. I was forged and beaten into being by others. I will hone myself.

I offered myself to the rain tonight. I gave myself up to the memories I have of my kids and danced in the rain and howled at the moon. No matter how well I cope, no matter how I move on, no matter who may come into my life, nothing will ever make me forget the perfect joy and pain it was, and is, to be the mother of my two amazing kids. It doesn't matter what separates us—death, murder, psychopathy—because what keeps us bound is greater than all of that.

My mother, my husbands, my friends—none of these ever brought out the best in me like my kids did-do. It's unfathomable, yet thoroughly known to me, how contradictory life is at all times. They brought out the best in me, yet the worst in me still showed itself and now the worst has happened. And now I am discovering the best of myself.

If Ella had lived, would she have suffered through the worst of me and not been okay? Am I better equipped for our next go-round after learning all I think I am this time? In my world nothing makes any sense. Sometimes I wonder if I make sense to others but, in the end, I don't care. There will come a day when my pain, my thoughts, and my sad, hard, contemplative soul can take no more and my body will die. This one will tell its stories in tattoos and words left behind. What will endure is what my soul leaves behind after this body of mine can take no more. It's much more beautiful than this current body can ever be.

When this body fails, the only two things I hope those who know me and truly love me know is this: (1) I *lived,* and (2) I *loved* them, every one of them. Paris. Ella. My mom. My husbands. My friends.

Frustration rips at my vocabulary. I have absolutely no fucking way to describe this to anyone other than myself; how hard it is to exist while becoming more horrified at the world in direct proportion to how amazed I am by it.

I've decided to live my life in segments for the time being. This segment will consist of enduring my son and my mother. Also, healing myself as much as I can, so that in the next segment I can plant the seeds of healing in others however circumstances present.

SEPTEMBER 15, 2009

I saw my son yesterday. As always, it was painful. He said he intends to terminate my parental rights. It won't happen. That's not my concern. That's not what hurts. What hurts is he still wants, is trying to, and is succeeding, in hurting me again. He didn't kill me; he didn't destroy me. So now he is taking a new approach. He is going after my motherhood.

I'm tired. Tired of being battered. Tired of being used. Tired of being unjustly reviled. Tired. Tired. Tired. Fucking tired.

SEPTEMBER 26, 2009

Yet again thrust into a world, and a life, I don't want, but have no choice but to participate in. In the two weeks since I last wrote, I've retreated almost wholly into my own existence to shelter myself. I'm disengaged from the world around me. Again. I'm overwhelmed. My pain buries me alive; I can't deal with even the most trivial detail outside of my own head. I carry so much spiritual and emotional pain; I'm physically breaking down. I've thrown my right hip out twice and have gone to the doctor twice unable to move my neck without pain.

I move forward through my life as much an observer as a participant. I feel so connected, too connected, to the life and pain around me, I don't want to feel a part of it anymore. It touches me. It affects me. I'm trying to cope with the awareness I'm something much more than I ever imagined, while less than nothing in the long run.

I don't feel like others do. I am not saying I'm unique or one of kind. I'm saying I'm odd, an aberration, something different. I'm an extreme in the way Paris is an extreme, but extreme in the opposite direction. Two sides of the same coin.

When I was a little girl I had a reoccurring nightmare. I couldn't see myself, but I knew it was me. In it, I am running. I am in fear, great fear, and I keep looking over my shoulder to see how close I am to being caught. I am trying to escape something, someone, not somewhere. The city looks like it's made of the newspaper's cartoon section. Flames surround me. Everything but me is on fire. I can't see the road, only ahead, above, around, behind me, but not below my feet. It isn't hot. I never see the monster I'm running from. I only know it is a monster and I have to run. There is no thought to being caught. The fear of that is too great to allow it to occur. In the dream, I was never caught.

That's it. Fire. Running incessantly. Fear. Evil. Fright. As I grew up, the characters would change, the setting would change, but the theme stayed constant. In one version of the dream, Billy, my mom's ex, chased me as I jumped over backyard bushes while Paris watched. My goal was to lure Billy away from Paris, although Paris wasn't afraid. I could not feel any fear coming from him; I just felt my own fear. I made it over bush after bush, a hurdle jumper. At some point, on some bush close enough for me to still see my son, I tripped and fell. I landed face down and frantically tried to roll onto my back. I wouldn't die faceless. Billy shot. I screamed. Paris watched. I woke up, before the bullet hit me, bathed in fear.

There are amazingly complex and sinister brownstones my dreams take me to. They're all connected by weird hidden passages in between floors. I have found in them Escher-style staircases, dungeons, dance rooms, stages, rooms made of glass, and school spaces. High schools. Gyms that double as theaters and assembly rooms when it's not pep day.

I have a dream that it is pep day, or at least a JV football day or something, because there are cheerleaders, players, in the gym, on the field. It's the uniforms that stand out. White with black lettering. There is a lake of blood in the gym and on the field. Everyone is dead but me and whoever did this. Again, the pursuit is on.

In this dream, I can taste and smell and feel the fear. I wade through viscous blood. I want to get away. There is no place that isn't covered in blood. I want to cry for these people and for myself. I tried to warn them back in the gym but they ignored me. I blinked and they were dead before my eyelids closed. I open my eyes and fight my way down the stairs onto the field. I want to cry. I want to vomit. Both take time I don't have. I have to run.

Unlike my younger self, I know why I run now. If I don't, I'll die. Violently. Painfully and beyond repair. Death will be welcome but may be withheld for the gratifications it gives. I don't see myself getting caught. There seems to be no choice in the matter. I've stayed true to myself over the years in this regard.

Amendment: I am *not* running from death. That's impossible in all ways. I'm running from evil, pain, fear, nightmares, betrayals.

Fuck. Another amendment: In one dream I am unable to run because the blood makes running impossible. God, I really want to, though. I'm stuck. I realize I am rooted to the spot by my own inability to move, not because of the blood. I'm so damn tired from running one step ahead of the evil in my life. I'm tired of contributing to it and being the victim of it. I'm crying and I vomit.

In another variation of the same dream, I can't run anymore. I'm knee-high in blood, soaked in it from head to toe. I can feel it cooling and coiling my hair. I sigh. In with the good, out with the bad. I turn around and that's where the nightmare ends.

I always question my sanity when I wake up, because my dreams tell me I will die by the hands of my Paris.

Now an adult, I dream when I am awake, and live while I am asleep. Same life, different place.

SEPTEMBER 28, 2009

The roller coaster goes up. The roller coaster goes down.

It was truly good to see my son yesterday. There are times my Paris shows himself, but the new Paris is always there, too. Today I got a copy of the grievance he filed on August 25, 2009, in response to his inability to get mail. He's gunning for me and it's so obvious the psychopath in him is getting smarter, more sophisticated, polished. Nonetheless, it's good to have moments with him where we can just sit and accept one another for who we are.

My time with him is running out. Two years and he'll be eighteen. Three and he'll be nineteen, headed to the hell that is a Texas adult prison. My baby, my Paris. I don't know how he'll bear up in a Texas prison with mean-ass motherfuckers. Although, he is a bit of a mean-ass motherfucker as well.

As long as he's locked up will I really be able to walk away at eighteen, at nineteen—anytime—if he doesn't want me to? Once he's out, I'm out.

OCTOBER 5, 2009

For the last week, I've had the worst nightmares. I wake up crying, covered in sweat. Dreams of destruction and running and hiding and acute despair. They take their toll on me. I'm worn out. I wonder, the more time passes, how I'm ever going to *live* again. My moods are uncontrollable. There's no steady keel in my existence.

I've visited my son twice in the last two weeks. Both visits have gone well. I have two years left with him. I want to be okay with him. I want to enjoy my visits, even though it's so obvious he is what he is. I want things to end on a good note if it must end.

I've now countersued my mother; I am finished with being pushed around by my mother and Paris, so I did the one thing she didn't expect me to do. Fight back.

I don't consider her my mother anymore. She's just the woman who gave birth to me. Along the way she forfeited her right to be my mom. Lots of people give up their birthright. She reneged on her mother right.

Just got home from a drive. Never a dull moment, I must say. After writing earlier, I had the need to take a drive. I'm not always sure which way I want to go on these drives. All directions away from here are good. Tonight, downtown kept talking to me, so I turned a corner and saw a man grab his girlfriend. It was obvious they were fighting. I slowed my car down then stopped beside them—with traffic behind me—rolled down the window and stared at the man.

He turned around all quick like, snatched his hand off her, and started smiling real nicely. I asked him if there was a problem and asked her if she needed help. They both said no, so I rolled up the window and left—slowly. Not one person honked.

Now I am shaking like a leaf because I recognize the glint I first saw in his eyes. It was rage, still building, but rage. My soul is attuned to it now. I know rage and what it can do. I threw ashes on his, but did I put out that fire or inflame it? Am I courting death by putting myself directly in the path of so much rage?

I'm a fucking rage magnet.

OCTOBER 9, 2009

I spent my day on the phone with lawyers in San Antonio and Hawaii who are getting paid hundreds of dollars an hour to decide if my mom could deliver a birthday card to Paris. It is more than that, but what she finally agreed to is to have a card hand-delivered to Giddings.

I know her game. I know her tactics. She's trying to make me go broke. She used to tell me when I was younger that "whoever has the most money wins." That rule applies to court as well as to life.

More power to her. I just want life. Power is overrated.

Just had one of those moments where you look up and have no choice but to chuckle at the insane reality you're faced with. I'm outside. In front of, and all around me, is music and color. I'm almost thirty-six. I'm covered in grief and butterflies. To my right sits a Walther PPK .380. I'm so worried someone may try to stop my life now I've finally found a reason for living it, I keep it close. A year ago, I kept it close in case I wanted to be the one to stop my life.

I'm catching aflame, shaking the ashes from my feathers, wounds healed enough to begin testing the stretch of the new scars.

OCTOBER 10, 2009

Today is Paris' sixteenth birthday. I was not planning to, but today I told him his gift is that I'll give him what he petitioned the courts for. I will voluntarily relinquish my parental rights. I'll give up my guardianship, split the money fairly, and walk away while I still can.

I'm not sure what overcame me. I hadn't planned on this turn of events at all. I'm tired of fighting; I don't want to do it anymore. I'm right with God when it comes to my children. I'm going to settle these issues, and then I'm going to Spain. If I like it, I'm selling everything and moving there. If I don't, I'm selling everything and moving out west somewhere.

It's time I find my place in the world again.

OCTOBER 11, 2009

I woke up today, expecting depression, anxiety, fear, and regret. Got 'em. What I didn't expect upon waking is I would also feel peace over/underlying it all. I'm okay with what I'm about to do—scared shitless, but okay. Paris called today. He's okay with it, too. Not just for his own selfish reasons, but also because he knows me and knows that I wouldn't say this unless I was going to do it.

Give me the last bit of strength needed to accomplish this one last act of mothering my son well and lovingly. Good-byes are so hard. Paris taught me—no, I taught me, with tons of help from life and love, good-byes are nothing but new beginnings.

OCTOBER 12, 2009

After I leave Giddings I usually stop at the Mexican restaurant in Lagrange, La Fuentes, to drink a margarita and eat chips. They have the best salsa—served warm. The act of doing something normal like stopping your car to eat is needed after stopping your car to walk into the prison of your son.

So here I sit almost smack dab in the middle of America and I'm what? What am I at this moment? Resolute and confident I'm doing the next right thing for all of us. The best way to win this karmic war is to walk away from the battle.

Tonight what I need is to sit alone in a crowd and write. Everything comes full circle. I remember a day sitting alone in a restaurant in Abilene and looking at the people convinced none of them could possibly have felt anything as horrible as I was at that moment. Now I look around convinced the majority of people, hopefully, haven't felt anything as horrible as what I've felt, yet they may and could, because they each have a life, a story, of their own.

OCTOBER 14, 2009

Love has no room, no matter what anyone may say, for the concept of deserving or earning. It just is. Life, no matter what anyone may say, is not about deserving or earning. It's about learning. Learning all you can about love will teach you everything you need to know about life. This I know, no matter what anyone says.

OCTOBER 15, 2009

"I have found the paradox that if I love until it hurts, then there is no hurt, but only more love." —Mother Teresa

What would I do without other people's words? Some I could live without. My words sustain me, yet I wonder, I hope, one day they may sustain others.

It's time for me to live my life the way I see it, not the way I wanted it but the way I envision it. I'm an orphan and I'm childless, but I'm at peace. I'm at peace with myself and at peace with my life. I have no idea where my life will end up— just an idea of where I'd like it to. I have embraced the fact that life *is* lunacy. That's all: lunacy. So why not believe it's still possible to create a life for myself? There is flame produced from the smoke of self-fulfilling prophecy.

My biggest fear, the one I thought I would never face or live through, was losing my kids—and I'm alive. As a result, I'm tired of living in fear and will now only live in hope. Hope I'll find love again. Hope I'll find Ella, which will be as beautiful as a *mariposa de la noche* landing on me. Hope I'll be happy again. Hope I'll be at peace. Hope. Hope. Hope.

If I'm Charity, I must also have faith and hope. I would be nothing without those two companions. Paris became faith. I had faith my love for him would see us through. Ella is love. My love for her gives me faith. There's no way to actually separate them out like that. Having kids requires both love and faith, sometimes more or less of one than the other.

It freaks me out, but moths and butterflies seem to have a thing for me. There is a *mariposa de la noche* perched on my hand as I write this. Ella talks to me all the time. Now it's perched on my right breast. Being breast fed for so long Ella always loved my breasts too.

Do you ever think there will come a day, Charity, that everything no longer reminds you of your daughter, your son, your motherhood, your love? I really hate to tell you this, but I don't think that day will come. You are Ella. You are Paris. You are Charity. And you are love.

It hurts, doesn't it? To love your daughter, to love your son, to love people despite the knowledge loving them may help them, but it won't change your world—just theirs. It's hard to be named Charity, to want to love and be kicked by it so many times.

OCTOBER 19, 2009

"The facts speak for themselves." —Demosthenes
Paris says good-bye just like I do. I just noticed that today while I was listening to one of his voicemails. I'm supposed

to save them, just in case, and I heard it for the first time. My son says good-bye exactly the way I do. Things like this, little things, hurt more than they should. I'm proud to see, hear, myself in my son. I just wish he inherited more than an accent and family defects, aberrations, and anomalous personality disorders.

I'm going to trust the reason Demosthenes' words are still around is because they are Truth. Lies have a built-in self-destruct button. They don't stand the test of time or truth. We've known this as far back as Demosthenes' time. We seem to always forget that fact when we lie.

The fact is I love my son. The fact is I haven't stolen money from my child regardless of all he stole from me and his sister. The fact is I believe I've always made every effort to act in his best interest despite my conflicting emotions. The fact is I'm at peace with my son, my conscience, and my heart.

My first appearance in court is Friday, three days before my thirty-sixth birthday. This is for one of three lawsuits my mother and my son filed against me. This one has to do with her allegation I have not acted in Paris' best interest financially, therefore I have breached my fiduciary responsibility as his Trustee. My mom may or may not be there. I have faith the facts do speak for themselves; if not for themselves, at least for me and the love I've held onto for my kids.

OCTOBER 22, 2009

Tomorrow morning, I wake up at 6:00 am to get dressed, put on my makeup, and go face my mom in court. I'm not even sure what to say. This is a pivotal moment in my life. Just how remains to be seen.

Three days after court I turn thirty-six. Paris has made no mention of awareness concerning my birthday in his now daily phone calls. I do well with him now. I let him talk. I hold my breath when he says things that reveal the psychopath in him. I respond to his dissatisfaction with his therapists by telling him only he knows the true extent of all that's happened to him, all he thinks and all he's done. I also remind him how hard it is for people to believe that if no developmental and attachment impeders happened to him, that means he did what he did out of curiosity and jealousy and found it gratifying.

His reply? "They don't understand but you do because you were there in our life."

It breaks my heart to be his friend and confidante again. It's so like before, when we would talk about all sorts of topics for hours. I loved his mind, the complexity of it. I worried about the sensitivity of it. To be his friend and confidante now means to see him let his guard down, hear him say things that show his lack of remorse and conscience. He doesn't even know he's giving himself away.

I look at my baby and know to love him is to love a psychopath, is to love the murderer of my daughter. It means loving him, knowing he won't ever truly love me back, knowing he may want to kill me. And knowing in the end, in the final part of this chapter, all of that makes no difference.

I love him. I'll listen until I've appointed someone else to listen and I leave.

Tomorrow, if my mother is there, I have a feeling I'll look at her and also know certain things: how wrong she's always been about me, how sad and racked with pain she must be, how bitter she is, how lonely she is, how afraid to face herself. I'm sure I'll feel anger and bitterness too. In the end, though, all I'll think is how glad I am not her.

So now I need to smoke a cigarette, brush my teeth, roll out my spine, and rest as well as I can. Then put on my face, make my ancestors proud, and let the phoenix show herself.

OCTOBER 23, 2009

My mother came to court. She walked by earlier with that fake pitiful look she does, the "I'm so sorry it has come to this, but what was I to do?" look. She tries to play the victim while being the predator.

My attorney says it's best to agree to a freeze on half of the assets since half are Paris' anyway. I was kind of looking forward to seeing her ass fry on the stage of public opinion, but cooking may take place better over a slow period of time.

OCTOBER 25, 2009

Court is over and after today I will never see thirty-five again. The best gift is one I gave to myself - freedom from fear of my mother. As soon as I saw her, I knew the day would be fine. As soon as court ended, I knew her reign of terror over me—whether it be real or imagined—is over. I've become a woman in my own right.

Once we women realize we are, and are not, our mothers, it makes living life as your own woman doable, regardless of whether our mothers see that themselves or not. I'm now able to view myself as her equal.

I wonder if Paris even remembers tomorrow is my birthday.

OCTOBER 27, 2009

Paris called and sang "Happy Birthday" to me. He remembered.

NOVEMBER 5, 2009

I finished reading my journals from 1992 and 1993. I've come a long way since then, but even then I had the wisdom inside me needed to mother Paris. I've never been as messed up as I thought I was; I just had no confidence in myself.

I'm not buying into anyone's perception of who I am or what I'm supposed to be doing with my life. I've made up my mind to get out of Texas and soon. If I don't like Spain enough to move there, I'll move to Portland and rent for a year. I want some breathing room, about five acres, forty-five minutes, maybe one hour, outside of Portland. I would have neighbors, but not up my ass. I want a simple and peaceful life. No more mental manipulations. No more murder. No more constantly wondering if I'm doing the best I can out of love for Paris.

Limbo is old.

FRIDAY THE 13TH NOVEMBER 2009

Paradoxes fascinate me. It's a beautiful day in Texas. It fascinates me that right in the middle of a beautiful day decay is occurring all around me and that decay is needed for growth, for life, to occur.

Yesterday I found out my mother is suing me for being an unfit parent. She wants the court to instate her as Paris' legal guardian. She wants to take the only child I have left from me. This makes the number of lawsuits she filed against me to two.

I'm not fighting this battle with her. I'm putting an end to it as soon as possible. I don't even care if I walk away from all this broke as hell. I have something more important than money. I have a heart. I love people despite what they do. I lost everything dear to me. In return I found out who I am, and even though I have my moments of doubt, I know I'm a good woman. I'm doing right by my son. My conscience is clear when it comes to how I've parented and loved him since he murdered Ella.

I will be okay.

Ella has been with me a lot lately. Last night I had a dream both Paris and Ella were standing on a shore across an ocean full of serpentine demons. I've had this dream before, but normally Ella is the only one standing on the shore. Just like the other dreams, I knew I had to find a way to get past those demons to reach them. I believe Ella is telling me there's still a chance for Paris; my love for him the last two and a half years may have helped in some small way. I'll keep swimming through the demons. I know I'll reach Ella, and I hope Paris will be on that shore with us when all is said and done.

While I was at dinner tonight I heard people complain about their kids' woes or the woes they think they have because they have kids. From the tone of their voice, I can tell they view their children as holding them back, holding them down. I can empathize. I remember moments of fantasizing about moving to Vegas, disappearing, be a cocktail waitress, and die young. I can even understand there's not really a way for anyone to know what they've lost until they lose it. What I don't know how to do is to help people see parenting is one-part magic, four-parts work—hard, hard applied work—and all love and sacrifice. I don't know how to help them see to me what they have is beautiful; how to love their kids, not see them as baggage, problems.

Why do people over four and a half feet tall seem to forget they fucked up all the time too—just like their kids? Too much gravity pulls at the auras of adults. Collectively we're becoming ambiguous and worthless to one another.

A five-year-old child was kidnapped in Florida. The man was caught on camera carrying her into a hotel room. When he was arrested, she wasn't in the room. He admitted kidnapping her, yet she hasn't been found. I looked at his photos on the Internet. I know she's dead. I hope Ella found her and helped her to know—know better—how to handle waking up knowing your last moments were so horrible.

I cried for this little girl as I cry for Ella. Too much hate. Too much pain and violence. Too much gravity. I refuse to participate in the negativity anymore. No more. Peace. Compassion. Depression. Love. Empathy. Ethics. Soul. Those are all I care about anymore. Those are what compose my character.

Losing your entire life forces you to hyper-examine your ethics. Life is no more peaceful, yet I manage to maintain my sense of right and wrong. If you don't look for the pieces of you that are left, how will you ever put yourself back together again? There's always one piece that's easy to find, and that is anger. Too many make the mistake of believing that's the only piece left because finding the others require so much work and pain.

I need sleep. I have a family reunion to attend tomorrow.

NOVEMBER 16, 2009

Ellaellaellaellaellaellaellaellaellaellaellaellaellaella ellaellaellaellaellaella...

I am so stressed out my neck is locked up and all my hand seems to want to write is *ellaellaellaellaellaellaellaella ellaellaellaellaellaellaellaellaellaellaella...*

Anyone who truly knows me and has doubts as to how much Ella is in all this with me: doubt in vain. This is hopefully going to be a more legibly written chapter of my life. This is no longer just a handwritten diary. This is now truly trying to be a coherent and peaceful reflection on all that has happened. To that end, it will get messy, I am sure. In fact, I am so sure it will, I'll chant more: *Ellaellaellaellaellaellaellaellaellaella....*

What fascinates me is how she can be written on and on eternally if you can manage to keep the pen in contact with the pages. All the loops and curves always lead right to her.

Ellaellaellaellaellaellaellaellaellaellaellaellaellaella.
Yes.

Charity. No.

Paris. No.

Ellaellaellaellaellaellaellaellaellaellaellaellaleeaella.
Yes.

I'm not mad yet. Rhyme and reason is everywhere, only it's more surreal and harder to recognize. I don't know how much I may write in the future. I may tell the present good-bye a bit in order to wrap up the past. From today I want to devote my time to ending my family on a peaceful note, healing, mourning,

Fuck it. I'll be writing just as much and just as messily.

NOVEMBER 20, 2009

I'm wound tight. I drove for hours. Nothing has taken away the edginess.

I met a money manager today. Blah … blah … blah. He kept trying to convince me how well he would do managing our money. I'm pulled in too many directions. I want this over. I'm wound too tight. It's storming. It's cold. I'm crazy. I'm sane. I'm no one and nowhere, yet I'm going somewhere.

That's what drives me crazy. This isn't my life yet, not the one I'm meant to live after losing it all. Patience has never been my forte. I'm tired of playing games with these people. I want peace of mind, as much as I can claim for my own. I want friends. I want a life. All I do and all I deal with has to do with Paris and my mother, murder, stress, drama, pain.

Breathe … now sigh.

As insane as it may seem, I must believe a happy life full of love and healing can exist. If I give up hope in that, I give up any hope left to me.

NOVEMBER 24, 2009

Hope is such an elusive feeling to hold onto. I'm in Seattle and depressed, crying, and altogether discontent, no matter what part of the world I'm in.

I HATE MY LIFE.

Now that I've broken one pen, thrown this book against the wall, and had a good self-pity cry, let's start over. Plain and simple, what all this feeling comes down to, is that I'm afraid. Not of life: of living. I am afraid of not be able to live again. Everything feels hollow and irritatingly meaningless at times. I feel unlovable.

Today is a bit better. My anxiety and depression have abated a bit. I ventured out in public. Physical needs trumped psychological pathos.

It's a grey day in Seattle (imagine that) and my mind is racing, trying all the time to make sense of the horrible, fascinating weirdness of my life. Needless to say, right upon the cusp of "getting it," it all begins to make no sense anymore, at all. I'm always trying to figure out what does and doesn't matter; what's worth karmic contemplation, and what's just fluff that fills in the gaps. Is every single thought we have, and every single action we undertake, going to come to bear somehow on our soul? If I notice one of my shoes is untied and I don't stop to tie it, do I get a karmic deduction for being lazy or a karmic point for not getting caught up in such mundane details that I have time to wonder if it matters if I tie my shoe or not?

My world is in my head. I spend more time with myself in the land of the spirits than I do in the land of the living. I really want to know what happens when we die. I'm more curious than afraid. It's hard to live in the moment when I'm always wondering what else there is in this existence, more than the one I see and experience now. I want to know the place Ella is in. I need to meet other souls who understand I'm not a freak. I'm not different.

Out of all the places I've been on this planet, the only place I ever felt I fit was with my kids. No place fits now. No idea what to do with myself. No idea which way to go next, what path to take other than the one that leads to peace, healing, and Ella.

I'm in a coffee shop with a homeless man to my right who is trying to warm up, munching on a roll of French bread, and writing, writing, writing his own words onto paper. Who is he? Why is he homeless and what does he need to say so badly? Everyone wants to be heard, to be understood, to at least feel acknowledged, if not approved of. So many of us seem frustrated and angry by the fact we aren't. The actions we employ to gain the recognition we seek reveal a lot about our character. People are not so hard to read as you think. Then again, we are.

For all I know, the homeless man sitting next to me could be the author of a Pulitzer novel who's gone off the deep end, a hero whose time has passed, or a child molester who's slipped through the cracks. To outside eyes, I could look like a grad student, a writer, a teacher, who knows? I'm pretty sure people don't look at me knowingly, and say to themselves, "Oh look! There's the progenitor of a psychopath and mourner of a beloved lost child. There's a woman walking in hell; look at the flames lick her feet, hear the demons suck on her soul, smell the decay she carries in her skin."

Humans should show their humanity to one another more often. It may not make a difference because as a race we're biologically and spiritually wired to operate in duality; life doesn't thrive if balance among the tensions are upset. Too much tension, we implode; too little, we rot.

NOVEMBER 28, 2009

Still in Seattle and I'm not sure what I think about moving to this town. The people are nice and don't seem all that pretentious. I love to see all the people walking around in nothing at all that looks like suburban America. It's almost as if you cannot—should not—live here if you're "normal."

But it's cold and wet. I've always said I didn't want to live anywhere cold. I love my house in Texas, but I know I can't stay. I have to go soon. I won't continue to build my life there only to have it uprooted once my son gains his freedom.

Having all this freedom feels like prison to me. I don't want to have to make all these choices again. What do I want out of life? Where do I want to live it? How do I want to live it? I already had all those choices made. Paris destroyed each and every one of them. I'm not sure I even know how to live alone, all about just myself. One place to start is by trying to go back to school—again. Social work. One door will lead to another. Maybe then I won't have to worry anymore about jumping out of windows.

DECEMBER 2, 2009

It's 1:00 am so I should be in bed, but need to attempt to write down a few conclusions I came to by the end of my Seattle experience. I'm not leaving Texas. I refuse to go into hiding. I won't live in fear of living *or* of my son. My turn now. No more limbo. No more having the rug pulled out from underneath me. No more trying to get away from people. I'm tired of moving; I like where I live - for now. I will have roots again. I will do all I can to help all I can.

I'm back from hell and ready to see the world with these new eyes.

I RSVP'd to an adoption seminar on December 10. Life has sent me three distinct messages dealing with adoption, so I may as well listen and learn. If I do adopt, it'll be another couple of years, unless Mariposa (I've already named my future adoptee) falls into my life. I'll know. Ella will let me know when and who.

I love you, Ella. All the time, every moment of every day. I'm working hard to earn my way to you, Singing Princess.

DECEMBER 3, 2009

Life never ceases to amaze me in its crazy, random, mind-boggling ways. I spent the day trying to jump-start my life, put it back on track, and keep it calm and even-keeled. Who do I hear from at the end of the day who causes me to wonder, yet again, what the fuck is going on and why?

Nic.

Evidently he can't be my friend because he's still in love with me, thinks of me every day yet can't have me. I'm still the great love of his life he holds silently in his heart.

As soon as I saw the text was from him I got excited, horny, shaky, so I came to the Cove to have a glass of red wine, calm down, write, and ponder. Who's here?

Nic—with his girlfriend.

Isn't life funny and weird as hell? Lest there be any doubt about it, life reminds you every day. He says he won't talk to me, but he will be in touch. He misses me; misses having someone like me in his life. I used to tell him I was confident he would always come home to me because I am the type to leave the gate open. Gates are open all around me.

Nic said in one of his texts he was never anything but a story to me. True and not. Life is nothing but a story, yet everything I feel is nothing but real. Stories help me cope with the realness. Evidently that story is not over.

Okay. Life on track info. I called school, took my house off the market, set up some shifts at SAPD, found a nursing home where I'll volunteer reading time. There's a mediation with my mother on December 17, so, hopefully, that will be out of my life soon.

DECEMBER 9, 2009

I had a dream this morning, another messenger dream. I'm standing in a very white room on the upper level of what I can feel is a rather huge house—strange it was so plain inside. Out of nowhere tremors rock the house and the roof slid off to let the sun in, and I do not feel safe at all. I'm panicked and terrified and notice the entire upper level of the house tilts when you try to walk on it.

I run downstairs to find my mother calm. I'm sobbing we have to leave, I have to leave, this house. It's not safe. I need to protect my kids—blah, blah, blah. She turns into some sort of wiry-haired terrier type dog and is acting bristly, so I grab the dog. I squeeze harder and harder while yelling desperately, "This place isn't safe! Can't you see this isn't safe?" while forcing the dog to turn her head to look around.

Right before my desperation turns evil, right before I squeeze the dog so tightly she dies, I see my Papasam, my grandfather, sitting on a bench across from me in an elaborate garden in a gazebo. He looks at me and shakes his head *no,* one time. He's not angry, not fearful, no panic—plain and simple *no.* I see his *no,* drop the dog, and walk out of the house.

That's it. I wake up.

Let go. It is time to let go of both emotions I feel for my mother - the wiry rat terrier. Let go of trying to get her to open her eyes in my world. Let go of hating her because she can't see; she just won't.

Papasam's *no* brought me back to myself. I love how my loves on the other side look out for me. I'm focused. My life's pieces are fitting back together. I finally found motivation in my emotional arsenal. My purpose doesn't seem as macabre or laughable anymore.

Houses. All my messenger dreams are set in houses. One on the back porch of a house with a cabin in the backyard. One with secret passageways in and under it. Now in a room. What do my houses mean to me? I'm starting to believe it's all the same house that I'm seeing in pieces.

Time to live and tend to my elaborate garden.

DECEMBER 10, 2009

My son had his guardian ad litem file papers today to remove me as his guardian and replace me with his grandmother. After all he has done, after all the love I've given him, he's still trying to get rid of me, hurt me. When I told him I would give him what he said he wanted for his sixteenth birthday, my parental rights terminated, he eventually said he changed his mind; said he was angry and wanted to hurt me. He has now symbolically stabbed me in the back

For the last time. I'm going to give him what he wants and what I need: freedom. He's pushed and pushed; I won't be pushed anymore. First, he wanted to kill me. Instead, he kills Ella. Then he tortures me psychologically for three years. If I'm not wanted as his mother, I'm only his victim. I won't be victimized any longer. I am done being his mouse.

I made it clear to him after this is settled, he's as dead to me as Ella. Death and money are the only things my son and my mother care about. They can have both. I walk away knowing I love my son. I'm a good mother and it's my time to live the life I have left.

DECEMBER 11, 2009

Nic finally broke down and had a conversation with me. I knew he would, but I don't know why I pushed so hard to get him to. I would be a fool to try to take him back. If he still loves me the way he says he does, it wouldn't be fair to hurt him again.

So, Charity, let's figure out what you're up to. First, I don't believe in being hateful towards someone I was once in love with; am still in love with. There was love, and after the anger and hurt fade away, why not let love and ethics be your guide?

He says he's going to have babies with and marry his girl, Debbie. I asked him why he is texting me if he wants a future with her. To get me out of his system he says; get the love out of his system. I never want to get love out of my system. I only want to get away from love toxic to my system. I suppose that's what he thinks of me; I'm toxic for him. I suppose I am.

After hearing he thinks he's happy, I know what I need to do: nothing. One of the reasons I walked away from Nic is because I knew he would never be happy with me. I expect more than he can give. I did/do love him, and I want him to find his happiness in life. He's young. He's not as far along his road as I am mine. He needs to do things like get married and have babies. And I need to do things like get my master's in social work. Find my own soulmate. Love and help as many people as I can.

Paris has called three times today trying to explain to me why he filed a motion to have me removed as his guardian. I listened with my heart turned off.

It's off because, as usual, it is a heart conflicted. Paris can do nothing to make me stop loving him. I have promised him I will be here for him no matter what. He knows this is his power over me.

Which has led to more circular thinking because, on one side of the equation, I want to keep my promise to him, my son. The other side of the equation is I need to take the chance offered to get as far away as possible from Paris, from all this, and in doing so, take back my power.

DECEMBER 13, 2009

But for the fact I spent the entire day in bed after going out to get ridiculously wasted, I would have written yesterday, because if ever there was a time I needed to write, it was then. It's time to face the fact my life is wasting away. I'm letting my soul rot.

Today I feel I am a hypocrite. I'm sure finding out your son, along with your mother, is suing you is enough to drive most people to drink, but if I keep letting him do this to me, I'll never accomplish anything good in the world. I will stay a broken human being.

I said good-bye to Nic—again—which contributed to my breakdown and drinking. It was good-bye, close the door, then sobbing, panic attacks, and the inability to stand up. There's no one in my world who helps me heal, so it falls again on me to sustain myself. Wait. That's wrong. I still have my spirits. My Ella, my dad, my Papasam. Today they're here without a doubt. I can feel them hug me from time to time. Ella sent a butterfly to sit on my shoulder, tattooed butterfly side, this afternoon, for ten minutes. She always goes to that side.

The only way I'll survive in this town is to make a clean break with The Cove, and all the people I hang out with from there. *Everyone* I know drinks like fishes. I went to Alcoholics Anonymous long enough to know what I need to change in my life to bolster my spirit. Sometimes it's nothing but finding the sheer will it takes to stop yourself.

AA would disagree with my methods, but fuck 'em.

DECEMBER 15, 2009

This is the week peace between warring parties will be made or full-scale battle erupts. Mediation with my mother is set to commence in T minus one day. T minus two days until court to thwart her attempt to take my motherhood and my son. I have, and will continue, to play nice when it comes to money. I will defend my character. My right to mother my son I'll fight for, because I am not going to let him take that away from me. It will be my choice when I "stop" being his mother.

I've finally reached my limit. There are certain behaviors and actions I'll tolerate no longer. There are emotions I won't let poison my life again. If I keep my son, or my mother, in my life, his psychopathy and her narcissism will erode my soul and kill me. If they get my soul, they hit the jackpot.

I am, in my own way, saying good-bye to this phase of my life—not my love, not the lessons. The toxins. Intense grief shall be returning. Every day I grieve for Ella. In the coming days, as I spiritually and legally let go of what's left of my family, I'll finally be able to deal with my rage and disappointment over the loss of who I thought of as family.

Paris is no longer the boy on the back deck in Spiderman underwear and Converse playing with Tonka's. He is a sixteen-year-old psychopath. We all forget that. Even me. Ella. Well, we all know what happened to Ella, but it seems we all forget that too.

Beaten. Strangled. Mouth covered so no one could hear her scream. Seventeen stab wounds, five of them in her back.

Seventy-five percent of the stab wounds nonlethal; the final twenty-five percent death blows. Her throat was stabbed after her heart had slowed enough or had already stopped, so there was no blood splatter. After he murdered her, he called a friend. Talked for six minutes. Then called 911. Lied. Pretended to do CPR. Picked her up "like a dead deer" (his words, not mine) and dropped her on the floor. He said he felt "disgusted" doing that because she was all bloody and he didn't want to get dirty. He was clean when the cops showed up.

Maybe Rebecca is right and my lesson in this life isn't to learn to love. It seems to me I've loved the 10,000 hours of practice needed to perfect a skill. Maybe my lesson is to learn to let go, not of love, but of my beloved. I've had a lifetime of losing beloveds in horrible ways. My dad was murdered, my mom was lost to spiritual decay, Ella, more murder, Paris murders and has the ultimate case of spiritual atrophy.

I swear to God if Paris kills me, the last two things I'll say to him are "I love you" and "I'll tell Ella hello for you, fucker." Even if he tortures me for days, weeks, months, years, it's all he'll get from me.

I want a happy ending, but that seems unfathomable. Happiness at death will be knowing Paris cannot hurt me anymore. My body is done. The pain and the trauma are over and Ella, and all those who are here for me now, are waiting for me on the other side of life.

Forget what you think you are and find out who you are— that's what I have to do. I thought I was a mother. Who I am is a nurturer, a lover, an empathetic and sympathetic wise soul stuck being human so I can learn more about love.

Fuck it all. I'm going to be okay. I am okay. Charity is back. I'm not letting either one of them take me away from me ever again. I set myself free. I'm taking off in flaming flight.

DECEMBER 17, 2009

12:49 pm

Technically it's the day I face my mother in mediation. I'm too keyed up to sleep. I can't go out for a long drive. All I have is me sitting here with knowledge that later today any hope I had, ever, of having a good relationship with my mother is gone. I still need a mother, but her time is past. Today is the day I become an orphan.

It's now the evening of the day I faced my mother in mediation. It's settled, legally anyway. Paris is now a sixteen-year-old psychopath with more money than any sixteen year old should have. His grandmother and all blood relatives have full access to him until he reaches the age of eighteen. After that he decides for himself who he wants around. He doesn't have the right to sue me in the future for anything regarding his trust. My mother's suit relating to the termination of my parental rights will be dismissed. That only leaves the motion Paris had his guardian ad litem file in Lee County to have his grandmother as his conservator. He says he called to have it dismissed.

What he doesn't understand is it makes no difference to me. I have to be done. I have to walk away. If I continue to put my love for my son above my need to heal, I'll lose Charity. I've dug too deep through too much shit to lose myself again.

If he has it dismissed—fine. I'll keep my rights and walk away, change my number, return to trying to do more than survive. If he persists, I'll walk into the courtroom and tell the judge I don't want to be his mother anymore, as all my son has done since he killed Ella is tell me how horrible I am, how fucked-up I am, how immoral and unacceptable my life is, that all I want is revenge.

All I've ever wanted is the ability to be my children's mom through thick and thin, good and bad. I so badly wanted a different relationship with my kids than I had with my mother. Instead, I get a kid who murdered and destroyed everything that made me happy instead of one who just yells he hates me and slams a door. There's no way to mother him that I can understand.

Psychiatrists have told me to walk away. He's a sexually-motivated violent offender, which means only one thing in this time we live in—there is no cure for him. He'll get out of jail; he'll lead life within its proper constraints for a while. Then he'll grow frustrated with someone, angry, bored. He'll see a Charity or an Ella and his "tentacles" will be free to play out those fantasies of his.

Forget Paris. This is what really bugs me. For seventeen years, I put my kid's needs above my own, most of the time. For thirty-something years, I thought about my mother in all my decision making. Ella is dead. Paris is about to be dead to me, and my mother is a nonorganic, robotic being.

Who am I going to be?

DECEMBER 19, 2009

I'm in Abilene for the first time since I left it behind me in August 2007. Justin, my tattoo artist moved back for family help, so this is where my phoenix tattoo is to be finished. All this full-circle shit never ceases to amaze me. I was destroyed in this town, and here I am back in this damn town so I can complete the symbol of my transformation.

When you take a trip down memory lane you find both the joy and the pain of life. How can memory be anything but bittersweet? I'm back in a place where memories are everywhere I look. I have no idea what's going to be brought out of me now. I have no idea if I should drive by their old school so I can see, in my mind, them running down the breezeway to the car again—or should I avoid all confrontation with any memories that could cause me joy, because pain will come and sucker-punch it right out of my gut? Do I go see the house I built for us? Do I go see the house she died in? Do I go sit and watch kids play soccer on the same field she did? Eat at the same Olive Garden?

All I can do with memories is remember, let them wash over me, and get ready to go the Christmas party Justin's parents are throwing That's what life is, right—functioning in the stickiness of the bittersweet?

Any way I look at it, anywhere I may look this weekend, Ella is all around me. For that I will always be grateful.

DECEMBER 23, 2009

Well, as I always say, life throws things at you, all the time, out of the blue. There is no such thing as control. There is no certain sense of what is right versus what is wrong, except what hurts, profoundly hurts, another is wrong.

I was arrested in Abilene this weekend. Class B misdemeanor for possession. Some ass at the hotel called the cops because they smelled me smoking. It's bullshit you go to jail for smoking pot. It's my first offense, but being known in Abilene was not helpful. Most likely the charges will be dismissed, but I will have to lawyer up to make that happen. If the charge is not dismissed, the future I want to build is already fucked, which is more bullshit considering all I have to give after all I've lived through.

After my arrest, I freaked out for a bit and almost committed to moving to Oregon, but I feel so much doubt about that decision, it's best to do nothing for now. As is chanted in AA: When in doubt do nothing. I need roots. I love my home. I'm tired of running and wasting money and starting over. I'm tired of limbo. I'm staying and embracing myself and my life, warts and all. I'll be reduced to tears some days. Some days I'll make a total fool of myself. Through it all I'll do my best to retain my heart of golden glass.

It is almost time for me to say good-bye to Paris, no matter if I stay in Texas or leave. I have to walk away. My mental health is a heavily guarded commodity these days. The last two, three times he called, I was so impatient to get off the phone. I'm almost ready to move on. I will never forget. I will never stop loving him, but I'll learn to let go of him. It's come down to my survival or his. He'll survive where he is and because of who he is. The only way I'll survive is to learn to act as he does: unemotional and unattached.

DECEMBER 25, 2009

I ruined Christmas.

Evidently it needed to be done this way, ended abruptly. That is how it all started for me. There's some justice in there somewhere.

I threw down the gauntlet. For Christmas, I asked Paris to write a story for me. He was having trouble coming up with a topic, so I suggested he write a story about a boy who kills his sister, but not a story about the murder; a story about the boy. What makes him tick? What led him to his crime? Who did the crime turn him into?

For so many obvious reasons he, of course, said no. I gave my solemn vow never to share his story with anyone. He said no. I would have kept my vow had he written me that story. After everything, I still just want to understand my son better. I want him to prove to me he isn't a psychopath. I can't understand and he can't prove it. So I left.

I can't help him, and as far as I can see, he doesn't care if I mother him. So how does this mother feel to know she's done with her son? Or maybe I should ask how does this mother feel to know her son never started with her? I'm in a daze, a fog. I don't know what I'm supposed to do after walking away from—on Christmas Day, no less—my son who killed my daughter. I gave him coldness, hardness. I returned some of what he has taught me. Like I said before, I have learned from the best.

I'm tired. I can't continue on with him much longer. I don't enjoy listening to him talk about himself, himself, himself, nothing but superficial bullshit. There's no deep, real emotion in there. I can't watch him perfect his mask with me as his model.

I made a pot of coffee. All I want to do is fall down, fall out, drop out, drop dead. Instead I'll drink coffee and sit in my daze, my fog, and wait for the sun to burn it off. Then I'll do what I've done for the last three years. I'll breathe and do my best to live despite, and because of, all this fucking bullshit. Life hurts obscenely, yet at times it's so beautiful to behold that it's undeniably holy.

Fucking paradoxes. Fucking life.

What does one do on the Christmas night one walks away from a limb of one's life? Carry on in a normal fashion? In my world normal is not normal. Fuck normal. Go with the flow.

I'm the mother of a psychopath and it's time to adjust to my new role. When you're the mother of a psychopath, you question reality on a pretty regular basis. It's time to stop worrying what other people may think, just let go and be whoever it is I've become these last two years and ten months. An adult who still likes to have fun, drive fast cars, and listen to loud music. A child at heart who's always known life hurts us as terribly as it loves us. An orphan with a family made of love and not blood. A damaged soul who's afraid of all my life has the potential to dole out daily.

"You can't be what you were, so you better start being just who you are."

—Fugazi

DECEMBER 31, 2009

Technically I should say it's now January 1, 2010. I am at San Antonio Police Department headquarters answering phones for the sex crimes/family violence division. So far it's a slow night in the station.

While I sit here I listen to the police scanner; what I hear amazes me. Outside the stations, gangs roam the streets assaulting people. Car burglaries are in progress. Someone's child has been sexually assaulted. Officers are chasing people down. It's a world within a world. It is a violent and degrading world. At least I'm someplace safe tonight. It's better than being out on the other end of that scanner, drunk and cold, pretending to enjoy myself. Even if others don't, I want to start anew this year.

In 2007, I decided to declare bankruptcy for New Year's. In 2008, I slept with Nic. In 2009, I slept next to Nic. In 2010—all on my own, trying to make the world a better place.

Time to head up to the station rooftop to watch fireworks with a bunch of cops. Never would have thought I'd be ringing in a new year on a roof with cops, but hey, life is always full of "I never thought" moments.

JANUARY 1, 2010

Happy New Year, Ella Lee. Even after all this time I miss you. If you'd been on that rooftop, standing next to me, or in my arms so you could see better, the fireworks would have reflected beautifully in those light-catching eyes of yours. Tonight they were nowhere near as bright.

I'm making it without you physically by my side, Ella. Somehow. I know you're here with me. I know I'll find you. This is the year I start keeping my promise to you, Ella Bella. I will live, and live well, for you. I will share the love you gave me with the world. No more just surviving. No more fear of Paris for now. It's time to heal so I can one day be with you again.

I will do all I can to keep you alive, Ella. If I can't see you, I need to see the light and colors you cast. Stay with me, Ella. Run ahead and back on the path when you will and must from time to time. My path is lit so you can find me again when you will, and you must.

It's been almost three years since you've gone. It makes no difference, time, in this new world of mine. The sort of love and pain I've endured since losing you has warped the edges of time, stretched the limits it imposes on the world.

You would almost be eight now—wow. I try so hard to imagine who you would be, fill in the unfillable gaps with an imaginary you. I would love and be in awe of you every moment of every day. Some things will never change.

Here's to 2010, Ella Lee. Mama will always love you. Like I said, some things will never change.

JANUARY 2, 2010

I have not spoken with Paris since our Christmas Day fight. I don't know what to say to him anymore. What's left to say?

It's hard to discuss the present. I don't want to talk about gangs, jail tatts, or who killed who and how. I don't want him to know too much about the life I've managed to build because I am scared the more he knows, the easier it will be for him to destroy it in the future.

It's impossible to discuss the future. Who knows what his future holds? He's safe for three more years. After that, I have a good idea what his future holds, and don't want to think of my Paris in that future. Refer back to my fear of him destroying my future to understand why I don't want to talk about my future with him.

That leaves the past. The past is off limits. The past will always be between us. The past is what makes the present and future with him unlike anything I know how to face.

In the days of certain blackness to descend in the days ahead, I am able to add to my list of litanies to life that I've overcome fear and found love. Life is ceasing to be an effort of Herculean will to bear and is turning into a fascination on par with that of any child experiencing life for the supposed first time.

My fascination makes sense. I *am* the baby darkly aware of the world I exist in. I may have the fascination of a toddler, but for a long time I've honed instincts needed for the survival of this soul. Every experience I encounter I appreciate because

I know how fragile all these experiences are. Life is forever going to be abrupt, strange, painful, and fascinating, as will love.

JANUARY 4, 2010

I've slumped. This depression is shallow compared to ones endured in the past. I'm not mentally reviewing methods of suicide, but I can't leave the house. I'm locked in today. I'm afraid if I leave my house on days like this, I won't be able to engage properly in the world. The insanity and uncertainty I push around will push back and expose how fragile and damaged I truly am. Am I insane or emotional? There's no real distinction for me anymore. I doubt every moment of my existence while having nothing but my existence as my faith.

How am I supposed to help the world when I have so many visits from my enemies: pain, loss, and grief? Always the Southern woman, hospitality must be shown even to my enemies. What am I going to draw on today to get through? What will keep me from sinking deeper into my muck? Where, if at all, will the motivation be found to put down this pen, get out of this room to bathe and put on my face, walk out the door of my holy prison, and face countless other realities? For what? Dry cleaning? Money? Gas? There's nowhere I want to go, nowhere I can drive that takes me away and gives me calm. Nothing, fucking nothing, to convince me "living" is worth all the effort today.

On days such as this, just the act of brushing my teeth becomes a battle. Here's the way it works: One simple thought, such as *brush your teeth*, pops into my head. Even though it's a simple thought it gets probed mercilessly, analyzed at every gatehouse, interrogated extensively as to its purpose, before finally released to fulfill it.

On days such as this I spend my time see-sawing on a tight rope above the abyss.

JANUARY 8, 2010

I'm floundering in the dark, lost. I'm not at all sure what to do with myself. Two weeks after Ella died I went grocery shopping. As soon as I walked in the store, I knew I was lost. I had no idea how to shop for one person. Without all the sugary cereals, magazines, and junk food arguments, what was it that I wanted? It seemed I hadn't thought about what *I* wanted to eat in fourteen years. Groceries started a panic attack.

Now the panic is dispersed, less pronounced, but it goes deeper. What if I fail? What if I can't put my life back together? The last three years I've done nothing but try to hold my pieces together. What if I can't glue them back? I believe life will never be anything but diffused and deep pain from now on. There's no closing my eyes once they've been opened.

JANUARY 12, 2010

I have, yet again, made a pact with my demons. At times they forget this is my mind they're fucking with. What they really want is attention. Then they quiet down. Even demons have stories to tell. After a week of listening to them, I made a decision, or at least came to a realization, about what I expect to teach myself and my demons this year.

This year we will learn what tranquility feels like. I'm not naive. I don't expect life to *be* tranquil. I do expect myself to learn how to maintain inner harmony: how to allow both my angels and my imps to tell their tales to me. I expect to learn how to give them all the proper amount of respect before reminding them, again, this is my head they're fucking with.

And if that does not work, I will just drag them kicking and screaming with me toward the light.

JANUARY 14, 2010

This is where I am today, right now, in my world. I'm on a dock, in the middle of a lake, mountains covered in snow all around me. Sunset fills the sky and the lake is placid. I am flat on my back, naked, spread eagled in the sun, absorbing the heat and light. I'm preparing myself to stand up, gaze at the serene surface, and then plunge into the currents beneath. Right now, I am content with the fact I am flat on my back, naked, and spread eagled in the sun.

JANUARY 18, 2010

I'm still floundering. I'm still floating through this life. I feel useless. These last three years I've had straws to grasp, but nothing to hold onto. All the small moments which bring me any pleasure or joy are just that, small moments, brief moments of second-rate joy. I'm afraid that's all I will feel now. Second-rate joy. Second-rate love. Second-rate pleasure. Pain has secured the top spot for too long, but what can I do? I can't shed it like I can my robe. I can't wipe it off my face along with my makeup. It's in me, of me. Pain loves me.

My friend Will, the Texas Youth Commission Ombudsman, recently left his job for another. A roast was thrown for him. I felt truly uncomfortable there. I was surrounded by people who are fighting for a cause, all ambitious, all moderately successful, all possess essentially good hearts, yet I can't identify with them.

All night long I was asked, "How do you know Will?" Always truthful, I speak about Paris and Ella, how that led to Will. Their thoughts about me shift in time to the shift in their eyes. Pity sets in, as does confusion about what to say when I am done speaking. Fear it will be the wrong thing. Then comes the "I'm so sorry for your loss; I can't even imagine what you've been through" speech. That's where the disconnect begins, because most of them are sorry, most of them do find it confusing, most of them do say the wrong thing because they begin to preach, to compliment. "You're so strong, so brave, so honest—it's an inspiration."

A woman at the party asked if I was an attorney. I laughed, told her no, and asked why she thought that. She said she saw me sitting at the bar looking classy and powerful, so she assumed I was a high-powered attorney. I told her who I really was. There went the eyes. I stopped being a creature of class and power to one of pity. How do I stay strong in the face of that? If everyone wants to feel sorry for me or make excuses for me, how do I stand up in the face of it all? I don't want pity. I want help.

I want someone to listen to the entire story I have yet to tell. I want them to listen so I can tell them they're wrong.

I'm not strong, or brave, or loving, or honest. I, too, am a Jekyll and Hyde, just like my son. My Hyde is not as evil, and my Jekyll is purer, but like all of us, I have my dual nature I fight to keep in check. There is a black hole in me that wants to eat me up, suck me in. I still have claws, so I dig in, hold on, scream in fury and pain, refuse to let go.

I must find my own unique way to change the world I exist in. I'm going nowhere, trying to follow in others' footsteps, or letting them dictate my path. I've been cast from friendly shores. I've held my breath when I couldn't keep my head above water. I'm the only lifesaver I have left, so I'm going to hold onto myself and drift for a spell. I'm so tired of trying to figure out how to deal with every moment of my life, trying to live it well despite all the reasons not to.

There are moments, if I had one wish, I would wish to give up, let go. Give up or let go? Which one? I don't know, because I'll never be able to do either until I feel I've accomplished the goal love has set for me. To give up, to lay down, to say, "No more, I need rest" is always beguiling. To let go, to say, "I don't know and who cares?" is selfish at best, cowardly at worst. Who am I to do either, when there are others out there in more pain than me, in worse circumstances, still making it day to day?

Nic is going to be a father. When I heard the news, my heart constricted because those days are past for me: being pregnant, thinking my future is great, thinking I'll have my love and my child forever by my side. The days of thinking, naively, life would never be cruel, lonely, or dark ever again.

How young and stupid I was.

It's time to start dealing in the reality of my moment. It's down to me to keep floating, down to me to find another viable meaningful life, down to me to find up-to-me again. Tonight, I drew on my reserves and went to a poetry slam. How am I to ever get up if I don't get out? I can live with myself. What I can't live without is others. I can't live without love or physical contact, or feelings. I can't live in isolation even though I can't live fully in this world.

I am not a poet, but I admire people for putting themselves out there, baring themselves in front of all the hecklers that come with performing at a poetry slam. Especially when it's obvious they suck. I love them for being up there anyway. They're trying. There's a lesson in that.

What I find so fascinating about the world of creativity is it's born out of decay, despair, and suffering. I don't know any musician, any poet, any writer, or any artist who expresses their satisfaction with life. All I hear, all I read, all I see come out of those of us considered creative starts with pain and ends with hope. Hope is what's left after the decay. The only problem with creative people is we're too sensitive. Decay hurts us to the point where all we have left to hope for is that we are able to convey the importance of decay to others more concerned with temporal concerns.

Even among this crowd I seem to stand aside, as though I have an invisible force field which stops people from approaching me. I see people look at me. I see their curiosity, but no one steps into my bubble. I'm too tired to step too far out of it. I believe I'll go to my grave not understanding what sets me adrift from others; why I seem to bump into many but engage or hold onto few. Another one of those things to accept about my life, I guess.

I should be grateful most people I encounter are positively affected by me. Most, not all. I should be grateful I'm still alive, that I don't give up, that I still feel, experience, and create beauty. And I am, except for the fact I have found nothing as beautiful as either one of my kids, motherhood, what I had. I'm struggling to create a moment and, hopefully, a future while still looking for the past.

Good luck with that, right?

JANUARY 22, 2010

I began my second set of PTSD treatment. This go-round my focus is Paris. In some ways the process is more difficult than when I focused on the night I lost Ella. With Ella, for now, the end is known, the trauma is complete. It ripples out and echoes back to me, but nothing new occurs. When I die, we'll begin again.

Paris is still here. Our future is dangerously unknown. New traumas pile on the original trauma, making it very difficult to know where to focus my efforts in order to process the damage.

I have a hard time imagining or planning anything past the moment because this moment is all I know I have to experience. I set goals, yet don't attach myself to them, because in a heartbeat that goal can be changed or eradicated. I can handle whatever it is the moment expects of me. If I think too far in the future, I don't know if I can handle what life may or may not hand to me. I've reached a back-ass-ward state of Zen. I'm not happy. I'm not at peace, but for now I'm giving in to being content, content to float my way into the next phase of my unknown life.

JANUARY 26, 2010

I was holding Thomas (my cat) tonight, like the big twenty-pound baby he is, and it brought another piece of Ella, therefore a little hope, back to me. Ella was a healthy baby, not too fat, not too solid, and big. She got heavy fast, and since she nursed until she was three, she was heavy a long time. She would pass out in my arms and I would hold her until I wanted to cry for the numbness in my arms. When you love someone, though, you want to hang on even when it hurts you to do so. As long as I had her to hold, the numbness meant nothing. Now it's not numbness, it's pain, but I still hold on. Holding Ella gives me hope even though she's gone for now.

Holding onto Paris hurts more than ever because the hope is gone. Still, I hold on because the love is there.

JANUARY 29, 2010

A girl, sixteen, was pulled out of the ruins in Haiti today after two weeks of being buried alive. Truly a miracle. Her brother said of her, "I think she has a special god."

Do we have a special god, those of us who survive the unimaginable, those of us who defy the odds? If we do, would that not suggest those who die have a regular god or no god? Would God really be that unfair if there is ONE? I understand why her brother thinks this, but I don't agree with him. God, man's God, gives us a black-and-white way to see this world. Good things—white, God things. Evil things—black, not-God things.

What I know is both are God things. God, if there is ONE, is not black and white, or black, or white. God isn't at all the God most think. God is more than we can think. Naming God constricts our ability to grasp the huge idea we wrestle with. God is life, and life is amazing, miraculous, and completely sadistic and masochistic.

What can you do but appreciate the grand irony of it all? Ironies such as Nic now having a baby and him wanting to sit and talk with me at the Cove. He still loves me. The only thing that keeps him going right now is the thought that one day we may be able to be together. So he says, as I appreciate the irony of it all.

FEBRUARY 1, 2010

Three days until the three-year anniversary of losing everything and already my old friend depression is here to sit on me. It's hard to move when you weigh a ton. What Paris did three years ago injected pain into my cells, pain that has caused permanent chemical changes in my body. If it had been anyone but her, but him, I wouldn't be reeling down corridors of thought about my mind/body connectivity and spiritual influences on my physical being.

Rebecca advises me to tell my girl depression just to be with me, but not overpower me. Like I have that option. When my girl is around, I am forced to scream so I have space to breathe. She doesn't listen to reason. She listens to whatever calls her out of her hole.

Three years. It can't possibly have been such a long/short time. Everything/nothing has changed. These days I can barely write. One thought after another runs through my head and that's the problem. These thoughts run and run and run. They go places I can't comprehend, much less describe. My hand can't compete with my mind, so it sits on the shore hoping to pluck one or two thoughts out of the rapids.

I grow concerned about the hermitic condition of my life. One of two things always happens. I want to get out of here, but I can't because dealing with the world outside my walls is unbearable. Or … I don't want to get out of here because the world seems so superficial, meaningless, and cruel. I'm thinking more about it since J.D. Salinger died. He chose a rather isolated existence. Or did he? Does anyone really choose to be isolated, or do you reach a point where withdrawing from this manmade world into your own seems the only "sane" thing to do? Not much of a choice, but still a choice I suppose.

FEBRUARY 14, 2010

My words may be brief. I feel rather stupid and clumsy with words and ideas right now, with no way to communicate the level I'm on; territory so new I'm waiting for new words of description. In the last three years I've seen and believed amazing and horrible things. Through that lens I've learned this. We are all immortal. Love does conquer all. Everything I do matters and none of what I do matters. The result of these three lessons is the binds that held who I thought I was in place have fallen away. I'm everything and nothing I was or am. I am vast, boundless, and immortal, and that overwhelms me. I am inconsequential, and that overwhelms me. But, I'm not worried. I'm curious—curious to follow this boundlessness and depth to whatever place inside myself it leads to. After two weeks of depression, I've made it to the point of being able to decide, tentatively, to live again.

FEBRUARY 15, 2010

A friend told me tonight he had the feeling I've always been different, special somehow.

I go to Portland again, in April, after Ella's birthday to be hypnotized, then regressed, into my past lives. I made a promise I'd love my children until the end. Well, it turns out there is no end, so I'm going back, to the past, to deal with the present. I find myself standing behind the gate of something vast so I'm going to open the gate. I have always been one to keep the gate open, remember?

I want to be in touch with the other planes of myself. I have to be in touch with them to focus on here again. Instead of having the spirits only in my world, I want to walk through their world to learn about what I am here to do. If I'm going to be different, special somehow, I'm going to be especially different somehow. Come what may.

FEBRUARY 16, 2010

The lawsuit my mother brought against me in now officially over. A Bexar County judge signed the final agreement today. My mother agreed to mediation. All of Paris' money was placed back in a trust for him and she dropped her attempt to have my parental rights terminated. When I asked her why she had made all those incredibly horrible, not to mention untrue, accusations about me in her lawsuits, she replied she wanted to win. When she wants to win, she is willing to do whatever it takes to do so.

I'm free ... for now. I'm not stupid nor naive enough to believe this cuts the real binds that tie me to my mother or my son.

I'll see both of them Saturday. It's Family Day at Giddings. I plan on three things occurring. One, I will completely enjoy my little sister's company. Two, I will enjoy my son's company. Three, I will let my son and my mother know they no longer call my shots.

FEBRUARY 20, 2010

It was a mistake ... going to Family Day. At least on this level it feels like it was. It could have been a good thing to do on some other level.

I didn't last two hours. My sister I could handle. Even Paris I could handle; I still enjoy seeing and being with him, most of the time anyway. My mother, though ... I sat there with an infinite scream reverberating through my brain. It grew louder and louder, and when she uttered even one word, it turned into a shriek. So I left. The further away I got, the "I am stuck in a rut" feeling returned, but that's better than the "you're going to explode, literally, from holding so much back" feeling.

I'm moving. My yearning for the west will be indulged. I feel better when I drive west so west is where I will go. I will not tell Paris or my mother I've left Texas. I'll let them think I'm here as long as I can. It's better that way.

FEBRUARY 21, 2010

I'm doing it. I'm leaving Texas, letting go of fear, embracing faith. My house is for sale. My time here is up. It's time to pull another layer of ego away to achieve another layer of evolution. My decision must be right because my tranquility and confidence levels have increased. I have no idea if this is the right thing to do. I have no idea where my life is heading. I had no idea I would ever have to live it without my children, no idea I would still be doing so after losing them, no idea I would love a psychopath or be moved to action via messages, sensical only to me, from my dead beloved.

Here's my plan. Sell the house. Sell almost everything I own. Go to Spain for three weeks. Move to Portland. I'll live downtown in a loft. I'll walk more, drive a modest car. I'll go to Portland State and explore international social work. I'll find out more about who Charity really is and what I can do, if anything, to help my son. Even if it means staying here and attempting to save him.

I'm tired of fear. I was pushed off a cliff into an abyss. Now I stare into another. My combination of fear, wisdom, curiosity, and faith have taught me all I can do is jump into the latest abyss to see what can be learned there. Such is the life of Charity. Love shines in all the dark places, so I have no reason not to look in them. As long as there's light, I can look and explore. Since I know it all comes back to the light, I should explore no matter how dark it appears. Darkness only seems; it is not. We don't fade into darkness; we go into the light. We fear darkness and allow it to keep us from our light.

Destiny opens the door. Free will walks through it.

FEBRUARY 28, 2010

I'm looking out my window and see one of my plants, in its world, in its flowerpot, blooming and facing the sun. One plant, three blooms. Two are alive and beautiful; one is dead.

Who's who of the three? Does it matter? The point, for the daisy, and most likely me too, is that even though the dead bloom is still attached, it doesn't stop, prevent, or take away from the growth and beauty of the other two. Like I said, though, who is who? They all come from the same plant.

MARCH 3, 2010

Today, at this moment and forever, I am in awe of how amazing life is and how beautiful my Ella is.

Yesterday, while working a career fair, I spoke with a woman about FACT. As she was about to step away, I noticed her necklace. It was a tiny silver picture frame on a chain with an angel charm. In the frame was a minute snapshot of a man.

"Is that your dad?"

It was.

"When did he pass on?"

Three years ago, this month.

Tomorrow Ella will have been dead three years and one month.

The woman and I spoke about our lost loved ones. She not only told me where to find the necklace, but how to reduce the photo to fit the frame. For a brief flicker of a moment my heart thought how nice it would be to have a butterfly shaped locket with Ella's picture. Me and my butterflies.

Life goes on.

Someone came to view the house today, so I followed Sam (my gun-removal friend, now tenant-of-my-rental-room friend) into the room, the one I finally painted pink for Ella, to make sure everything looked my kind of neat, not his. And there it was. On Sam's wooden chest. My butterfly locket. I picked it up and asked Sam if he'd found it for me somewhere. No. He swore he had never seen it before, swore it was not a gift he found for me. He would not lie about something like this to me.

Ella. Plain and simple. It's a gesture of love and faith on her part. She gets stronger as I do. She's learned to talk to me; I've learned how to hear. I'm Alice falling down the rabbit hole. I have the sense I'm about to occupy an entirely different world, yet again, after my past lives come into the light. A much wiser and kinder world.

How do I explain what I feel when I find gifts left by my daughter for me? A daughter who no longer occupies a physical body, yet so clearly exists. I rejoice. I yell out my love to her and all that has been, is, and will be. I say thank you—of course. Not to acknowledge and revere a moment of bliss and oneness with life is you learning nothing and not understanding just how beautiful life is.

What happens here, in this daily life, is our path to pure being, pure light, love, and energy. I am overwhelmed. Physically, I am alive to the tip of every nerve. My soul and my biology slide into harmony. Every single moment of these glimpses of what is in me and in front of me sows hope. Hope is the partner of love. Anger partners with pain.

I have found my groove again. I decided to be, so I became. In becoming, I decided to show the kind of woman I am to all who look and listen. I'm an open book. My spine is broken, my covers have been ripped off, my pages used as toilet paper and kindling, but words have souls and souls cannot be destroyed.

MARCH 4, 2010

Today it is three years and one month since Ella died. I'm better than I imagined. Today, at this moment, I'm at peace with myself and life. Beyond all shadow of any doubt, Ella is still with me.

MARCH 9, 2010

Life continues on its seemingly random path and I am okay with this. Despite everything that happened, or because of what happened, I now face the future with curiosity and patience. I fully enjoy every moment of the present. I'm slowly reining my grief in and kicking my ability to love in the ribs. Now that I understand I'm immortal, I begin to understand how unstoppable I can be. Call me crazy if you want. Delusions lead to harm. I don't love to harm.

I weaned myself off half of the antidepressants. I'm working on the other half. I drink and smoke less. Am I scared of diving into life again? Yes. Am I scared of loving as much as I did before? Yes. Am I scared I'll fail and not leave the world a better place or myself a better person, never see Ella again? Yes. Yes. And yes again.

Have I learned fear is nothing in the face of faith?

Yes.

I know things now I never knew one could. I've seen and experienced things I'd only read about with a fascinating familiarity and deep revulsion. There's no way I can give up now. I'm too aware of what is truly at stake. I'm far too engaged and involved in my story to not see where it goes, where my soul goes.

MARCH 12, 2010

Nic came over Monday because he attempted suicide Friday. Debbie left him. What I am supposed to do? I can't turn him away, yet I can't make him happy. It's obvious he could use some happiness. Every time I look around, I wish I could convey to those I see that it's possible to achieve peace in the hell of life. I can't, though. All I can do is keep smiling and loving and hope those who see me are positively affected.

Is there ever going to come a day when I meet someone who tries as hard to make me as happy as I try to make everyone else? That would be exquisite. Point-blank exquisite. They are out there. I know it.

Earlier tonight a girlfriend of mine said how nice it would be to find a guy who "understood" her. I don't need understanding. Understanding is a bit too much to ask for. Acceptance is nice. "Honey, I don't get you sometimes, but I certainly do love you." Because, really, what chance in this hell do I have to find anyone who could begin to understand or comprehend what I go through daily? Does it matter if anyone understands me as long as I try to?

Sigh. To be stuck in this body really makes life more complicated than it needs to be. This constant struggle between the physical and the spiritual takes its toll. My soulmate needs to find me soon. No matter how much I change this world, it won't be fulfilling until someone changes mine. Forgive me, feminists. I only speak the truth for myself. No matter how many I help, how many I love, one of these days, I'll have to find someone of my own, to love personally. It's part of my wiring. Love to the masses while devoting myself to one man, woman, or child, makes no difference to me.

MARCH 22, 2010

Hello, Charity Lee. It's been a while since I've been able to think deeply. I can't write if I'm not deep in thought.

Last night I was on patrol with SAPD. I work as a trained interventionist providing support to victims of crime. I stopped a man who had been stabbed repeatedly in the neck and head from staggering any further down the street. He was completely covered in blood. For a nanosecond the image of Ella's dead body flashed before me and then blinded my eyes.

How could it not? Blood jolts me, but this time that image set me in motion rather than slam me into a wall. When I could see again, all I saw was him, so I jumped out of the car, held him until the paramedics arrived, and then kept as many people as I could out of the crime scene, calmed as many people as I could.

A switch is flipped when I find myself in a moment of crisis. I don't need to think about what to do or say. What is needed comes out when it's needed. It seems I now possess the ability to see underneath what's expressed in a moment of crisis and intuitively grasp how to help. I'm with people in intense pain and am able to be totally present in the moment. I help them the way I wish I was dealt with the night my life fell apart.

In a violent crime, the victims aren't the only wounded. Those who know and love the victims are wounded too. The violence, the trauma, affects everyone who comes into contact with it, is exposed to it: family, friends, lovers, the community, those who read of it, those who witnessed, those who participated, those who chose to bury their heads in the sand, those who tried to do some right. Violence resonates, harsh, shrill, and, depending upon the singer, can sustain its note indefinitely.

My phoenix tattoo is finished, and it couldn't have been completed at a more auspicious time. I'm solid again. I'm back. I'm all new and always old. This Charity has earned the ability to burn bright and true. My core is calm and certain. I feel there isn't much I can't accomplish as long as I continue to live by love, service, and sacrifice. I have no idea where I'm going. I'm eagerly looking forward to discovering that. I'm ninety-nine percent sure I know how to get there, though. That I can get there. That I *have* to get there. I can't fail to learn what I came to learn this go-round. Too much hinges on my learning this lesson, remembering my purpose.

APRIL 1, 2010

Life weaves itself into a new design, not as beautiful to me as the tapestry I once had, but beautiful, nonetheless. I've been in contact with my mom twice. I never thought I would be able to say this in reference to my mother, but I believe she's trying to love me better. I believe she just doesn't know how. I won't be running into her arms anytime soon, but neither will I turn my back on someone I love, no matter how they lack the comprehension of the concept or expression of love. That's not who I am.

Charity.

Remember.

With the proper amount of focus, love, huge amounts of survival, and full-on sacrifice in the form of hard work, I know I'll make the world I inhabit more loving and humane for as many as I can. That's my purpose, why I came back to this existence in the first place. What other path is there for me to take?

APRIL 9, 2010

I've opened a can of worms, or maybe it was caterpillars. It may take a while for them to crawl out, but they will.

I changed the focus of my blog *Butterfly Flits*. From now on I will tell the story of falling in love with my son and the hardships I have dealt with. My goal is for people to know us as a family before they know us as victim, victim/mother of murderer, and murderer. I've made two postings and each one has triggered a tremendous amount of emotional catharsis. I've given myself until August to tell our story, 1993 – 2006. I'm determined to tell the story unedited, but for the names.

To be honest, I'm both excited and terrified of the response I may get. I don't know too many people who are willing to expose to the public their innermost thoughts, make them open for commentary, but at this point, I don't know what else to do.

All I do is think and feel and write and read. There's too much in my mind to stay in my head. This journal, my blog, are the only places I can empty myself out.

The only story I feel I am worthy to tell is the one about my family. Maybe people will understand my thoughts and position better if they know more about how I arrived here in the first place. I'd like to see others on the long and winding road with me. I don't understand, fully, my compulsion to tell this story. There's a huge part of me who wants to put it behind me, live well, and fade into some sort of normalcy. I know that isn't how my cards must be played. To keep this experience, this life, to myself, would still cause some kind of growth in me. But how would it ever help someone else to grow too? There are too many words here for them to be for my consumption only, so I do the one thing I have always been able to do, no matter what cards I've been dealt.

Write.

APRIL 12, 2010

Ella's eighth birthday . . .
Fuck. It's Ella's eighth birthday.
Yes. It's Ella's eighth birthday.
I promised myself I would not ...
I can't ...

APRIL 18, 2010

I don't know what I promised myself on Ella's birthday, but it must have worked because I'm still here and still writing.

APRIL 24, 2010

Surprisingly life progresses in a fulfilling direction, for now. *Butterfly Flits* is taking off and the Facebook group is growing.

People I don't know are following *Flits* and leaving comments, encouraging comments—nothing nasty yet. I expect some nastiness when the group grows larger. To expect everyone online to be nice is naive.

I'm exhausted but I'm doing what I was born to do. Last night I spent the evening on patrol with SAPD, three family violence calls. I slept five hours then spoke at the Children's Shelter. Tomorrow I go see my baby.

I am grateful for the friends I have but have reached a point where I know I would keep going if I didn't have any. Family—that's another matter, but I love them. My love life is nonexistent, but time will tell how that develops.

To keep a long story short, I'm spreading the love. It's the only thing I'm still here to do.

APRIL 27, 2010

Life steadily moves forward. I move forward with it.

Just finished having lunch with a friend at the Cove, and as always, it was pleasantly enjoyable. I spent the morning at the FACT office answering phones and helping someone fill out their Victim's Comp application. I'm scheduled to give tours at the Family Justice Center tonight, but I'm on the edge of frazzled, so I'm not sure I'll be able to make it.

The best thing I did today was make an appointment with a foster care agency for a home interview. I'm going to try to become a foster parent. It's time. I've gotten myself back together enough to begin to be able to think of myself as a mom again. I'm not wired to live alone; have the focus of my life be only me. I love people too much to be content to help on such an anonymous short-term basis as I do in FACT, so I'm going to try. It's all I can do. I told the man who interviews potential foster parents about my situation. He didn't seem fazed, or, at least, it didn't seem to make a difference.

Yet another ride on my emotional roller coaster today. I'm not sure if I'm depressed and disassociating or content with doing my own thing these days. I feel the need to be around adults but not necessarily interact with them. The idea of adopting a child I can embrace. The thought of talking to my peers not so much. I don't want to be in my house too long without human interaction, but I've no mind for small talk or revelry. It's hard for me when there's no drama in my life, when life is just drifting along. It's not what I am used to because there is no such thing as "normal" for me. The life I'm trying to create is being built without a blueprint. I'm not sure how it will hold up because I've never built a life out of serenity. Chaos, yes. Loss, yes. Peace, never.

I met yesterday with two employees of a foster placement agency. They came to the house because they wanted to meet me, because of what Paris did, before I filled out the application. After meeting me, both say they believe I would make an excellent foster parent. But they aren't sure Child Protective Services will approve me.

I've been in a funk ever since they left. I don't know for sure I won't be approved. I do know for sure others will never look at me the same because of what Paris did. I know cognitively life is never fair, but it still makes me cry.

How long will I suffer the consequences of *his* actions? Some would answer as long as I choose to be victimized, but the truth of being a victim is you have no choice in a lot of matters. As a victim, you can choose how you react to all the shit thrown at you, but you have no choice over what shit is thrown. Because of what my son did there will always be those who believe I don't deserve a child, another chance to love.

Back to hell for a visit. The last five days have been a blur of crying, family drama, and mind-numbing grief and depression. Today the cloud began to lift. I need to start back on meds. I'm better, but I've not healed, no matter how I interpret the word. I'm certain the tailspin began after the visit with the foster parent group.

May 7, 2010

I leave for my road trip in two days. I'm going to see friends from elementary, middle, and high school.

Paris, by now, received my card that let him know he's no longer welcome to contact me. As of right now, I feel okay with my decision. I've told my sister I can't be her Facebook friend because I don't trust our mother not to snoop into my life through her. I think my mother is a heathen for using my sister to get to me. I hope she will contact me when she's an adult. Cutting her out of my life is the only way to keep my mom out of my life, the only way to stop my mom from using my sister to get to me. It is also the only guilt I feel concerning my family. My mom spent thirty-six years sowing seeds of bitterness. Let her reap what she's sown. My son failed to learn his lesson this lifetime, fell into violence and hatred again. He thinks love is weak. Let him reap what he has sown, too.

I am done.

I find myself at the Cove again on a Friday night. I like the fact I've gone through so much drama with so many of these people, but I can still sit here, have a glass of wine, feel comfortable and at home. Some of them have been kinder and more honest than my own blood has been. While it's been brutal at times, there's a feeling of acceptance and community here. No one here pretends to be perfect. It's obvious to all we're flawed.

For instance, as I write this, I'm sitting at a table with an alcoholic whom I have grown to love, and a woman older than me who is totally speeded out. I'm sorry for them and want to laugh at the same time. Not out of hilarity but absurdity. I think I come here sometimes because it comforts me to see there are so many mistakes I'm not making which I could still easily make. I'm not drinking too much. I'm not doing speed or coke. I'm not getting mindlessly knocked up. I'm not hating on people. I'm not running in circles. I'm not trying to keep up with the Joneses. The only mistake I continue to make right now is I still smoke Camels.

MAY 18, 2010

I'm back in San Antonio and I don't know if I'm bored or depressed. There's no drama in my life right now, and to be honest, I don't always know what to do with myself when I don't have to spend every second dealing with my children or trying desperately to hold my head above water. The sea is calm after the tsunami, and I'm floating where I've been cast.

I try telling myself I'm using this time to heal, but I get depressed every time I come back to Texas. I feel oppressed here. There's so much I can't do in this state because of what Paris did. I can't work with any agency that works with kids because Child Protective Services found me negligent because they concluded that any "reasonable" person would have known better than to leave Paris with Ella. It did not matter I had a babysitter that night. It did not matter she left before she was supposed to. It did not matter that Paris had never hurt Ella before. The only thing that mattered to them was that Ella was dead. I can't teach because after what Paris did to Ella there is no way I can be around pre-kindergarten/kindergarten children all day. I can't foster which means, most likely, I can't adopt. I would never pass home inspections because CPS has already decided that I am not capable of being a good mother.

Texas has brought me nothing but misery. My mom had cancer. Twice. I relapsed on cocaine. Paris killed Ella. Now it seems that because the impossible happened here, nothing is possible here.

"Just living is not enough," said the Butterfly. One must have sunshine, freedom, and a little flower."—Hans Christian Anderson

MAY 20, 2010

And another day in the life of Charity has transpired. It was another day of mind-numbing boredom and depression. I feel useless and pointless in this existence of mine. No matter how many hours of volunteer work I do, it's not enough to feel I'm really giving back to the world, to feel I'm making a difference. I'm not comfortable with the idea of taking this break to heal. I don't know how to do life without drama. I'm certainly not going to court drama. I have no choice but to learn to live without it. For the first time in thirty years I'm not being bombarded with murder, betrayal, drug addiction, narcissism, disappointment. I'm only having to live with the fallout of it.

I don't understand how to do "normal," so I'm going to keep doing what I do best: hold on against all odds. It's my specialty. I don't know how to give up. I don't always know how to live in a manner conducive to healthy mental functioning, but it doesn't matter because I've never known how to give up. I continue to put one foot in front of the other and hope it turns out for the best.

Hope. What a loaded concept. If it wasn't for hope, I wouldn't be alive while at the same time I wouldn't be in as much pain. Double-edged swords form the heraldic crest of my life.

Everyone I've told I didn't pass muster for the foster parenting said I should have my own child. I don't know about that.

MAY 22, 2010

I had an epiphany about men today, or more specifically, the men I dated. They were mirror reflections of everything I didn't like about myself.

The reason I choose them is to hate them instead of myself for my own flaws. Actually, I find and date men who are a little worse than me in the areas of motivation, ambition, focus, drive, and intelligence. I've never dated a fellow caretaker, because that's one of the qualities I like about me.

And then there's the flip side. Part of me truly doesn't feel worthy of being loved. Not hard to figure out where that idea comes from is it? *Thanks, Mom.*

So where does this revelation leave me? It leaves me thinking two things. One, I need to have more respect for myself. Two, I must consciously choose to walk away from the bad boys and instead gravitate towards those who match me, complement me. No more lovers who are mainly used for self-hatred reflection. Like the other countless revelations I've had since this re-birth—easier realized than done. But, like the plethora of my other epiphanies, it puts me one step closer, hopefully, to a more fulfilling life.

MAY 28, 2010

Another Friday night at the Cove and Nic and I are not together … .

HA! I had to say that for old time's sake. We actually get along quite well now. He seems always to be by my side when we're both here. We're able to talk now about emotionally touchy subjects. He asks for my opinions again. I try to give impartial and objective advice despite what I personally think or feel. I still love him without wanting to be with him.

My life is on an upswing most likely due to the fact I am back on meds. What Paris did permanently altered my chemical blueprint; it's a hard fact to deal with. On the other hand, trying to deal with what he did without medication leaves me focusing all my time and energy on convincing myself life is worth living and it's okay to leave my house. It's a trade-off. I take meds to be able to live an enriched and fulfilling life.

JUNE 3, 2010

Paris and I used to play a game concerning mind maps. The sole point of the game was to answer the question, "If you drew a map of your mind, what would it look like?" My answer at the time was Hogwarts Castle. His was a road map. He emphasized the number of off ramps his mind map held. If he were to ask me now—which he would never do—my answer would be different. Now I would say my mind map consists of an old dilapidated but clearly beautiful house. With a lot of love and care it can be restored. The house is surrounded by a field of flowers. That's my mind.

JUNE 10, 2010

I was naughty. I'm riddled with guilt.

I called Nic on Sunday night and we met. We talked. We went to the park. We soaked our feet. We ran from the cops. We came back to the house. We almost slept together.

I'm in a funk.

JUNE 11, 2010

I've returned to an uneasy peace within myself. I'm cognizant of how precarious my grip on my sanity and well-being is; how the slightest setback can kick my ass back to hell. I'm also fully aware the only way to counterbalance this is to fight like hell to live until I die, to have faith because life has always given me doors and windows to choose from. The entire point is to keep on choosing.

As soon as I woke up Monday morning I knew the only thing left to do is to stay away from Nic. He's not the only one who makes bad decisions when it comes to the bond between us. Obviously, for reasons I grasp yet which make no sense to me, we're connected. This attraction of ours is more than what most people think. We knew one another before, and our paths will cross again. We didn't get it right this go-round, this lifetime, but I believe we made progress. It's time for him to work out his karma with his baby's mama and his son.

It's time for me to look forward, stop looking over my shoulder all the time. My new future is beginning to unfurl. I finally received word UTSA approved my change of major and I can register for classes. The LSAT class is paid in full and ready to be aced. That one door cracking open is all I need to distract my attention from the damn windows I'm stuck looking out while in my depressive episodes.

It's been three years and four months since I lost my children. There's still not one day or minute that passes when I do not think of them. It comforts me to know even though I can't have either one of them in my life the way I want, at least I still have them. They continue to be the only reason I struggle to be the best I can be. I tell you, without my children, I would have been no one.

JUNE 14, 2010

I prefer having my weekends on weekdays. The explanations for this are very simple. One, there aren't as many people out and I still have a very hard time dealing with crowds, especially on my own. It seems I'm on my own for the time being.

Two, the people I encounter out on a Monday night are much more interesting than those I encounter on a weekend night. Weekenders try hard to follow the rules society attempts to impose on us. Get up. Go to work. Raise your family. Do it all hoping you will be rewarded—with what? All that to stave off the underlying feeling of hysteria until, one day, it doesn't.

Those of us who take our moments when they happen tend to be more fucked up and consequentially more interesting. Sad, tragic, and true.

So. Monday night. San Antonio. 10:49 pm. Broadway 50/50. Why am I here? Alone? Writing in this damn journal instead of making sure my kids are not only in bed but asleep? Wait. It's summer. Why aren't we having a movie marathon? A slumber party? Why am I not waiting up for Paris to get home from a date?

Instead of doing any of those things, today I registered for my first two MSW classes, did some writing, and took comfort in the fact that if I can't have my kids, at least I can fulfill my destiny. The degrees will be earned. People will be helped. I'll do my best to be a light in the abyss for others to focus on. I'll continue to trust people, give them the benefit of the doubt, until they prove my trust ill placed. I won't become bitter or allow my heart to become jaded. Anger may be my companion, but it will never be my guide.

If I've proven anything to myself in the last thirty-six years, it's that I'll do what life expects of me, even if I have no faith I can. I'm no longer scared of death, so that fear no longer stops me. I know I'll always exist, so the fear of nothingness doesn't stop me. I'm scared of physical pain if Paris ever gets to me, but if that ever happens, it's the last thing I'll ever be scared of in this life, so who cares? The only thing that truly, completely scares me anymore is that I'll fuck this life up so bad I won't get to be with my Ella. This is why I'll always do what I'm called to do, regardless of whether I think I can or not.

JUNE 17, 2010

There will always be a part of me that feels the need to skirt along some edge.

When it comes to Nic, I'm flirting with disaster. At this moment he's behind me, at the Cove. We've talked, and chemistry still courses between us. I promised him I'll behave;

no more throwing myself at him. Well, what I really said is, I'll do my best. I don't want to cause problems for anyone, but why does it seem I'm always giving up my pleasures in life to make someone else happy?

I need to forget the drama and pain caused by having Nic in my life. Maybe what I need to do is take a lover, not someone I'm intent on being with, someone who will do for now. No expectations, just good company when I need it. Maybe, at this point, too much emotional entanglement would distract me from healing, writing, and studying. I'm not the type to take a lover, though. I was born incapable of superficial thought or feeling. My entire existence has been an exercise in introspection, excavation, and investigation. To all of a sudden change my spots for stripes is impossible. If there's no passion, there's no feeling. If there's no feeling, there's no passion.

Nic just played the song he wrote about me, about the time I broke up with him in London, when he left and came back to San Antonio. It's not the love song I thought he would write, but it's still a love song about me.

It's time to stop all this. It's time to earn my master's, get my JD, maybe publish a book. Staying in these circles, talking to the same people, watching the same games and dynamics played out is too easy. I need a challenge. I need someone to challenge me. I'm bored with the people I know. I want a partner who stands up to me, teaches me something about myself I don't know yet.

What don't I know about myself yet?

I don't know how to give myself fully to a lover. I never have.

JUNE 22, 2010

I've been catching a lot of hell from people lately. It seems people's opinions of me change after knowing me awhile. They like me when they first meet me. My honesty is maybe refreshing or weirdly morbidly fascinating. But then, I think, there comes a point for some when honesty becomes too heavy a burden to bear. When that point comes, my honesty has made me an arrogant, heartless, condescending, cold, blah, blah, blah. I've made it to the point in my life where I can't care anymore what everyone thinks. I did that and look how life turned out for me and my loved ones. The only person left to please is me, and it pleases me to speak my mind honestly and to let my conscience be my guide when I do. In my opinion my conscience is typically very wise, when all is said and done.

JUNE 24, 2010

I've discovered another lesson learned these last three years: how to put everyday occurrences into perspective. When Paris killed Ella, all the blinders, all the chains, all the half-truths my culture, my government, my mother, my schools, my husbands, my lovers, my friends laid upon me were shown to be the false realities they are. For the first time I saw underneath all these trappings. What are we? Animal? Human? Angel? I'm no philosopher, certainly not a real writer, so my means of explaining what I've seen are limited.

People fail. This civilization will fail because too many people stay focused on too narrow a view, mostly of themselves. Ultimately nothing material or tangible I create in this life will last as long as I will. Memories and markers of me will fade while I still burn bright. The only thing I do that matters now, and will follow me into infinity, is the love I spread. Not the amount I have, but the amount I'm able to share.

Alas, this is also the crux of the problem. In order to share as much love as I feel for this world, this life, all those blinders and chains had to be ripped off of me. I've learned that to truly, completely, love another, I can't live in fear, in hate, in anger. I will, via my curse of hyper-emotionality, feel all of them often, but I'll never navigate by those stars again. The only way to truly love is to drain all the poison out of your heart and actively pursue the art of filling it with love.

I make a lot of mistakes. I'm no doormat, and I know I'm sometimes a bit too fierce and too fiery. I am moved to sadness with all the pain I feel, by all the pain Ella felt, for all the pain Paris feels living in that psychopathic hell of his mind. I feel the pain everyone around me carries. It motivates me to try to generate as much love as I can on par with the pain; to try to create a karmic balance.

Want to know what's fucking ironic? Paris is a Libra. He is supposed to be the diplomat, the one who brings balance, the righter of the scales.

Astrology is shit.

JUNE 29, 2010

Here I am in Abilene to finish another tattoo. The only way it will get done is if I come here. Justin can't come to me. I hate this fucking town. Being here brings me as close to vitriolic as I can become. I hate this place. The bad memories are painful to bear; the good ones excruciating.

This is the last time I have to be here until 2012. Paris will be eighteen years and six months then, and I'll finally have to take a stand, on the record, under oath, in court. Then he will have a hearing at which the juvenile system will make a recommendation to either send him to adult prison or release him to highly supervised parole. It will be time to stop drawing such blurry boundaries between us. I will have no choice but to let the court know that I know my son is dangerous.

Have I mentioned how crushing it is to be the mother of a psychopath?

JULY 1, 2010

I made it out of Abilene in one relatively intact psychological piece, but I had to get out as quickly as possible. While I'm there I imagine myself physically building a Berlin Wall around the worst of my memories. The only way not to drown in my memories is to willfully pretend they're not there. It's heavy work. Now I'm tired and grateful to be alive.

I spent the weekend on patrol with the SAPD, Saturday and Sunday, 10:00 pm to 6:30 am. Sunday is the Fourth of July and I ride Westside, the hardcore part of San Antonio. I expect it to be intense, but I'd rather work than be out celebrating freedom. There are still too many not free, so why celebrate?

There are so many moments in life when it feels absolutely nothing of any importance is occurring. Yet every moment we experience is the most singular important moment we have ever experienced, including the ones spent in supposed boredom. Every moment our synapses are firing is a moment you had the opportunity to learn something and a moment you cannot get back. There's no going back, no staying in the moment, no holding onto the future.

JULY 10, 2010

I'm still in love with Nic—I know … it makes no sense. I don't know I want my life to make sense. Since I was a young girl I've tried to make life make some kind of sense, but the only time I got anywhere close was being a mother to Paris and Ella. I miss my children. Immensely. I want them back. Eternally.

Twenty minutes ago, Nic asked me if he's as bad as Ella's father was to me or for me. What he doesn't understand, and what I did a horrible job of conveying when Nic and I were together, is I've never felt for anyone what I feel for him. Believe it or not, he's the best of them, all the men from my past. No doubt about it he's crazy, but he has the purest heart I've encountered, other than my own. There's never been any distrust. I knew he would never cheat on me. We didn't fail because we don't love one another. We failed because we let our emotional instability and the opinion of the world matter more than our love.

The dog days of summer progress. I hate Texas more than usual in July and August. I volunteered to go on patrol again this month. That gives me to a total of five shifts, forty-five hours in one month, if the shifts don't go overtime.

What can I say? During those hours, I feel at ease; it's the only time I feel I'm keeping my promise to Ella and living the lesson I was meant to learn in this lifetime.

I received a letter from Paris two days ago. After taking time away from him, his tone with me has changed completely. He's worried about me, wants to know how I'm holding up, wants a note to know I'm alive. He claims to be sorry for all the pain he's caused. Oh, yeah—he's also acquainting himself with God.

In my heart I know it's all bullshit, another attempt to feel me out and see how much power he still has over me. Honestly, I have no idea what to do. Obviously, if I was dead, he would know by now. As for his concern, I'm not sure he's actually capable of feeling concern for others, other than to know where his "possessions" are—as people are objects to him. On the other hand, because I'm his mother, there's a small percentage of me that wants to believe his words are sincere.

I find it beyond sad that in order to get advice on how to deal with my teenage son, I can't talk to friends or family. I must talk to psychiatrists who specialize in juvenile psychopathy, lawyers who specialize in juvenile criminal law.

There are days now, at most three in a row, when I can forget, almost, what tragedy has occurred in my life. Three days I can pretend I'm happy, content with my life. Then a letter or a thought wondering how my son is comes along and shatters my fantasy again.

What Paris never calculated was that I'd survive all he's done. He assumed I would die of heartbreak without my children. He was right, almost. He doesn't understand how sustaining love is in your darkest hour because he's incapable of feeling love. He didn't destroy me. He helped to forge me.

JULY 19, 2010

I can tell already it's going to be one of those days. My wake-up call from Paris' caseworker set the tone. The follow-up call with Dr. Ferrara, the forensic psychologist who performed the assessments of Paris, sealed the day's fate. It's 12:30 pm, I've been awake two hours, and already this day has worn me out. Waking up to hearing all about your son's psychopathic behavior and deviant thoughts tends to exhaust you. I want to go back to bed, but I won't. Ella won't have died just to indulge Paris' fantasies and cravings. I'll make sure of that. I have to make sure of that.

JULY 25, 2010

Something's happening to me I don't feel at all comfortable with; something I thought would never happen again. I'm finding peace and comfort in my life. Not happiness: peace and comfort. I have begun to enjoy pieces of my life in this hell. I have moments when everything actually seems okay, even though it isn't. I've grown attachments to this place, this city, this state, this cause. I've dug deeper into it, using the sewage as fertilizer for my soul. All wonderful, yet unexpected, results of surviving my own personal hell.

Great! Right?

Right. Great. But what happens to this life, this peace, this comfort, these attachments, in ten, twenty, twenty-five years when my son is free to come find me? I want to put down roots; I'm tired of running, but wouldn't it be easier to run while my baggage is still manageable? I don't know I would survive another of my son's attempts at demolishing all I've built. It's not like he would just burn my house down and that was that. If he did, I'd be burning inside it.

I should accept the fact there will never again be too much peace, too much comfort, in my life. Never again. Ever. I don't know why fear has me in its grip again. Maybe because occasionally I can't help but think I'm living on borrowed time. I need to make the best of the time left to me.

I've always wanted normal. I accept now there is no normal, and if there is, it was never an option in my life. Now all I want is not too strange: since I can't have happiness, I want my peace and comfort. Since I can't have my family, I want friends better than the family I had. Since I can't shower my children with love and affection, I want to bathe the world in love and affection.

I just want to be good, to leave the world a better place once I'm better.

Simple. Right?

Right. Simple.

JULY 29, 2010

I must have really bad karma to work off in the state of Texas. Every major event in my life since moving here has been a negative. My relapse. Ella's death. Paris' transformation. Being sued by my mother and my son. Can't foster parent. Can't adopt. Can't. Can't. Can't. Can't …

Now UTSA may not be a possibility. I received an email last week instructing me to check my financial aid status. When I did, my loans were cancelled. The department of social work at the university admitted me as a special nondegree seeking student. It took me a week to get my advisor on the phone. Today, when I did, I was informed UTSA at first wanted to deny my application because they aren't convinced my personal issues won't prevent me from enacting social justice, so they admitted me on a conditional basis.

What fucking bullshit.

The committee of professors who decided my mental fitness never met me.

What if all these *can'ts* are life's way of telling me to get out of Texas? Maybe it's time to throw all caution to the wind, sell most of what I own, and start fresh on the West Coast. Who cares if I lose money? Who cares if I may never be able to afford a house again? At least I'll have peace of mind. Everything I do here is an uphill battle. I'm thirty-six and life has already worn me out. I'm tired of paying the price for what Paris did. I didn't kill anyone, but I may as well have.

JULY 31, 2010

Come hell or high water, neither of which would break me, I'm selling my house and leaving Texas for Portland. I don't care if I lose money. I don't care about school. I just want away. I've thought, and balked at the thought, of leaving long enough. The issue with UTSA pushed me to certainty. I still want my MSW. I may still want to go to law school at some point, but not here in Texas. Texas is a prison.

I won't lie; I am afraid, and not overly excited. I don't know that moving will be a good event, but I know it won't be a bad one. Nothing can be worse than what I've lived through here. I do feel at peace with my decision.

AUGUST 2, 2010

Nic became a father today—another reason to leave San Antonio.

AUGUST 3, 2010

It's official. My faculty advisor emailed today to inform me UTSA won't change my admission status. Without the change I get no financial aid. I'm leaving Texas as soon as I can.

All this time after Ella's death, I thought the obstacles I faced in Texas were only more hurdles to jump over. I believe I misinterpreted the signs. These trials haven't been hurdles, but obstacles. My life isn't meant to be lived here. For two years my heart has yearned to leave this place. For the last year, it's wanted to be in Portland.

Time to follow my heart. I'm ready to move on, to remember and honor my past without letting it drag me down or ruin all chance of future happiness. There's an entire world out there, and for the first time in my adult life, I'm completely free. I have no strong ties to anyone. I have a little money. I have only myself to live with, so I may as well make living an activity conducive to mental health. To thine own self be true—right?

Another new, and unexpected, chapter in my life is about to begin, and this time, all the changes are of my choosing.

AUGUST 13, 2010

Friday the 13th. So far nothing even remotely scary, demonic, evil, or bad luck-ish has happened. In fact, I just spent a very enjoyable fifteen minutes with sixteen-month-old Layla, a little girl at the Cove with her parents. When they put her in her highchair she started to fuss and throw herself around. Because I'm me, I had to go over to talk to her. She instantly calmed down, ate her lunch. She grew fussy again, so I offered to walk her while her parents finished their lunch, to give them a chance to talk a bit. All parents deserve a break, and I'll take any chance I can to love a child, so we walked and checked out the art on the walls, said hello to all the regulars, played the drums, and had a tickle session.

I have a way with children I don't have with most adults. I'm glad to have it. Small moments of happiness are better than no moments at all, yes?

My fears in regard to leaving Texas plague me more often now, but I don't let them sway me. I must make the effort to get out of here, create a life conducive to healing rather than hurting. If I don't, the idea of leaving will become a regret rather than a memory. Life will change despite my fears and concerns. What choice is there but to be an active agent rather than a passive victim?

I know now today won't be a bad day. I had the opportunity to help someone and I took it. These opportunities surround us, but most people are interested only in helping themselves. I know there are people in the world who believe it is nothing more than codependence to try to help others be happy so you can be happy. Personally, I believe it may be that way for some people, people who can't, or won't, be happy on their own. I *can* be happy on my own, but I'm happier helping others as opposed to helping only myself. It's why I was born - to love and help as many as possible.

Life has fallen into a peaceful groove these days. I'm awake by 9:00 am to get the house ready to rent. I come to the Cove, drink some wine, write, talk to people. I'm doing what many would consider nothing but, in my book, is healing. I know I can't do this forever, but I also know this is exactly what I need to do right now.

AUGUST 22, 2010

Today I want to yell at everyone I encounter. Instead I yell at the heat because it reminds me of how oppressed I feel in this damned place. It's better than yelling at the people I care about. Everything in this state wears me out, wears me down. I know experts say geography changes none of the facts of your life but fuck the "experts." Geography can change your perspective. That can change your facts.

I need both a change of perspective and a change of facts. I've never been content in one place too long. I sometimes wonder how well I really would have done as a long-time mother. Then again I also know "mother" is only the role I played in this lifetime to both Paris and Ella. In the long term, I'm always with Paris and Ella. Just not right now.

SEPTEMBER 4, 2010

I've learned that talking to clouds about your concerns and fears puts you in touch with either God or your subconscious. One and the same, either way. This is especially true when answers are formed in response to your prayers. And no, I don't take hallucinogens, nor am I drunk. Although, being in touch with life often makes you feel that way.

Today I find myself appreciating life in Texas, but I know it's because I'm leaving. I'm gathering my best thoughts of my time here. I want to keep the good thoughts. I can only hope for the best. No matter how much I learn or appreciate, what I'm left with I'm unsatisfied with, because once I reach one point of acceptance and understanding, I have to go to find more—what more there is.

As I write this, I am out, in public, where someone just told me how inspiring I am. Whenever someone says this, I can't help but think myself a fraud. Everyone seems so inspired and amazed by my life. I hope I make them feel better, but I'm not inspiring, not to myself. I'm not amazing. In my world, I'm barely hanging on. But they don't live in my world, do they?

I miss you, Ella. I miss you, Paris. I miss you, Charity.

SEPTEMBER 16, 2010

You think I would have learned by now life is full of surprises. I should have learned by now that life is full of pain. I've had my share of both today.

This morning I learned I've been nominated for the Phoenix Award. It's given to those who have gone above and beyond the call of duty to help victims of family violence. The award ceremony is on my birthday. I hope I win, but if I don't, I won't be devastated. I'm truly happy to have been thought of for the honor

This afternoon Paris' caseworker called and asked me to come to Giddings on Monday. Paris says he has things he *needs* to tell me about the night he murdered Ella. She asked me to bring someone to drive me home. It's potentially that devastating. Great.

Joy and pain. Two sides of the same coin.

SEPTEMBER 17, 2010

So much for the pure life. I decided to get drunk to try to forget about, or at the least not dwell on, thoughts of what I may hear Monday. It worked, but not as I expected. I cried, I ranted, I completely broke down. I got it all out of my system and woke up feeling somewhat better balanced and ready to face whatever is coming my way.

It's time for me to let go of who I thought I was; time to let go of some of my rigid morals and expectations regarding social interaction. I can't and won't condone violence, but I see now all people are flawed. None of us can live our ideal. The point is to continue striving for it, continue trying to become the best reflection of yourself.

SEPTEMBER 19, 2010

I am trying very hard to hold onto my sanity today. I have not seen my son since March. I haven't talked to him since May but for one line telling him I'm alive and he's still loved. It seems he wants to test, again, if both are true. Tomorrow, after three years and seven months of lies and manipulations, he wants to be "honest" with me about the murder of his sister. I know so much of the truth already, and it almost killed me. How much more truth can I handle? Because, when it comes to Paris, you can never really prove when he's lying.

This is how the part of me who believes he's a psychopath interprets what will take place tomorrow. After all this time, all the emotional torture he's put me through, he knows it's do or die time, so to speak. He's soon to turn seventeen and begin the Capital Offenders program. He has to come clean and show proper insight and remorseful behavior to have a snowball's chance in hell of not going to the Texas Department of Criminal Justice, big boy prison, when he's an adult. If he confesses to me, is "honest" with me, he looks as though he's changing and maybe, hopefully, I may even buy it. Even if I don't, he still gets the pleasure he experiences seeing me in more pain. This "honesty" session is only a win-win for Paris. I'm being toyed with while everyone else is hopefully being swayed. Of course, TYC would like to be able to declare Paris a success story. What great PR for the agency!

The part of me unable to stop loving him and hopes I'm wrong, the mother part, is who's going to this meeting, senses intact. If this is truly a chance for him to change, who am I to take that away even if it throws me deeper into this psychotic world of mine? He's my son. I love him. I miss him so much. I can't wait to hold him again tomorrow, even though it may be the last time I'm able to bring myself to touch him.

I'll never get away from the facts of my life. I'll never be able to wrap my mind around those facts. Every time I try to move on or put it behind me, something happens and here I am – reminded this is my world. The population consists of Paris, Ella, and I.

The weight of the universe is centered and carried in this world. This is the school of my life, this world. When I enter here, more and more of what matters in so-called life means less and less. Here I face my demons, my shortcomings, my mistakes. Here is where I experience the power of love. Here is where it matters I exist. In all this, with my son and my daughter, I find my true self, someone I find very difficult to deal with. The only way not to be constantly pulled into pain is to consciously pull myself away from this world, retire my thoughts of Paris. But to do that would be to lose half of what I've loved about my life.

Fuck fuck fuck fuck fuck fuck fuck fuck fuck fuck fuck fuck fuck fuck fuck fuck fuck fuck fuck fuck fuck fuck …

Mantras can be so soothing. I'm so scared of what I'm going to hear tomorrow. I've spent years imagining every horror, every stab, every hit, gasp for breath, every scream for help, every feeling of terror Ella felt; everything I thought could never exist. What if there is more I haven't thought of because, even though I know my son better than anyone, I'm not a psychopath? What if I learn there are worse places than hell?

*   *   *

It's 1:00 am. I can't sleep anymore, because in five hours I leave to go hear my son say God knows what; to tell me the "truth."

I dreamed of stillborn babies. I wonder if I am about to give birth to my son again, this time born dead to me, this life dead to me. What I don't want to face is that tomorrow may be the last time I see my baby in any setting beside court, parole hearings, or the day of my death.

Maybe if I change my perspective of this upcoming conversation, it will make it easier to cope with. Let's see … tomorrow the universe is giving me the end of this chapter. I don't have to stop loving my son or give up my chance to live life again just because I am, will be, periodically destroyed by him in some way. I'll lose one more night's sleep, have one more day of hell added to my pick of hellish memories to relive, and I'll find a way to turn shit into fertilizer. It's what I do best in this situation.

Nope … still thinking this conversation is going to hurt.

In four hours, I must be prepared to face his confession. I should focus on a happy moment with Paris, bring something less painful than the present to mind … here we go, here's one …

I'm seven months pregnant. I'm scared because Paris hasn't moved all day. I have to ask him to give me a sign, because I'm scared I've lost him. *Wham!* He kicked the hell out of me. He's alive. My fear dissipates. Love for Paris washes over me along with awe at the connection we share.

Please. Let that be my tomorrow.

Paris kicked the hell out of me again. He called me to Giddings to let me know he was molesting Ella since early 2005, before I became a concert promoter, before I went crazy with the cocaine, before anything he said was his reason for killing her had even happened. He killed her so she wouldn't tell on him. He sexually abused her that night, and he admitted the more violent he became, the more excited he became, ending in death for her and climax for him.

I walk into these meetings steeled to hear the worst. I must be somewhat numb and guarded before he even opens his mouth if I have any chance of remaining sane after he does. When Paris drops his bombshells on me, I do my best to keep my cool, to act therapeutically rather than destructively; to be his parent rather than his victim.

I do not want to give him my pain. I do not want to give him my rage.

It took everything I had today to hear him out, tell him I love him, and walk away without choking him out of existence. But I did it. Barely.

Where does this leave me? The bubble I put my anger in during the meeting has burst. The pieces of myself I worked so hard to gather and put back together are shattered and scattered again. For the last two days, I've been sick, mentally and physically. When I hear his words repeating in my head, I vomit. My entire life with my son was a lie; a lie I swallowed hook, line, and sinker. I thought I'd heard the worst a parent can hear the night I was told my son murdered his sister. How stupid of me to think there aren't worse levels of hell. A whole new can of worms has been opened, and they're eating what's left of my sanity.

Never again will I feel I fit in the world others occupy. I fit in the world of lies, murder, pedophilia, incest, secrets, and violence. No more sunny days or carefree thoughts for this Charity Lee.

Paris is dead to me. I don't want to hear anything else he has to say. No more visits. No more birthdays. Nothing.

Dead. Like Ella. Like me.

SEPTEMBER 28, 2010

My God. I've been sick ever since my last experience of Paris. Physically, I have an absolutely ridiculous upper respiratory infection. I need to stop smoking. Mentally, my mind has become the gutter in which my son dwells. I'm sure my body is sickened by the poison my mind had to absorb this week. I know, at this point in my ordeals, neither my mind nor my soul will fail me. My body—that's an entirely different story, one I'm not very interested in. I'll try to keep it going as long as it takes me to finish this story, but my body isn't my primary concern.

My only concern right now is getting the hell out of Texas, flying away to live another day. Life is helping to make that happen. I have been renovating an apartment in the carriage house behind my main house for additional income and it is almost finished. Today I found the right tenants for my home, my oasis. I'll find a place I want to live next week in Portland.

I have nothing but full faith that everything is falling into place for me to be the Charity I'm destined to be. I am, yet again, standing on the brink of the abyss. This time no one is pushing me in. This time I am jumping myself, catching the current, soaring as close to the sun as possible before losing the view.

The only favorable comment I can make on the amount of pain I feel, and carry, is it has enabled me to feel and carry a proportionate amount of bliss on my back also. In plain, less descriptive English, the thing I am trying to say is this: I know, in the bones of my soul, this move is what I need to move ahead.

For the first time in this thirty-seven-year life of mine I have to worry only about making sure I'm okay. I know Ella is okay.

I know Paris is, ultimately, the only one who can choose his path. I know my mother is poison to me. It's my time to shine. Let me amend that. It's time to shine again, brighter than ever before I think.

After the last three years seven months, my mind is what the general public could describe as, and would consider, a really bad trip, brown acid style. It doesn't matter what I put in my body—alcohol, music, drama, words, whatever—my mind trumps all. My mind takes all input, no matter how instructive, destructive, or constructive, turns it inside out, flips it, twists it, wrings it dry, and fluffs it up all to arrive at this: me, Charity.

OCTOBER 5, 2010

I rented an apartment. I met with Portland State University's social work department admission's advisor. I'm doing this. Moving. Walking away. I'm doing one more thing in this life I never thought I could, or would, have to do. I'm choosing to walk away from my son. In order to live I must defy death as long as I can, so it's time. I'll be in Texas three more weeks.

Paris stabbed Ella seventeen times. I know the exact placement of each puncture, every bruise, every detail of what he's capable of. I hurt in every one of those points. To walk away from my son means I must pull a knife out of each and every one of those wounds and fill it with love. I have no idea why I pretend distance will have much effect. Thoughts of those two will always reign supreme. They are both everything and nothing. I'm what's left of the best of us now.

Imagine that.

How to describe the amazingly beautiful light at the end of the tunnel? All I can say with confidence is it *is* there. It's always been there. I'm grateful to have almost reached it. I will never be the same after my time in this state. That's probably a good thing. I can breathe again. I look forward to life again. I'm ready to *live* again. I have a chance many aren't given; I have the chance to rebuild my life exactly as I want it to be.

I'm not squandering this chance; I'm making the most of it. I'm going to will my life into being a bowl of cherries.

OCTOBER 16, 2010

Life in Texas isn't as unbearable now that I know I'm almost out of here. Two and a half more weeks and this chapter of my life has been written and finished.

Packing is progressing. There have been a couple of stumbling blocks along the way. I had to force myself to put Paris and Ella's things and photos in storage. Not all of it, but a lot of it, because it's time to move on. I won't pretend they never existed. I've done well putting away clothes, schoolwork, art, and framed photos, but I had a breakdown the other night when I tried to box up their books. The thought they no longer have need of those stories, or that I would never have need to read them again, broke my heart. The reality of boxing those stories showed me the reality of putting this part of my life behind me.

This story is almost over. And I know it's the best, most important, story I will ever tell.

I must keep reminding myself my kids were, are, real, no matter how many, or how few, physical mementos I have of them around me.

NOVEMBER 5, 2010

All my planning and building and setting up shop in Portland was rendered moot by my "last Friday night at the Cove."

It's Friday; I'm here. Still. I have two broken feet.

It was my last Friday night at the Cove, so I went out drinking with my Cove family. On my way home I decided I was too tipsy to keep driving, so I stopped at a friend's place to crash on his couch for a bit. When I arrived, the apartment's denizens were locked out and engaged in deep drama, so I decided to go home. It was at this point my ankle rolled and I surfed down an entire flight of stairs. Of course, no one was still around. I managed, somehow, to hobble back to my car and drive home. I had no idea my feet were broken. Sprained, yes; broken, no way. At this point, I still thought I could move.

When I woke up Saturday morning I had the feeling I wouldn't be moving, no pun intended, but only for a couple of weeks. I lost my phone somewhere in the night, so I had to crawl out of the house—literally—to my car. I somehow drove here, to the Cove, and found my best friend. He took me to the emergency clinic. It was there I learned both my feet were broken.

I didn't know how bad they were broken until Monday.

My left ankle has a hairline fracture and is severely sprained. It will need four to six weeks in a walking boot to heal. The arch of my right foot is "destroyed" (so says my highly paid and well educated orthopedic surgeon). Surgery was last Friday, and it took three plates and numerous pins to rebuild it. I have Terminator foot. It will take three to six months to heal and I'm stuck in a wheelchair the entire time. If I mess it up and it doesn't heal properly, I can be permanently disabled, walk with a limp, and my leg can possibly turn either in or out. I'm not going to take that chance with my foot. I'll be in my chair until I'm told I can get out, because one day I may need the ability to outrun a violent death.

For now, I'm stuck in this wheelchair trying to grasp the reason and lesson in this latest setback. I was so damn close to getting out of here. Now I find myself, literally, unable to walk away from Texas. Again because of some sort of trauma. Fucking A, already....

At first I thought it meant I'm to stay here, in Texas. Not now. I still have to get out of this place. I can't see myself here long term. Since my latest fall, my problem has become I can't see myself anywhere. When I try to look forward, all I can see is uncertainty. I have no visions of where my life is headed right now. I'm once again left without the safety net a false sense of security provides.

Add to this I learned my mother is very interested in moving to Oregon for law school. She had only a subliminal idea this is I where I want to be and she co-opted my dream, yet again. Why? Do I confront her? Is this part of the message? Or is breaking my body meant to stop me from being where she is? A warning? A very obvious warning.

Easy to see why I'm crazy. Nothing is ever just simple and straightforward for me. I take for granted how intense and surreal my everyday existence must be to most people. All this bullshit becomes par for the course, my new normal. A life, like mine, should never be the "norm" for anyone. It's too visceral, too violent, too sick and perverted to be normal, yet here I am, grounded by a life I don't want.

What is it I am missing? What have I overlooked that forced life to ground me so thoroughly? What is it I'm supposed to sit here and think so hard on? Again, where the fuck is this life taking me? How much more out of control must I be in in order to finally feel engaged again? I'm clueless. I've no choice but to sit and absorb all this shit. Wait and see what oozes out when I'm full.

Time to start exploring myself again, it seems … .

NOVEMBER 17, 2010

I will be going *nowhere* for the time being. My cast comes off in three weeks, but I still won't be able to go anywhere. I was able to cancel the lease on the apartment in Oregon. I will live in my carriage house until my renter's lease is up. Texas has me in its grip yet again.

Essentially what it comes down to is I cannot, will not, don't seem to be able to, or allowed to leave my son. I know he's sick. I know he's dangerous to me, but as long as he's locked up in an institution, I have to know how he is. I can't leave my son to rot in a Texas prison. Before he killed Ella, before he molested her, before he thought about cutting my head off, he was my baby. As long as he's locked up, he's no danger to me. As long as he's locked up, he lives in danger's lair.

I don't have to stop living and I don't have to see him all the time. If my son is sent to the Texas Department of Criminal Justice, no one will fight for him like I will should something happen to him. I have to do the same thing I've always done - let Texas decide the punishment and make sure he stays safe by holding Texas to task.

I tried to move to Portland because I fantasize I can leave here and have a "normal," happy life somewhere else. I can't. This is my life. It's not normal. It's not happy, pretty, or neat. It's ugly. It's violent. It's bloody and painful. And I navigate it better than anyone I know, which means I must be on the right path. As much as I want to run, I can't. When I try, life literally knocks me down the stairs to remind me of that fact.

Paris and I aren't done with our lessons yet.

Believe it or not, I'm okay with this change in plans. I've finally chosen to accept the choice I wasn't allowed to make. Like I said, this is my life, my place. There could be more to it one day, but it will never be without all this. How naive I can still be at times, despite all the pain I've lived through, to think I could actually go 1500 geographical miles and magically turn into a mystery woman with no past.

There's no way to explain who I am, what I do, if none of this ever happened.

I spend too much time embracing my demons. No more fantasies about leaving. It's time to bite the bullet. When faced with the choice of being selfish or selfless, it goes against my entire being to choose selfish or be self-seeking.

I will be here as long as Paris is locked up or he pushes me out of his life. Whichever happens first—time always tells.

My entire life is related to crime. My past and my present are defined by criminal acts. My future is to be defined by criminal acts. There's no escaping the violence or reality of how badly people hurt and degrade one another. My job is to show people they don't have to be degraded or degrade others to get what they want out of life. I know I won't win the fight against human nature, but I know I can, and will, make a difference.

I will, in the long run, change my world for the better. People may not like my reality, my delivery, or my honesty, and that is their right. Though hopefully even the ones who think I'm crazy will still have been inspired to think outside their box, if only for the moment I registered in their reality. If I have to be labeled, label me thought provoking. I won't stop violence and pain from happening. What I can do is provoke as much thought as possible about how senseless violence is.

I'm in my element in this world. I truly believe in the power of love and, at the end of the day, good trumps evil. Somehow I'm still full of hope. My life is proof miracles do occur and angels exist. At least for me. Whatever life throws at me, I'll calmly catch it and throw it right back in play. This time I will not be one who loses this cosmic game.

NOVEMBER 18, 2010

I've joined the ACLU and will start attending monthly meetings. I also found Compassionate Friends, a support group for parents who have lost their children, but not necessarily through violent crime. Since it seems I am doomed to be in Texas, I decided to create a program for the San Antonio Police Department, an expansion of the FACT program. I want to create a group of specially trained volunteers who accompany homicide detectives to visit the victim's families. Once the family is notified, the volunteer will be there and will stay there, with the family, to offer comfort, mediate with officers, educate them concerning support services, etc. In other words, specially trained volunteers who advocate for the extended victims of homicide.

Once I get that program in place, I want to add a twist. One day I want specially trained victim advocates there for offenders' families too. That may be a harder sell, but it would be groundbreaking. SAPD can claim all glory. I'll just do the work.

As painful and nightmarish as my life is, I love life. I love the process of it, the unfolding of it. I don't like all the details, but I love the plot. I remain curious as to how the story evolves. I'm engaged in my own story. As long as I remain an active participant, I'm alive.

NOVEMBER 26, 2010

I'm so ready to walk again, drive again, and be independent again.

I am impatient with this literal sitting around. There are plans I need to enact. Silent screams build in my head as I sit here hour after hour either reading news, doing online research, chronicling my past, enduring my present, and willing my future into being. Very hysterically-toned silent screams. I always manage to swallow them. Draw a deep breathe. Move on. All while sitting absolutely still. One has to love the paradoxes.

I finished the preliminary research on victim advocacy programs. I picked seven cities which have programs similar to the one I want to create. What I want to do is visit each cities' police department's programs to either go through their training or stay a couple of days to learn about the program. After that I'll have a better idea in which direction to head next.

DECEMBER 1, 2010

Still in the damn cast. Stir craziness increases. I feel exactly as I did when I was close to Ella's due date: so close to getting something you want so badly the end is finger-tippingly out of reach. I want the damn cast off. Five more days, after which I'm still technically not allowed to drive. It will beat sitting on my ass all the time. I crave the freedom of movement. I crave hot water on a smoothly shaved right leg; showers that don't require the involvement of garbage bags and duct tape.

Five ... more ... days ... .

I've progressed in contacting police departments concerning their victim advocacy programs. I can go to Miami and Denver next year. Still working on the others.

To create this program for the SAPD, I'll have to call up all the emotions, lessons, and experiences of the last three years and turn them into a compassionate logical aide. My passions must be tempered by logic if I'm to accomplish this life's goals.

Logic trumps my ability to write well. Writing is much better suited to insanity. But I'll do my best to keep up with it, the writing and the insanity, just as always.

I've spoken with my mother lately—once or twice a week. Most of the time I still enjoy talking with her. On the other hand, if needed, I can just as easily cut her out again if she even thinks of fucking with me, my son, or my life. I've had it with bullshit out of her. If she wants to be in my life, it will be on my terms. I may not be able to hold a grudge, but I can hold myself firm. Neither she, nor Paris, will ever again hurt me as much as they already have.

Time to make Ella proud.

DECEMBER 3, 2010

I'm now steadily reading research on crisis response teams (CRTs): theory and real-world application; boring, yet necessary.

There are some very cool cities I can go to shadow and/ or train with CRT units: Miami, Denver, LA, Sacramento, Portland, Seattle, DC. It's going to be an adventure; one I eagerly look forward to. It will allow me to get out of Texas. I'll meet a few new interesting people, maybe have an affair or two (though I highly doubt that), learn tons more than I already know, and cap it off by putting together a beautiful program to honor my Ella. The only life that could be better is the one I had.

I see a life of caring in front of me. I see a life of work in front of me. What I have a hard time seeing in front of me is a life of being loved. I imagine, I know, there's someone out there, two someones: a lover and a child. I have a hard time seeing when we will find one another. At times I'm disheartened to think my life will be ultimately fulfilling but, finally in the end, lonely.

I was born to love and crave family, but I must live without and still live to inspire others to crave them too. Cosmic irony is often a karmic buzz kill. I take comfort in the truth if I don't find someone else in this lifetime who loves me fiercely, at least I loved this lifetime fiercely. I may die alone, but not without making the world more loving and manageable for others.

Sigh.

I could totally be a mother again. Time will tell.

I'm seriously considering creating my own nonprofit foundation, because I need money to create this program. I want to call it The ELLA Foundation. Named for Ella but stands for Empathy, Love, Lessons, and Action. Amazing how Charity and Ella both seem to be names of destiny for us both, almost as if they were foreshadowing, warnings, and signs of what was to come.

DECEMBER 7, 2010

Tonight, I'm a very happy woman. Finally. I no longer sport the damn cast. Finally. I can move and use my body again.

Six weeks in the damn wheelchair made me remember how much I enjoyed my physical self before Ella died. I know my body is damaged after all my hells, but I want it back. I want to be strong and firm again. My outside needs to match my inside. I'm older but sexier, in my opinion. Confidence is sexier than firm any day, but if I can have both, why not?

DECEMBER 9, 2010

I can walk again. Sort of. I find myself wanting to keep to myself. I am in creation mode. I want my program to be born.

I have to be careful, though. Creation mode can also be PTSD mode which can convince me I'm an island when, in fact, I'm only mired in shit.

DECEMBER 19, 2010

My mother and sister arrive for Christmas in three days. My mom and I are trying, yet again, to love one another more than we dislike each other.

I'll see Paris on Christmas. I'll be with one of my children. It's better than none.

DECEMBER 26, 2010

It soothes me to have my home to myself. It's recuperative to have time to myself, relaxing to have only my adopted family to deal with. Though, this Christmas wasn't as bad as the last three; a little life crept into the day. I would be lying if I said it wasn't tense at moments with both my mother and my sister. There were also moments we were family again. I made sure to get away on my own a little each day.

I won't pretend to know how to write an accurate overview of my feelings for my mother now. I love her as much as ever. I like her a lot less, but I feel sadness and sorrow, not so much for our relationship as I do for her, for everything she's lost or missed in that life of hers. I don't feel any happiness in her, only resignation, boredom, pain, anger, and sadness. She said she enjoyed her visit, but I sense there's little she truly enjoys anymore.

The gift of her visit wasn't the ride to see Paris. It was the chance to see a similar version of who I would have become had I not fought the good fight, held tight to my faith in the power of love to save me more than it can hurt me. I'm okay. I've passed my test and know, from this point on, I will live as Charity. I'm so relieved to have earned a reprieve from a future state of being easily mine had I given in to the pains of love and losses of life. There's no way or place to hide from them. May as well live with them. May as well love despite them.

Conflicting emotions make it difficult to know where to begin describing Christmas with Paris. It was the best visit we've had in a long time. He was Paris. He was my baby and the son I remember from long ago; no trace of the other Paris, even when we talked about Ella. We laughed a lot, gossiped, talked politics, science, music, and gang hierarchies. For three hours I could, almost, pretend we were at home, sitting around the kitchen table, a boy and his mom having a special moment. Almost. If we'd been home, Ella would have rushed into the room with her own need for a moment, and that moment would have broken without being bittersweet.

In the end, any and all moments end cherished.

DECEMBER 30, 2010

This is officially the last night of 2010 for me, because I work tomorrow night. I'm ringing in the new year with the SAPD, doing what I love. I see no better way to spend New Year's Eve. I've repeatedly had the feeling, a premonition, something bad is going to happen tomorrow night. I keep seeing an ambulance, lights flashing, no siren—so they aren't in a hurry, and a woman whose hair is falling around her face, screaming. She has on a black hoodie and grey sweats, capris. I hope I'm wrong. I hope this possible future stays just a feeling.

I can't see things that *will* happen. I think I see things that *could* happen. But I'll never know for sure. When my phone rings, I know when it's Paris calling. Every time. I know when there's a letter from a friend in my mail. I know how a person will most likely react in most situations. This could be psychic ability. It's no coincidence, but it's not psychic necessarily. I only know things about people whose paths intersect with mine. If what I see really happens tomorrow night, it was meant to be, and I'm meant to be there to help.

2011. New Year.

On February 4, Ella will have been dead four years. On October 10, Paris will be eighteen years old. On October 26, I will be thirty-eight. Life will still be a life I never could have imagined I'd be living. I will continue to prevail, as usual.

I hope to do two things this year: create the homicide crisis team for the SAPD and adopt a little girl. No matter what has happened, I know I'm a better human being when I love someone that completely. I would be remiss to preach all this, do all this, and not live all this by opening my home and heart to another child of mine. Come what may, once I've adopted that little girl into my life and heart, I will have proven love does conquer all.

As far as whatever else may happen in life this year, I'm not so worried. School may or may not pan out. Paris may or may not have more to throw at me. My personal life is a tragedy and my professional life will be born of tragedy. I am bound to tragedy. I will be okay. I've learned that much. And if I forget that lesson, I still have my faith in life and love, so I'm good no matter what 2011 has in store for me.

Every day of 2011 I will do my best to make one person per day feel better after meeting me than they were before we met.

JANUARY 5, 2011

For five days I was foolish/hopeful enough to believe this new year would be less insane than the last three. Or at least I would be. Of course, my foolishness has to do with my so-called family and my foolish belief that love can conquer *them*.

Yesterday I learned my mother looked me in my face and lied to me, yet again, about something pertaining to Paris. His best friend in Giddings was released. Paris, of course, asked his grandmother to break the rules for him to facilitate letter exchanges between them. His grandmother, of course, complied with his request. (But, she protests, only once, which must make it ok.) During her Christmas visit, she told me about the request but said she told him no.

He manipulates and lies. She manipulates and lies. I end up their fucking patsy, Paris' illness is further reinforced, and my mom continues to prove she doesn't love, like, or respect me, Paris, or herself.

I was unsure how to proceed yesterday, so I decided to put it out of my mind as best I could and sleep on it. Another foolish thought. I spent the night with nightmares. At dawn I made the decision to call my mother, ask her side of the story, and proceed from there. Enter the next foolish thought: the belief I can call my mother and have a conversation about my son which is rational and respectful. I called her.

She readily admitted her involvement and, true to her nature, immediately presented her defense: she didn't lie, she just didn't tell me everything. See the difference? She told me to go fuck myself at least six times because she's apparently tired of being pushed around by me all the time. Per her, I've also had Paris put in solitary confinement by cutting off his contact with the outside world. According to my mother he gets bored, so he obviously should be allowed to contact whomever he wants. Also according to my mother, it's evident to everyone that everything wrong with our family is my fault.

I hung up on her twice. She was hurling accusations, blame, and "go fuck yourself" so loud I could have put the phone down, walked outside, and still been unable to get her out of my head. Third time always being a charm, during the last phone call I gave her one week to inform TYC what she has done. That only got me another round of "go fuck yourself Charity."

I hung up again.

At some point, while hoping I was fucking myself, she did find time to call Paris' caseworker to leave a message about her infraction. So she said. To ensure against the high probability of that being a lie too, I called the superintendent, not the caseworker, and told him the latest situation. Needless to say, they're both in trouble. I'll be at Giddings tomorrow for another meeting about my son, my mother, and their constant manipulations.

In the midst of telling me to go fuck myself, my mother also managed to convey her belief that I'm overreacting, because the letter is "benign" (such an amazing woman, my mother, to use *benign* and *go fuck yourself* in the same breath). Her ability to grasp the reality of our situation is as inadequate as Paris'.

JANUARY 6, 2011

I spent my day at Giddings with Paris, the Superintendent, and Paris' caseworker, having a two-and-a half-hour circular conversation. The exact same conversation we've had just shy of four years now. I'm tired in so many ways.

Some days I have trouble holding onto the dragon's tail. I had an hour-long detailed conversation with my son and his caseworker about his sexual abuse of Ella. Apparently he enjoyed "stroking" her vagina. I'm supposed to believe he only tried to penetrate her once, during one of their showers. It never fully dawned on me until today as he described the various things he did to Ella, as I watched the barely perceptible grin of pleasure lurking and tugging at the right corner of his mouth, that we aren't just talking about sex abuse.

We are talking about incest. We've been talking about incest the entire time.

I now know that by the age of thirteen the following crimes and transgressions had been committed by my firstborn, my baby: vandalism, theft, assault, incest, torture, sadism, and murder. I also know that at the age of seventeen he has, to date, shown no true remorse for, or meaningful comprehension of, those actions.

I'm someone I never even knew could exist. I fight a war I know I can't win and where there is a very viable potential for death, either directly via Paris' hands, or indirectly via the insanity he's sown into my soul. When you give birth to a child, no one in their right mind ever dreams or imagines they will one day discuss his attempted rape and brutal murder of his little sister.

The only way to survive days like today is to split myself in half, one half Ella's mother, one half Paris' mother, and then shut both halves down. Days like today I suspend all feelings high in my mind and allow small drips, measured doses, of pain into my system. Pain overdose is too unstable to risk.

My son is very sick. My daughter is very dead. It is a very hard time for me to move this pen across this paper, but as long as I can write, my thoughts are forced into focus. If I can't write, my thoughts will fly out in all directions with no pattern, a rudely constructed net. If that happens I'll be trapped in my thoughts and then in my own private hell. All this will be wasted time if I can't write. All this thought is wasted time because all my thoughts always end with the same conclusion.

My son is a psychopath. I can't help him. That may not matter in the long run. What may matter is I can't, not at this point, give up on him either. He's caused me unimaginable pain and virtually inexpressible suffering, but I can't give up or walk away from him while he's locked up. Tragic and stupid as it is not to.

I'm not sure how many more times I can convince myself of this. Psychopaths tend to stay frozen in time. They repeat the same patterns, over and over again. The psychopath's cycles are so fucking debilitating to those who deal with them on a regular basis. Therapists who treat them experience higher burnout rates as opposed to, say, treating clients with PTSD.

Imagine how it must be for their moms. No need for me to imagine. I know life's not easy for anyone who's raising another human being, but sometimes I look around and want to weep because so many people don't seem to realize how great they do have it. They waste life; they complain about it, disdain it. I'd take a kid smoking meth or fifteen-year-old pregnant daughter any day over what I've got. At least those parents can still have hope for change.

I have to force my head to sleep. It's time for the awake nightmares to clock out and the sleep nightmares to clock in.

Paris called today to tell me of his decision not to cut his grandmother out of his life. He had discussed doing so at our last meeting when he realized TYC staff don't think too highly of their joint toxicity. His reason for changing his mind is he'll prove himself strong by keeping her in his life, recognizing his weakness for manipulation, and using his new strength of character to help him not to give in to his weaknesses. At this time, he "chooses to believe we are not toxic to one another." They've been toxic together for years, lifetimes, eons.

He also informed me he's spoken with her and instructed her (I swear he talks exactly as I write) to no longer bad mouth me when they speak. He never said if she agreed. He then asked me to do the same and began to explain he was asking this of me because he's tired of being stuck in the middle of us and tired of being our victim. Well ….

I told him to save the speech. I don't want him to choose between his grandmother or me. I want him to choose to discontinue a relationship that feeds his dark side rather than make the effort to thwart it. TYC has yet to make theirs. I have yet to make mine. I told him never again ask me to censure my speech or my actions for his benefit, because I'll not forgo saying or doing something I feel needs to be said or done at his request, because it's obvious his reasons for asking only ever suit one purpose: his. I told him how obvious it is he's a psychopath. I told him his arrogance leads him to believe he has this situation under control and that same arrogance blinds him from seeing how his actions reinforce the belief in so many that he truly is a psychopath.

The last thing I told him was, "It's time for this to end."

I don't know what I meant, exactly. Time for what to end? My decline into insanity? Good luck with that one.

His character to stop degrading? Even better luck with that.

I truly believe one of those two—Paris and my mother—will be the death of me one day, if I don't figure out a way to stop caring what happens to them. If I don't stop hoping they will (1) care about me; (2) ever understand how insane they are. If I don't find it in myself to let go, I will die. I will wither away to nothingness, drink and smoke myself to a slow death, die a death of stress, go insane, clinically, not the functionally eccentric way. I wish I could forget them both. It's my fault I'm still in this position. I've been mentally and emotionally unable to cut them out of me.

I'm not saying what I want to say very well. It's a problem I have so often now when I retreat into my house and my head to talk mostly to myself, smoke too many Camels, and drink a bottle of wine a night, all so I can sleep with bad dreams rather than nightmares.

Even so, on the cusp of four years, I have better balance on this tightrope. Being on a tightrope, I'm still liable to fall off at any moment. The art of staying upright is a gradual process. There will always be that moment when I fall into the next abyss.

I tell myself the worst has happened—but has it? Paris is fascinated with serial killers. Was Ella's murder just the beginning for Paris? He called it practice once. It's not the end for him. I'm not at the end of the marathon. The last four years have been nothing but a warmup lap before the race begins. If I say it's time for this to end, Paris most likely will see this as one round of a hotly contested competition.

I've got to go back to therapy before I once again become unfit for human consumption. Welcome home, PTSD. Hello again, depression, betrayal, disappointment, worthlessness, pointlessness. Time to patch myself up. Yet again.

Let go, Charity. Let go. You're dying and losing the battle by trying so hard to win. Listen to yourself. Save yourself.

JANUARY 10, 2011

Something is taking over me. What is taking over is a damn world of murder. My life is bookended by murder. There is no way around it but to write, then read, the damned books in between.

I've grown obsessed, not only with my own son's actions, but my mother's murder trial and my genealogy. I send emails to various researchers who study psychopathy. I'm searching for whatever records I can find concerning my mother's trial. I hired a genealogist to see if I can find some of these spirits of mine. I need to know them better, remember them.

I don't know that I'm not leading myself down the path of madness by embracing Paris' world. I know I can't focus on the world outside the one in my head long enough to stay functional in it. Something keeps telling me to stay in this rabbit hole and see where else it leads. I'm not sure I really even have a choice. I can't "work" because I can barely leave my house. I'm incapable of having light or superficial social interactions because inevitably someone asks if I have children. Nuclear fallout typically commences. The countdown, reflected in the eyes of the listener, consists of incomprehension, then horror, then pity, then gratitude it's not their life. Sometimes actual personal derision or disgust for me crops up.

I live in a mad, mad world. I've grown tired of trying to get others to understand it. They won't. They can't. You have no idea how happy I am they most likely never will. No more trying to get people to understand.

I'm just sharing a story. It may not be important to anyone but me to have it told. It may hurt a lot of people, but no one will die for feeling the pain of it, except maybe me. But then again, that's always been the case.

Every compulsion, every fear, every panic attack, every lawsuit, every revelation about Ella's sexual abuse has left me in a place where the only ability I have left is to write and no choice but to focus on this story. The only logical conclusion I can come to is to forget about doing anything but telling this story. If I'm going to go mad, it makes sense to go mad in familiar territory. Finding a way to go public, flaying myself for love, the quest for truth and science is the only course left to take because it's the only one I can motivate myself to walk down.

It's my turn to throw caution to the wind. I will find a way to go public. It's time to accept my son is dangerous. It's time to plan for the worst and shelter hope through the storm. After all we've been through, all it has done to us, if I'm ever asked, point-blank, if I think my son can kill again, my answer will be yes. If I'm asked do I think he will kill me, my answer will be it's a possibility.

If I'm asked how do you live with all this, my answer will be: "painfully with love."

Just when the caterpillar thought the world was over, it became a butterfly. – Unknown.

TWO YEARS LATER ... 20TH
BIRTHDAY LETTER TO PARIS ...

OCTOBER 10, 2013

Dear Paris:

Twenty years ago, on the day you were born, I took one look at you and two things simultaneously occurred: a feeling of fierce love unlike any I had ever experienced before took root in my heart and the realization, and accompanying fear, finally hit my brain (which had been engaged until that very moment in blissful fantasies of mom and baby always in perfect harmony) that I had absolutely no idea how to be a good mother.

I had no good example of how to be a good mother, but I figured I knew two things I hoped would work in my favor. I knew what not to do, how not to be, and I knew what kind of mom I wished I had had.

Armed with that knowledge, I set about making you two promises that day, October 10, 1993. One of the things I knew not to do was make promises to your child you never intended or could not keep so, despite the fact you blissfully slept through me whispering my promises in your ear, I considered my promises the foundation of the house of love I wanted to build for you to live in.

The first promise I made to you was to love you always, no matter what, unconditionally. I know too well what conditional love feels like; what damage is done to your heart and soul when you are judged unworthy because of your mistakes instead of loved for your existence. We all make mistakes. We should all be loved despite those mistakes. Then we should be loved even more because we make mistakes. Being loved through our mistakes is what gives us the confidence and will to learn from those mistakes to become a better person.

I have kept my first promise to you. I can say with great certainty I will continue to keep this promise to you for as long as I live. I continue to hope that loving you unconditionally will give you the confidence and will to be the best person you can be.

The second promise I made to you was to be the best mother I could be to you and for you. This promise has always been, and still is, a bit harder to keep, for many reasons. As a parent it is hard to figure out what is the best thing to do to your child and/or for your child in "normal" circumstances. I think we can both agree many of the circumstances I have tried to keep this promise in are about as far from "normal" as one can be.

At times I know I have failed miserably in keeping this promise, but I hope the love I feel for you and have shown you has, or will, trump any damage my failures cause you to suffer. There have been times I believe I am doing the best thing for you, and you (most likely) think I am full of shit and wish I would back off or stop doing whatever it is I am doing that you disagree with.

In these times, please reflect back on all the years I have kept promise one and try to love me as unconditionally as you can now that you are old enough to understand this concept better. We won't always see eye-to-eye. I will never stop being your mom, but I am doing my best to make the transition to be a true friend to you now that you are growing up. It is confusing at times to determine if your child needs a parent or a friend.

So here we are on the cusp of your 20th birthday. I can't even begin to describe to you how it is possible, how emotional and overwhelmingly surreal it is, for me to look at you and see both the baby I held close to whisper my promises in his ear and the full-grown, extremely easy-on-the-eyes, brilliant man who could (if he was allowed to) pick me up as easy as I used to pick him up. The best and simplest way to sum it up is just to tell you that, in spite of the passage of twenty years and all that has transpired between us, I still look at you and feel the same fierce, no ... fiercer, love that swept me away the moment I first laid eyes on you.

The Texas Department of Criminal Justice will not let a mother help her child celebrate and acknowledge the passage out of his teen years into his young manhood. I can't bake for you, send you a gift, see you on your birthday because it does not fall on a normal visitation day, or sing you Happy Birthday unless you decide to call me on October 10th. I am left giving you what I hope you consider a gift and is something that no one, not you, not TDCJ, NO ONE, can ever take away from you.

For your 20th birthday, I make you two more sacred promises Paris Lee, my first born, my first love.

I promise I will always be by your side as long as you are locked away from mine. No matter where Texas sends you, no matter how much time passes, no matter what you have to do to survive, no matter what I have to do to get there to see you... I will never turn my back on you while you are incarcerated. You will never be one of the forgotten ones. You will always know someone in the free loves you, thinks of you, and misses you.

People often ask me how I can continue to stand by you after all you did and all the suffering it causes me. I always respond the same. I tell them when you were a toddler I had to take you to daycare so I could go to class and work. I hated to leave you. It was so hard to walk away and a part of my mind and heart was always with you at daycare. Every afternoon I would walk into the classroom to pick you up and you were fine, playing and content, so I would sit on the floor and wait for you to notice me. As soon as you saw me, your eyes would light up with a look of pure happiness, you would drop what you were doing, run across the room, and jump on me. That was the best part of my day, every day.

Almost every time I have come to visit you since you have been incarcerated I still see that look in your eyes when you first see me. It may be for a split second, so quick I have to really be paying attention to see it, or it may linger the entire visit. Sometimes it has been replaced with a look of anger, hatred, or contempt but it has never been entirely demolished. This is how I know that MY Paris is still in there.

I promise I will never give up on MY Paris; never give up my hope and belief that the Paris who got locked in the underground room inside you the night you killed Ella will find a way to survive both prison and that underground room. I know you are still in there. You may forget sometimes. Your environment may force you to hide him away. But when you are with me, you can let that boy out without any fear. I will love him the same way I have loved the other boy that lives inside you ... unconditionally, no matter what.

Happy 20th birthday, Paris Lee. Since I can't give you a cake, I guess you have to settle for unconditional love, a mom who tries her best to be a good mom and a good friend, loyalty, and unwavering faith in the man I know you can be.

All in all, not a bad gift to get I think ...

EPILOGUE

As I write this, nine years after where this memoir left off, I wish I could tell you that I no longer have to ask myself, "How now, butterfly?" I would be lying to you if I said I had. The book may have ended, but my life has not, so the issues addressed in this memoir still affect me.

What I can tell you is that I am much better at answering the question of what to do when a challenge born of these experiences forces me to ask, yet again, what the hell am I supposed to do with all this? I can also tell you that all answers lead to more questions. I have reconciled myself to the reality of this tragedy, reconciled myself to the fact that because I am the mother of a sociopath, decisions on how to move forward through this ongoing tragedy will never be easy decisions to make.

I can also tell you the life I have built since 2011 is the life I desperately wanted to create when I wrote the words that became this memoir. Against all the odds stacked against me, despite my ongoing bouts of depression and grief, I did find meaning again. I kept my promise to Ella to make her death meaningful. I have found a way to put myself back together again, and in the process of doing so, I can now look in a mirror and see my friend, myself, again.

In August 2011, my dream, of creating an agency where both victims and offenders could find the help they need after trauma has occurred, became a reality. Over the years, The ELLA Foundation's programs have provided emotional support, community classes in psychoeducation, designed to educate others about mental health conditions, and advocacy efforts on behalf of thousands of victims, prisoners, and the general public.

In the past we have held writing workshops for children of incarcerated parents so they can reframe the stories of their lives into narratives which are free of shame and full of empowerment.

I have personally taught classes in prisons all over the United States and in Canada in an effort to help inmates better understand themselves from an emotional and psychological perspective and to help them foster empathy for those they have harmed. We have also developed and implemented programs for correctional officers and law enforcement agencies which help them to better understand the emotional and psychological needs of themselves, their colleagues, and those they encounter in the performance of their work.

We have created a support group called Forgotten Victims which offers emotional support and education about grief to the families and loved ones of incarcerated individuals.

We facilitate a program called Seeking Safety (an evidence-based program developed by Lisa M. Najavits, Ph.D.) for victims of trauma.

We have a community education program called Let's Talk in which we address various topics pertinent to today's issues surrounding criminal justice and mental health. Topics in the past have included childhood trauma, intergenerational trauma, mental health in people of color and the LGBT+ communities, and mental health and faith.

As the founder and Director of The ELLA Foundation, I have traveled the world to deliver keynote addresses at conferences dealing with victim and prisoner rights, family involvement in the criminal justice process, and advocacy training. My family, and our tragedy, was featured in the award-winning documentary *The Family I Had* which premiered at the 2017 Tribeca Film Fest. In 2019, our story was documented by CNN's Chris Cuomo in a one-hour program called *Inside Evil* and by Piers Morgan in his program called *Psychopath*. I have been interviewed by the BBC and numerous other national and international media outlets. I have received awards for my work with family violence victims, prisoners, and victims of trauma from various organizations and police departments.

I continue all this work today, still with the hope that my story will convince and inspire others to find their voice, find their meaning, and, most importantly, use their experience to help others and make the world a better place.

To learn more about The ELLA Foundation and the work ELLA does, please visit our website at **www.ellafound.org**.

By the time this memoir is published, I will be enrolled at Georgia Southern University's Master of Criminal Justice program, after which my plan is to obtain my Ph.D. in Clinical Psychology.

The work I do with The ELLA Foundation is good for my soul and has helped me through my own mental health journey. But what keeps me motivated, keeps me sane, and brings joy and peace to my life, are the events that have transpired in my personal life since the end of this memoir.

In 2013, I gave birth to a son, Phoenix. I'm not going to lie to you. His birth brought me back to the land of the living, but our journey, his journey, has not been all rainbows and celebrations.

Twelve hours after Phoenix was born, I learned he was born with a congenital heart defect. Critical aortic stenosis. At six days old, Phoenix had to have open heart surgery. The surgeons had to completely remove his aortic valve and replace it with his pulmonary valve. They then implanted a bovine vein to act as his pulmonary valve. He was unable to eat by mouth, so he had a G-tube inserted at four weeks old. His prognosis was not good.

For two months I stayed in the NICU with him. For three years he was under intense medical supervision. Four days a week, he had to participate in feeding therapy sessions and sensory integration sessions. He had daily in-home nursing care. It was both a time of great joy and great fear.

I am happy to report that today Phoenix is a happy, affectionate, intelligent, stubborn, and opinionated six-year-old. He faces more surgeries in the future to replace his pulmonary valve as his body outgrows the bovine vein. He takes all of this in stride, making others laugh as he tells them he is part cow and moos for them. When they ask about his scar, he tells them he fought a lion and won.

When I give a speech, I tell the audience that when I gave birth to Phoenix, I had one foot in the land of the living and one foot in the land of the dead. Giving birth to him brought me fully back into the land of the living. Ella's death and Phoenix's birth have taught me how to stay fully present in the moment I have, because each of them taught me that we never know how much time we have on this Earth, so we better make each moment we have count.

I am honest with Phoenix when it comes to his brother Paris. He knows his brother is in prison. He knows why his brother is in prison. He knows his sister is dead because of what Paris did, but he does not know exactly what Paris did to Ella. He knows I love his brother while hating what he did. And I am glad he knows these things, because he knows it means I will also love him, no matter what, under every circumstance.

Phoenix and his brother don't have a relationship. Paris is not allowed to have visitors under the age of 18, so they have never met. They do occasionally speak on the phone, a few words every now and again. Critics of mine like to disparage me for allowing Paris to speak to Phoenix. They tell me what a horrible mother I am for allowing the child who murdered my child speak to my other child.

They are certainly entitled to their opinion. My opinion is that I am setting an example for Phoenix. An example of how unconditional love and forgiveness look and behave. I believe parents, using age-appropriate conversations, should always strive to be honest with their children. I also believe that parents should not force their own agendas on their children but should help them learn how to navigate the complicated business of living so they will hopefully grow into confident adults who are capable of making decisions based, not just on their emotions, but also by employing critical thinking skills.

As Phoenix grows older, I am sure he will have questions about his brother, about my feelings for Paris, about what the future holds when the day comes that Paris is released. As he asks these questions, I will answer them. Honestly. I will be as honest and transparent with my son as I am with the thousands of people I share our story with. As honest and transparent as I have been with you, the reader of this memoir.

One day Phoenix will be an adult, who I hope will utilize the emotional and critical thinking skills I hope I am teaching him to reach his own conclusions about Paris, as would be his right as an adult. One of the many things Paris has taught me is that we can only do the best we can to raise our children, hoping they will take those lessons to heart. But there always comes the day when our children must begin to make their own decisions about how to live their lives.

I bet you are curious as hell about my current relationships with my mother and my oldest child, nine years after this memoir has ended. You may be surprised to learn that my relationships with both of them are the best they have ever been.

At the time of the conclusion of the memoir, I had stopped speaking to my mother. I did not speak to her again until the end of 2016. At the beginning of 2016, I was working at an agency which provided supportive housing to women with drug addictions. These women were involved in drug court and were required to participate in counseling, psychoeducation classes, and attend school or acquire jobs in an effort to have their children returned to their care and custody. My job was to provide case management and facilitate psychoeducation classes. During one of the classes, which met weekly for six months, the women and I spent much of our time discussing our childhoods. I found it interesting that all of them, including me, had mommy issues.

I hope the classes were as beneficial for them as they were for me. At the end of the series of classes, I came to the realization that I would be a hypocrite if I did not attempt to practice what I had spent the preceding years preaching: forgiveness. I had forgiven my son for murdering his sister. It was time to forgive my mom for all that had transpired during my childhood and in the period after Ella was murdered. So one day, after not having spoken a single word to my mother for several years, I called her to tell her I would like to try to build a better relationship with her. After years of not speaking to me, she was ready to try again too.

Making that phone call was one of the hardest, and best, decisions I have made in recent years. The relationship my mama and I share now is loving, respectful, and intimate. She is my best friend, my confidant, and my biggest supporter. We don't always see eye to eye (especially about politics!), but we have learned how to disagree without hurting one another. We have learned how to see each other from the vantage point of love rather than through the lens of dysfunction. In the past I thought a future without my mother was the best option. Today I can't imagine a future without my mama in it.

Paris...my relationship with Paris will always be a complicated one, but some things never have, and never will, change. I love my firstborn with as much intensity as I have since the day I found out I was pregnant with him. He no longer intentionally attempts to hurt me emotionally. We are as honest with each other as each of us are able to be, due to who we each are and how our individual minds work. He is still a sociopath, but I have learned to accept him for who he is, both the good and the bad. Paris will always be Paris. He will always be cerebral, only capable of intellectual empathy and remorse. His narcissism is firmly hardwired. He will always be capable of choosing to do acts of kindness. Along with all of us, he will remain conflicted about his true nature and the ramifications of his actions. Consequently, he will always process those thoughts and feelings much differently than the majority of us do. I hold onto the hope he will one day become part of the majority. A full-fisted hold on a very slim hope.

I believe he has learned I am near impossible to destroy and I think, in some way, this has engendered in him a respect for me he did not have in the early days of this nightmare we share. He "loves" me as much as he is able to.

What the future holds for us, I cannot say. We both know there will come a time, as his release becomes imminent, that I will have to decide if I can still be in his life. When that time comes, I will do what I promised him I will always do when it comes to him: I will love him no matter what and I will always try to be the best mother I can be for him, to whatever extent I am able, no matter where I am living.

But for now, we do the only thing we can do. We focus on the moment we have. As for all the rest, we will cross that bridge when we get to it. I am just happy the bridge is there and was not burned down in the destruction brought about by his decision to murder Ella.

Before I go back to living my life, loving my children, and running The ELLA Foundation, there is one last issue I want to address. I often receive hate mail accusing me of capitalizing on the death of my daughter and the destruction of my family. Of all the hate mail I receive, these are the messages that bother me the most, so I want to clear this matter up once and for all.

I have never made, and I never will make any money off the murder of my daughter. Every speaking fee, every royalty from this memoir, every donation received, has gone, and always will go, straight to The ELLA Foundation to support the programs we provide, free of charge, to all who participate in them. I have never paid myself a salary. ELLA has no paid staff, instead relying on amazing volunteers who give their time, skills, and passion with no expectation of compensation. When speaking fees, royalties, and donations are not enough to support what ELLA does, I make a donation of my personal funds to keep ELLA going. To date, I have spent over a quarter of a million dollars of my own money to make sure those who suffer because of trauma get what they need, because in my opinion, everyone who suffers needs a little ELLA of their own: Empathy, Love, Lessons, and Action.

There is a tale told in many cultures of the two deaths a person experiences. The first death is the physical death, the death of the body which removes one from the daily lives of those left behind. The second death occurs when the last living person who remembers your name experiences their physical death. At this point, when the memory of you no longer exists, you die your second death.

Thank you for helping me to keep Ella alive in the memory of each and every one of you.

For More News About Charity Lee and Brian Whitney, Signup For Our Newsletter:

http://wbp.bz/newsletter

Word-of-mouth is critical to an author's long-term success. If you appreciated this book please leave a review on the Amazon sales page:

http://wbp.bz/hnba

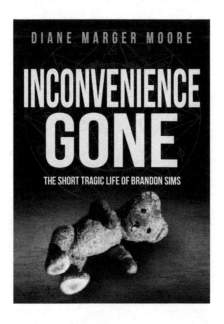

See even more at:
http://wbp.bz/tc

More True Crime You'll Love From WildBlue Press

A MURDER IN MY HOMETOWN by Rebecca Morris
Nearly 50 years after the murder of seventeen year old Dick Kitchel, Rebecca Morris returned to her hometown to write about how the murder changed a town, a school, and the lives of his friends.

wbp.bz/hometowna

BETRAYAL IN BLUE by Burl Barer & Frank C. Girardot Jr.
Adapted from Ken Eurell's shocking personal memoir, plus hundreds of hours of exclusive interviews with the major players, including former international drug lord, Adam Diaz, and Dori Eurell, revealing the truth behind what you won't see in the hit documentary THE SEVEN FIVE.

wbp.bz/biba

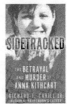

SIDETRACKED by Richard Cahill
A murder investigation is complicated by the entrance of the Reverend Al Sharpton who insists that a racist killer is responsible. Amid a growing media circus, investigators must overcome the outside forces that repeatedly sidetrack their best efforts.

wbp.bz/sidetrackeda

BETTER OFF DEAD by Michael Fleeman
A frustrated, unhappy wife. Her much younger, attentive lover. A husband who degrades and ignores her. The stage is set for a love-triangle murder that shatters family illusions and lays bare a quiet family community's secret world of sex, sin and swinging.

wbp.bz/boda

CPSIA information can be obtained
at www.ICGtesting.com
Printed in the USA
LVHW011747300620
659399LV00015B/1429